Music In Our Lives:
Rethinking Musical Ability,
Development, and Identity

Music In Our Lives: Rethinking Musical Ability, Development, and Identity

Gary E. McPherson
Jane W. Davidson
Robert Faulkner

OXFORD
UNIVERSITY PRESS

KH

OXFORD
UNIVERSITY PRESS

Great Clarendon Street, Oxford OX2 6DP

Oxford University Press is a department of the University of Oxford.
It furthers the University's objective of excellence in research, scholarship,
and education by publishing worldwide in

Oxford New York

Auckland Cape Town Dar es Salaam Hong Kong Karachi
Kuala Lumpur Madrid Melbourne Mexico City Nairobi
New Delhi Shanghai Taipei Toronto

With offices in

Argentina Austria Brazil Chile Czech Republic France Greece
Guatemala Hungary Italy Japan Poland Portugal Singapore
South Korea Switzerland Thailand Turkey Ukraine Vietnam

Oxford is a registered trade mark of Oxford University Press
in the UK and in certain other countries

Published in the United States
by Oxford University Press Inc., New York

British Library Cataloguing in Publication Data
Data available

Library of Congress Cataloguing in Publication Data
Data available

Typeset in Minion by Cenveo, Bangalore, India
Printed in Great Britain
on acid-free paper by
CPI Antony Rowe, Chippenham, Wiltshire

ISBN 978-0-19-957929-7

10 9 8 7 6 5 4 3 2 1

Whilst every effort has been made to ensure that the contents of this book are as complete,
accurate and up-to-date as possible at the date of writing, Oxford University Press is not
able to give any guarantee or assurance that such is the case. Readers are urged to take
appropriately qualified medical advice in all cases. The information in this book is intended
to be useful to the general reader, but should not be used as a means of self-diagnosis or
for the prescription of medication.

6/28/13

Foreword

Gary McPherson and Jane Davidson are both well-known figures in the psychology of music education: Gary has published widely on musical development, motivation, and performance, as has Jane on the physical, social, emotional, and cultural aspects of communication in musical performance. They came together to jointly undertake this large-scale longitudinal study on the musical development of a sample of 157 young Australians over a 14 year period (between the ages of 7 and 22); this must surely be the largest such study, not only in terms of the number of participants involved, but also as it is the longest-running, and so there is a great deal to be mined from the wealth of data which was collected. The study was supported by two large grants from the Australian Research Council.

Following her doctorate, Jane had worked as Research Fellow on another very well-known and widely-publicized longitudinal study on '*Biographical determinants of musical excellence*', which investigated the family backgrounds and musical lives of pupils at several specialist music schools in the UK; although these schools devoted a good deal of time to pupils' musical studies and activities, they also covered the full range of the secondary school curriculum up to age 18. This project was funded by the Leverhulme Trust, and co-directed by John Sloboda of the Department of Psychology at Keele University, where Jane was based, and by Michael Howe of Exeter University. The legacy of this project lives on in the many publications, still widely cited, which arose from it, and in many ways provided the basis for the project reported in this book.

This new project has already given rise to various academic publications, but I am very pleased that this book has also been written in order to pull all the threads together, and thereby to provide an overview of the enterprise as a whole. It is clear from the acknowledgements that Robert Faulkner, who worked as a PhD student with Jane at Sheffield University and who is now Associate Professor at the University of Western Australia, has played a vitally important role in this process. It is impossible for me to do justice to the many different facets of this huge project in the few words available to me here, but what I like most about this book is the way in which the three authors (McPDF) have managed to weave theory into the wide range of empirical findings and case studies throughout. Amongst others, they draw on theoretical models from positive psychology (e.g. Deci and Ryan's self-determination theory), from sports psychology (e.g. Abbott and Collins' model of the development of sporting expertise), from educational psychology (e.g. Trautwein's multilevel modeling of processes involved when children and adolescents complete school homework), and on McPherson and Williamon's adaptation of Gagné's differentiated model of giftedness and talent to music.

Perhaps the most central theoretical foundation lies in McPDF's adoption of Sameroff's transactional approach to their participants' interactions with significant family members, teachers, peers, and community members as predictors of their self-perceptions and musical development. This is summarized in a very elaborate taxonomy of the 'regulatory sites' at which the nature of the musical transactions with these significant others are negotiated; the extent to which these transactions are either promotive or demotive of specific musical developments is at the core of McPDF's conceptual approach, on which they elaborate further in four flow-diagram-type models of the transactions which are needed to meet the psychological needs of *competency*, *autonomy*, and *relatedness*. This is probably the main way in which McPDF have moved beyond the theoretical conclusions that were reached in the Leverhulme project by Sloboda, Howe, and Davidson. To return to my mining analogy in the first paragraph, this engaging and accessible book is full of gems and nuggets for the reader to discover. I congratulate the authors on producing it, and am confident that the mining process will continue in the years to come.

David Hargreaves
Applied Music Research Centre, Roehampton University, London

Acknowledgements

Our 14-year longitudinal study has been enriched by the participation of many close friends and associates. During the first 5 years a number of undergraduate music education students at the University of New South Wales helped with data collection, especially during the end-of-year sessions with students and their parents. Among the most important are Amanda Brown and Jasmin (Pesic) Jones, who coordinated and led teams of undergraduate students across the early years of data collection. Their persistence and hard work meant that we were able to keep track of all the participants and process the hundreds of hard-copy questionnaires and interview files onto an electronic database. We thank also Dr Stephanie Pitts (University of Sheffield, UK), who visited Australia as a research assistant in the third year of the study, and helped to analyse parts of the qualitative data that were important in identifying various aspects of children's instrumental practice.

We are indebted to the New South Wales Department of School Education and Training for allowing us to undertake the study and to the school principals, school administrative staff, and classroom teachers who worked around the many individual and group research sessions when students were taken from class.

The study was funded by two Australian Research Council grants (A79700682 and DP0770257), without which we would not have been able to undertake the research.

There are three colleagues in particular whose insights, support, and enthusiasm have meant so much to us during the past 14 years.

Associate Professor Emery Schubert (University of New South Wales) provided invaluable assistance in the early years, especially helping to gain the support of participating schools and to devise efficient techniques so that we could process interviews directly onto an electronic database that could then be used to analyse our results. His help with statistical analyses was invaluable.

Dr James Renwick (Sydney Conservatorium of Music, University of Sydney) provided wise and carefully considered suggestions during many phases of the study, and we are grateful for his collaboration and extensive knowledge of self-regulation and self-determination theory that proved influential in helping us frame our findings.

Dr Paul Evans (University of New South Wales) undertook postgraduate study during the second phase of the study when the participants had left school and were either studying at university or had entered the workforce. His extensive review of literature combined with his IT skills enabled us to devise online surveys and separate individual interview techniques that could be used to compare participant data from various stages of the study.

Our most special thanks go to the 157 students who participated in the study plus their parents and music teachers. As we reflect back over the years, it seems remarkable that there were so few instances when the participants, parents, or teachers were not able to make themselves available to answer questions or participate in research sessions. We wish to convey our heartfelt thanks to all of our participants, their parents, and their teachers for being so generous with their time, and for their continuing interest and participation across the 14 years of the study.

Finally, the book is the result of much hard work over an extended period of data collection, reflection, and writing. Gary McPherson and Jane Davidson wish to pay particular homage to Robert Faulkner, who was able to pull all of our thoughts together during the writing process, and especially during the final months when we were developing our theoretical position. Although we regard our contributions as equal, without Robert this book would not exist.

Contents

About the authors

Gary E. McPherson studied music education at the Sydney Conservatorium of Music before completing a master of music education at Indiana University, a doctorate of philosophy at the University of Sydney, and a licentiate and fellowship in trumpet performance through Trinity College, London. Before arriving in Melbourne to take up his current position as Ormond Professor and Director of the Melbourne Conservatorium of Music, he worked at the University of New South Wales (where the study was first funded), and then the Hong Kong Institute of Education and the University of Illinois at Urbana-Champaign, where he held the Marilyn Pflederer Zimmerman endowed chair in music education. He has served as national president of the Australian Society for Music Education and president of the International Society for Music Education, and has published extensively in various books and refereed journals.

Jane W. Davidson studied musicology, classical singing, contemporary dance, education, and psychology in the UK and Canada, completing several postgraduate courses, including two masters degrees and a PhD. She worked for 13 years at the University of Sheffield before taking up the inaugural Callaway/Tunley Chair of Music at the University of Western Australia in 2006. Her research includes projects on reflective performance practice, vocal production, musical expression and emotion, expressive body movement in performance, musical skills acquisition, and therapeutic uses of music. She has published widely, is the former editor of *Psychology of Music* (1997–2001), was vice-president of European Society for the Cognitive Sciences of Music (2003–2006), and president of the Musicological Society of Australian 2010 and 2011. She is deputy director of the Australian Research Council Centre of Excellence for the History of the Emotions.

Robert Faulkner is a graduate of the Royal Academy of Music in London and holds a licentiate in singing teaching from the same institution. He went on to postgraduate music education studies at Reading University and later completed an MA in music psychology and a PhD from the University of Sheffield. He lived in Iceland for over 20 years, where he worked at all levels of education from early childhood to tertiary, played a leading role in national curriculum development and was inaugural deputy chair of the Iceland Music Examinations Board. He was the postdoctoral research associate on the ARC DP0770257 (2007–2010), the topic of the current book, and is now Associate Professor in the Graduate School of Education at the University of Western Australia.

Chapter 1

Frames of reference and the origins of the study

The current volume is situated in Western musical learning contexts. Its roots stretch back over 20 years to when we began to ask fundamental questions about how and why some beginner musicians persist to competency whilst others cease playing their instrument within a few months of first receiving tuition. As has been the case for many decades, the overall involvement of the average Western child in musical instrument learning for performance continues to display myriad outcomes: some children progress quickly, moving from group to solo lessons, with some individuals gaining more and more performance experiences, while others achieve only piecemeal learning with *ad hoc* experiences taking place both informally with friends or through formal one-on-one private instrumental lessons. Even within these limited contexts, outcomes for music learners appear extraordinarily variable.

Our aim in this book is to investigate the gamut of achievements of the Western music learner from continuous to sporadic, from persisting to quitting. We will include an analysis of the ever-increasing gap that has developed between engagement with Western instrumental performance skills and music's role in everyday life. The music industry represents a significant part of the Western consumer economy and statistics provide strong evidence of the significance of music listening in everyday contemporary life. In the USA, for example, around 75% of young people between 8 and 18 years of age owned personal music systems, such as iPods, in 2009. Just 5 years previously that figure was around 8% (Rideout *et al.*, 2010). The same USA study reports an increase in the average amount of time 8–18-year-olds spend listening to music from 1½ hours a day in 2005, to 2¼ hours in 2009.

For the vast majority of young people, soundtracks can be personalized through selection and arrangement to accompany, configure, and regulate their personal and social lives, everyday work and recreation, mood, movement, and identity at the push of a button (Bull, 2007). Yet, in spite of this consumption of music listening products, more active forms of engagement such as performing music seem by comparison to be low.

Across our professional lives as musicians and academics, we have continually sought to explore different ways of thinking about musical engagement and development, ability, and identity. Much of our current thinking has been shaped by the longitudinal study that forms the basis of this book. The study, which traced participants' musical lives from their 7th to their 22nd birthdays, has helped us think more deeply about a number of important issues: definitions of musical skills and abilities; assumptions that continuous engagement for performance is the sole way in which those skills can be developed; and the consequences of trends and behaviours we observe amongst the general public and their listening consumption.

Popular views of musical abilities in Western contexts

The gulf between music listening consumption and active music participation is reflected in popular views about the acquisition of instrumental music and listening skills and the capacity people possess to acquire them. So whilst levels of consumption testify to an unquestioned capacity to listen to music, ideas about performing music or composing it are often tied up with flimsy notions of 'gifts' and 'talents'. When asked to express an opinion about musical capacities, people often place an emphasis on an innate view of musical talent: individuals are born with a 'gift' that makes them special and particularly able in the domain. A good example of this popular view is found in a survey by Davis (1994), who asked educational psychologists, secondary teachers, primary teachers, and members of the general public to identify activities that they believe require a 'talent' or 'gift'. Davis reports that 75% of the professionals interviewed reported that playing instruments, singing, and composing music were the result of a special innate gift or natural talent. Reasons for their responses included the very young age at which 'talent' emerges and can be demonstrated (such as the talent of child music prodigies) and the observation that many youngsters try but often fail to develop musical skills (Winner, 1996; Walker & Plomin, 2005; Lehmann *et al.*, 2007; McPherson & Hallam, 2009; McPherson & Lehmann, in press; see also Sloboda *et al.*, 1994a,b; Gagné *et al.*, 2001)

In general education, 'gifted' and 'talent' are terms often applied simply, and per-haps misleadingly, to those individuals who have been identified as demonstrating skills and abilities in the top 10–15% of their year group in any particular subject or curriculum area. As far as music is concerned, a growing set of neurological studies reveal that we all have the capacity to generate and perceive musical information, indicating that music is a human capacity that all of us posses, and is certainly not limited to special 'gifted' individuals (Münte *et al.*, 2002; Altenmüller, 2011). Investigations into infant–adult interactions demonstrate the hard-wired impulse for musical communication for regulated comfort, nurturance, and expressive purpose (Malloch & Trevarthen, 2009; McPherson & Hallam, 2009).

Over the past 20 years music psychologists have also compiled evidence showing that successful musicians are conscientious learners, rather than being mysteriously 'gifted'. Musicians consistently put a great deal of effort and practice into developing their craft (e.g. Sloboda & Davidson, 1996; McPherson & Williamon, 2006). Even the achievements of child prodigies such as Mendelssohn and Korngold can be explained through environmental influences, exceptional time investment in practice, and stim-ulating musical interactions (Davidson & Faulkner, in press; McPherson & Lehmann, in press). Nevertheless, the 'innate' or 'natural talent' view of music still translates into misconceptions about the purpose of music education and contributes to an unwit-ting self-fulfilment of prophecies about musical 'giftedness'. Its presumed presence or absence emerges in early adult representations of and family scripts about children's musical abilities. Thereafter, it impacts dramatically on parents' and children's commitment to learning music and upon some of the arrangements that are made for teaching it.

Reconciling specialization, amateuring, and music in everyday life

Confusion about the nature and acquisition of musical skills may also have emerged because of the levels of specialisation predicated by large social and industrial systems (Cooke, 1998; Small, 1998) and from modern Western education's entanglement with them. In spite of the phenomenal growth of the arts, entertainment, and creative industries, there is still a strictly limited demand for professional performers. So whilst the commercial rock and popular music industry, and even their classical music counterparts, offer high financial rewards and celebrity status, the pathway to success as a music performer is often seen as one littered with the debris of broken dreams. Parents, teachers, and career advisors seem unlikely to encourage young people to pursue aspirations as professional musicians. Nor are institutions likely to make music a high priority in formal education planning and curriculum. The often politically motivated rhetoric of education needing to 'return to basics' reinforce a hierarchy where literacy and numeracy are considered essential for life, and prerequisite to long-term security, wealth, health, and happiness.

Creative skills, and the arts in particular, remain at the bottom of the list of educational priorities in spite of the lip service paid to the importance of creativity and the overwhelming evidence in support of its significance across all learning areas (Schellenberg, 2006). There is not, currently, a general entitlement for children to learn music in schools, even in many Western countries like Australia, where our research has been based. Highly valued outcomes of schooling such as self-discipline, being able to work with others and in a team, problem solving, and creative thinking are all effectively learned and enhanced through musical participation. Even though a review by Hallam (1997) illustrates the compelling case for music's impact upon the development of a wide range of human competencies or intelligences, there is still little evidence to suggest that music is likely to be seen as contributing significantly enough to these general outcomes to justify systematic institutional commitment to music itself (McPherson & O'Neill, 2010). Other recent research that indicates the potential of music listening and active participation to improve senses of wellbeing and make a genuine contribution to the health of young people and elderly alike have yet to make any noticeable impact on the value attached to music education at political and policy levels (Stegemann et al., 2010; Davidson, 2011).

As children progress from primary school into high school, their goals and curriculum objectives become increasing dominated by desirable and attainable career pathways. In such circumstances young people are unlikely to find themselves encouraged to pursue their musical talents as vocational pathways. Even if instrumental music learning and performance enjoys a place in the primary/elementary school curriculum, and there is no guarantee that it does, it finds itself competing, sooner or later, in an extra-curricular arena focused on social-capital, recreation and relaxation, health, and wellbeing. Young people's decisions to persist or quit with instrumental music learning is based upon a personal attachment that balances benefits with costs to other recreational and social opportunities, academic achievement, or vocational ambition, and finite financial resources and time. Parents may be willing to make significant sacrifices for, and investments in, their children's musical activities, just as they do for, say, sporting activities or some other site of interest, achievement, and enjoyment. They are unlikely to do so, however, in the absence of real and sustained personal commitment on the part of the learner.

At the same time, musical specialisation and the extraordinary increase in everyday listening opportunities may also have undermined the status of the amateur musician, and added further to doubts about the usefulness of formal music education. As an amateur cellist and chamber music-maker, Booth (2000) highlights this phenomenon in his book *For the love of it: amateuring and its rivals*. Even here though, a uni-dimensional view of active musical participation would be misleading. Research into informal music-making among popular musicians (Green, 2001), participation in Gilbert and Sullivan festivals (Pitts, 2005), the garage-band (Westerlund, 2006), and karaoke phenomena (Xun & Tarocco, 2007) all illustrate how music performance is still highly relevant to some people's lives, whatever the impact of formal instrumental learning.

The consumer phenomenon and what is often, if questionably, defined as passive participation is not unique to music. It is evident in all the arts, and it is particularly prevalent in sports, where performance is experienced vicariously in the socio-emotional ambience of the lounge room or sports stadium. Even if we accept that few young people will gain full-time employment in the performing arts, what are the outcomes that we may be looking for in educating our children musically and in providing instrumental lessons in particular? If a career as a musician is not the learner's goal, what is it? Is doing music 'for the love of it' or to regulate mood and movement, work, play, and socialization a sufficient reason for learning? What, if any, impact does music education have on longer-term musical engagement as active participators and makers of music, as appreciative listeners or concert goers, or as purposeful and discriminating users of personal music systems?

The context for this book

In 2005 Oxford University Press produced an edited collection of the writings of John Sloboda that spanned a quarter of a century (Sloboda, 2005). The text outlines the directions of music psychology investigations across the timeframe. It notes that despite some important work on perception and cognition of music that took place through the 1980s, by the start of the 1990s very few research clues had been offered as to why people are motivated to develop the intense involvement with music that is observed in such a wide range of human cultures. One part of that story would require a better understanding of the musical development of children and young adults. This is where our story begins, in the early 1990s, with a focus on the theoretical and empirical work of that time. In 1991, Gary McPherson was in Australia, engaging with his own doctoral study, looking at the skills required to successfully learn and perform music. In parallel, Jane Davidson was in the UK, beginning a 3-year post-doctoral fellowship with John Sloboda and Michael Howe, investigating the biographical determinants of musical excellence in western classical music learning, especially focusing on children who had been labelled as gifted and talented. These two studies emerged from interests of the time, namely, the focus on the nature of skills acquisition. The underlying principles driving both those studies, and other research in the 1990s, brought McPherson and Davidson together in 1997 on a collaborative longitudinal study tracing children who began their very first music lessons aged 7–9 years old.

Musical beginnings, 1991–1997

When Sloboda and Howe first met in 1990, they discussed their frustration with the strongly held folk belief, outlined above, that 'musicians are born not made'. Since it was impossible for them to examine biological similarities of those achieving musician status, their focus was on the environmental factors surrounding the lives of children who had achieved prodigiously in music. The data obtained provided important preliminary information. From a small sample of 42 young people in receipt of specialist musical education, they discovered that those with the most successful musical profiles undertook more practice, possessed a more pervasive sense of music's function in their lives, and had parents who supported their practice activities (Sloboda & Howe, 1991). These findings laid the foundation for a major project entitled 'Biographical determinants of musical excellence' for which Davidson became the research fellow. In this work, Davidson interviewed 258 children who represented a spectrum of abilities: (a) those who had received a minimum of a year of lessons and then given up playing, (b) those who sustained music learning in their lives, but for whom it was considered inferior to, or at best on a par with, other hobbies such as dancing, playing soccer, horse riding, (c) those who were serious players and who rated music as an important part of their lives, and had considered attending a specialist music school, (d) those who had auditioned but failed to achieve entry to a specialist musical education, but who still possessed high attainment goals for music, and (e) those who attended one of England's leading specialist music schools. Comparing these five groups with their sliding scale of successes, engagement, and ambitions, some key results emerged.[1]

The findings were extensively reported, for example see Howe and Davidson (2003), Howe et al. (1993, 1995, 1998a,b), Davidson (2002), Davidson et al. (1995/6, 1996, 1997, 1998), and Sloboda et al. (1994a,b, 1996). Overall, they revealed that the students in receipt of a specialist musical education had sung spontaneously some 6 months earlier than the children in any other group. This could have been because the parents engaged in more musical activities and so stimulated this facility sooner; equally, it could have been that these children were self-engaging in their early music-related activities more extensively than other children.

The quantities of practice undertaken by all students surveyed produced starkly contrasting results. Indeed, those in a specialist musical education did four times the

---

[1] Some outputs included contributions from Derek Moore, who offered statistical input at the analysis stage of the project.

practice of the non-specialists, quantities in line with those surveyed by Ericsson *et al.* (1993), who found that students at conservatory on a professional performer trajectory had achieved an accumulated 10,000 hours of formal (scales, pieces, technical exercises) practice by 21 years of age. These huge differences in investment in formal practice were apparent from the start of the learning process.

Examination achievements in the study cohort also provided contrasting group differences. The specialist group progressed rapidly through these examinations, at a rate proportional to the amount of practice. Indeed, looking across all groups, the participants actually took the same amount of practice time to achieve a musical examination grade level, irrespective of group. So, someone doing little practice may achieve grade level 1 after 3 years, whereas someone doing regular daily practice might achieve the examination in 1 year with the total practice time being the same for each person.

Parents/care-givers' involvement in the learning and progress showed that those students who were most successful did indeed have more parental involvement in their lessons and practice: speaking to the teacher, taking notes for practice tips, and then assisting with listening to or guiding practice. These successful learners did not come from more musical homes. Rather, the parents did no more than listen to music at home and in some cases the parents took on the musical activities of their children by becoming involved in band committees, concert organization, and so on.

In addition to parents, family dynamics were also examined by considering the role and influence of each sibling on the students studied. The majority of the student participants noted that their siblings were often positive influences: taking up the same instrument having been inspired by the sibling example. In a handful of cases, the siblings had bullied/teased or tormented the students investigated. But in all these cases such potentially negative experiences were turned to a positive by the students who went on to be successful: they regarded the bullying as a sign of jealously and so were all the more stimulated to do well in their own area of musical interest.

Inspiration and support from others in general was found to be very important. For those in specialist education, attending the school had facilitated their musical involvement and through being with like-minded peers they were assisted in focusing on their music-making and were able to overcome prejudice or a lack of understanding about musical involvement they may have experienced in their previous schools. These students were also often inspired by an older role model; a practice supervisor who was often a tertiary level student at the local conservatory or a visiting artist to the school. Teachers were also highly important.

For the students who ceased playing, the whole support mechanism of family, friends, and teachers had an interactive role in the decision to cease: parents were less supportive, friends less interested or engaged, and teachers simply less involved. Students who ceased tended to have a rapid turnover of teachers and had far more group than individual lessons. Those students who persisted and gained musical learning success had more one-on-one lessons and only changed teachers an average of 2.5 times over the period surveyed (8–18 years of age).

Generally, students reported that a warm, friendly, and supportive teacher was the norm. Whilst subsequent teachers of those who continued to learn were also perceived to have warmth and generosity, those who were more successful in their learning experiences seemed more able to differentiate between personality and abilities. For example, one interviewee was very clear that whilst his very first teacher had not been a particularly good musician, she had been ideal for the young beginner. As he progressed, he realized that being a kind and supportive person was a crucial quality for the teacher of the young child, whereas for the older, more experienced, and successful player, it was important to recognize that lots can be learned from a teacher who explains things well and who presents role-model musical abilities, even if that person is not particularly kind and agreeable socially.

This brief summary of selected results demonstrates that motivation, attitude, and the nature of social interactions and behavioural norms, such as establishing a practice routine or sitting examinations, had highly interactive roles in determining the student's musical progression. Overall, the study examined the students at only one time point and so real-time emergent influences from first musical contact or the impact of increasing independence in the transitions between childhood, teenage years, and adulthood could not be accurately traced. By the time Davidson and McPherson met, they were both eager to trace in detail the first 3 years of the learning process for students receiving regular school-based instrumental ensemble programmes. They were keen to see whether the same types of results would be found when tracing students from their first lessons.

In parallel to the British study, McPherson, working in Australia, was finding that children develop musically more efficiently when instrumental instruction incorporated an orientation towards aural and creative forms of performance from the beginning. The child then develops a greater readiness for the introduction and learning of notation, and a more equitable balance of visual, aural, and creative forms of performance skills in latter stages of their development (McPherson, 1995a,b; McPherson *et al.*, 1997). As depicted in Figure 1.1, this balance between visual, aural, and creative forms of performance is seen as essential for students to reach their full potential as musicians, and develop the aural, technical, kinaesthetic, and expressive skills necessary to perform in a wide variety of styles and idioms.

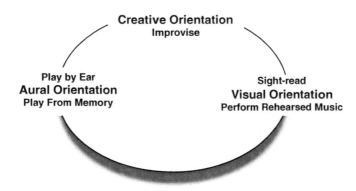

Figure 1.1: Visual, aural, and creative aspects of musical performance.

A key part of the research helped to clarify the types of skills that explain various aspects of performance ability (McPherson, 1995a,b, 1996), given that authors in the late 1980s and early 1990s often defined these skills differently or used them interchangeably. For example, Priest (1989) defined playing by ear to 'include playing from memory and all forms of improvisation' (p. 174).

Up until the early 1990s, much of the literature had focused on visual aspects of performance, and especially the skill of performing rehearsed music from repertoire books. In a number of Western countries, this approach was often seen as the *sine qua non* of instrumental teaching (Priest, 1989), partly due to the fact that many teachers themselves are unable to perform aurally and creatively, let alone help their students acquire these skills.

From his analysis McPherson was able to model instrumentalists' ability to perform music visually, aurally, and creatively. In the testing of his theoretical model, as shown in Figure 1.2, a number of relationships were shown to be statistically valid. In the simplified path diagram coefficients are represented visually, so that broken lines indicate a weak relationship and thick lines indicate a strong one. The skill of playing by

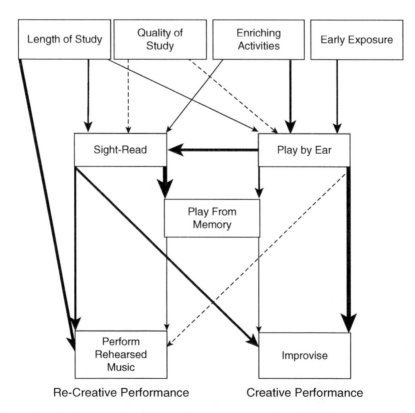

Figure 1.2: McPherson's (1993) theoretical model of relationships between musical skills and conditions of study.

ear was strongly related to the capacity to improvise, and sight-reading ability related strongly to the level of skill on performing rehearsed music. In addition, the skill of playing by ear emerged as being strongly related to sight-reading and both playing by ear and sight-reading to the students' ability to play from memory.

Some of the results confronted commonly held beliefs. For example, there are some instrumental teachers who believe that instrumentalists who spend time playing music by ear and improvising rarely become efficient sight-readers. The results of the study indicated that this was not the case, with most of the finest sight-readers being students who scored high on the tests of playing music by ear or by improvising. Likewise, the reverse was also often the case.

Another important finding of this initial work was that students exposed to a traditional, visually oriented approach to learning a musical instrument were typically inefficient in their ability to audiate (i.e. comprehend) music from notation or aurally; a finding that added weight to the importance for early instruction to emphasize playing by ear and improvising so that beginners can develop their capacity to 'think in sound'.

McPherson's research provided a neat description but one that needed much more extensive explanation through other forms of data analysis. One significant extension occurred in 1996, when Sloboda and Davidson (1996) presented an explanation of how individuals who had not been given systematic formal opportunities could achieve expertise. They based their analysis on Louis Armstrong, the jazz trumpeter, and Noel Patterson, a young autistic adult who had astonishing musical performance skills, despite never having received any tuition and having profound mental disabilities. One of the most important findings of this work, which had been missing from the earlier biographical studies, related to the defining of five essential characteristics of high-level expressive music performance: automaticity, systematicity, communicability, stability, and flexibility (Sloboda & Davidson, 1996). Above all, this research indicated that these qualities had been learned regardless of whether they had been taught formally or not and that they related to a high level of domain-specific structural knowledge and significant memory span increases.

A picture had emerged of a long-practising musician tuned into the social and cultural rules about musical expression that was offering personal fulfilment for engagement. The key question for music educators then was, if these qualities can be learnt, how might they be most effectively taught?

Over the past 15 years educators have paid increasing attention to the interface of formal and informal learning, and provided rich insights into some informal music learning practices (Green, 2001, 2008; Folkestad, 2006). Indeed, culturally specific cases have shown that peer learning or learning through being immersed in a cultural context can provide highly positive learning environments (Green, 2011). We believe that despite this more recent research, the importance of Sloboda and Davidson's discussion from 1996 has still not been fully recognized or adequately developed. It has great significance for music psychologists and music educators, not just in exposing the characteristics of expert music performance, but in pointing to the qualities of sustainable and significant musical development and, therefore, of effective music teaching and learning. This hypothesis is central to our study. We shall return to this and other principles as our practical and theoretical ideas unfurl and as we attempt to account for the musical journeys of 157 young people from childhood to adulthood.

Our cohort

Our study[2] was initially set up to examine young learners in eight primary school instrumental music programmes in Sydney, Australia. Contacts were made with music teachers from the schools to recruit students who were about to start learning an instrument. We organized information sessions to talk about the study and to distribute information so that parents and their children could make an informed decision about whether or not to participate. As a result of these sessions and the information supplied, a total of 157 students, made up of 87 (55%) girls and 70 (45%) boys, and their parents agreed to take part.

At the beginning of the study, the students were all in school grades 3 and 4, between 7 and 9 years of age. The participating schools represented a range of inner city and suburban primary schools within Sydney, Australia. Instruction on the ensemble instruments for the eight schools normally involved one or two music ensemble rehearsals each week plus a small group or individual lesson on the instrument. All eight schools taught the students using popular method books and this material was often supplemented by additional technical and solo repertoire that was covered during the individual or small group lessons on the instrument.

The study involved a wide variety of data collected over a 14-year period. In the weeks before the students received their musical instrument and began lessons, we interviewed all the students and their parents to gather descriptive data about the student and collect information concerning student and parent beliefs and attitudes about music learning. Individual student interviews focused on previous experiences and exposure to music, the reasons why they wanted to learn music, why they had chosen their particular instrument and the degree to which they were satisfied with their choice, and their beliefs and feelings about music learning, especially their expectations and valuing of the activity.

Likewise, the initial parent interview (mostly undertaken with mothers) focused on: gathering background information on the child, the child's early experiences and interests in music (from infancy), any musical interactions in the early years, reasons why the parent was allowing or encouraging their child to learn an instrument, whether any other family members had previously or were currently learning music, parental beliefs about music as an area of learning, plus predictions of the child's potential to learn an instrument. A set of questions attempted to situate the child's music learning within all other activities, both at school and outside of school.

During the next 3 years of the students' primary school education, parents were interviewed by phone at regular intervals. Some of these interviews were short and lasted only a couple of minutes, collecting information on how much practice the child was undertaking or if there were any problems such as diminishing motivation

---

[2] The project was the first Large Australian Research Council grant awarded for a project in music education (McPherson & Davidson, No. A79700682).

or family circumstances that might impact on their child's progress. More extensive interviews were undertaken at the end of each year of the child's learning.

Similarly, all the students were interviewed personally at the end of each of their first 3 years of learning. A comprehensive set of questions was asked across a number of dimensions. The students also undertook, on an individual basis, a battery of tasks aimed at assessing their progress on their instrument according to a range of visual (sight-reading, performing rehearsed music), aural (playing from memory and by ear), and creative (improvising) aspects of their progress. In addition, many of the students had their home-practice sessions videoed on a regular basis, enabling the triangulation of survey reports from parents and students about practice habits with empirical evidence.

During the first 3 years additional information was also collected annually from interviews with the students' classroom teachers, their instrumental teachers, and their ensemble directors. Students' school reports and results in their system-wide literacy and numeracy tests (which were administered at the time to all students in school grades 3 and 6) were also collected.

Whilst at high school, the students still playing and their parents were contacted less frequently. Data was collected during the period between years 9 and 10, a crucial time for those who were still playing, when they were making choices about which school subjects to focus on for their final year 12 examinations. More recently, Davidson and McPherson were awarded a further Australian Research Council Discovery Project Grant (DP0770257) to follow up on as many of the original participants as possible. Immediately after leaving school and taking a gap year, employment, or going to university, an online survey was administered and further phone interviews were taken with students and their parents, along with additional face-to-face interviews and, where appropriate, individual sessions to assess the current performance ability for those students who were still playing. Well over two-thirds of the original sample were still engaged in the research project at this stage. A comparison of earlier data for these ongoing participants with those individuals with whom we had lost contact or who had declined to continue in the project suggested that there was no reason to believe that there was any fundamental difference between them (Evans, McPherson, & Davidson, in preparation). It would not seem unreasonable to think that those who discontinued in the research project by choice were unlikely to be high achievers. As we shall see, however, even the definition of high musical achievement is controversial and it is not unlikely that people with very interesting musical lives may have disqualified themselves from the project because of preconceptions about the technical and cultural nature of musical achievement. Regardless of the length of participation in the project, we owe all the young people, their parents, and their teachers a huge debt of gratitude for sharing insights into their musical lives.

The extensive data we obtained is a combination of quantitative information about frequency and consistency of musical practice, scores from test batteries, plus a host of qualitative information about student, parent, and teacher beliefs and opinions on musical engagement. While most of the information was solicited through face-to-face sessions and phone calls initiated by the researchers, there were many occasions when a parent or child would provide information of their own volition.

Much information was gathered using these informal contacts, particularly when the family was moving to another location or when the child experienced a particularly positive or negative influence, such as doing especially well on a music examination or being about to cease instruction.

It is not the aim of this book to report or discuss all the detailed findings that have emerged from this array of data: many individual research report papers have already been published by the authors of this book and other collaborators on the project that examine some of those individual threads and themes. Nevertheless, the next three chapters provide an overview of some of those findings: first, by looking at participants' learning, practice, and progress in the early years of the project and, second, by looking at the gradual fall-out of participants from instrumental music. Subsequently, we will review much more recent data about the musical lives of the participants regardless of how long they stayed in the initial instrumental music programme. From Chapters 6 to 10 we consider the need to rethink some of our preconceptions about musical development by looking at this rich and wide-ranging data through the lens of individual lived experiences. This book tackles the challenging task of presenting a holistic, summative view of the study, and its theoretical interpretation and implications. Our final two chapters, 11 and 12, attempt to provide some frameworks and interim theory for further investigation and discussion. In doing so, we hope to make a contribution to the understanding of musical development in the dynamic and vital context of music in our lives.

Transformational, translational, and transpersonal approaches

One of the keys to our journey as researchers in this project, and to our efforts at unlocking some of the secrets of the everyday musical lives we have been following for more than a decade, has been the wider psychology literature about motivation, education, and the development of expertise or talent. Several key theories have emerged since the publication of our early findings that have enabled us to unearth frameworks in which we can situate and make better sense of so many of the musical lives we have been carefully observing. Whilst these theories will be discussed, developed, and adapted later as they help explain our data, it is appropriate to engage in a brief exposition of some of the key theoretical principles and themes here.

Essentially the process of writing this book has been guided by an approach that can be described as transformative, translational, and transpersonal. It has been transformative in the sense that we have attempted to question the validity and/or appropriateness of existing conceptions, not least our own, for defining students like those we studied. This included a consideration of different ways of thinking about and defining musical development, skills, and achievement, and the role of music in people's lives. Our approach has been translational in the sense that we have attempted to bring together the best ideas and insights from other research studies and theoretical conceptions with our findings to use as a basis from which to advocate an updating and redefining of practice within music education. Finally, it has been transpersonal in the sense that we have attempted to examine as far as possible holistic longitudinal and multi-perspectival musical journeys and not just key sites and events in musical lives. In doing so we have sought to draw together traditional quantitative and qualitative music psychology frameworks towards emerging phenomenological approaches to understanding real lived experiences.

In terms of mapping out young people's skill development on the musical instrument that they were learning, the philosophy underpinning our work was influenced by our unease with conceptions of musical achievement that focus on students' ability to perform repertoire from notation which they have practised at home. The problem with this concept is that it is possible to learn a piece of music through mindless drill and practice with little or no understanding of the task (Lehmann & Davidson, 2002); what Schleuter (1997) refers to as 'button-pushing' students 'to whom notation indicates only what fingers to put down rather than what sounds are desired' (p. 48). More than 60 years ago Mainwaring (1933, 1941, 1951) argued for a broader view of musicianship that included not only being able to perform from notation, but also being able to play by ear and improvise. As noted earlier, McPherson used these ideas to define five aspects of music performance relevant to understanding children's abilities to perform music (McPherson, 1993, 1995a,b; McPherson *et al.*, 1997).

> *Perform rehearsed music:* Using notation to provide a faithful reproduction of a pre-existing piece of music that has been practised over multiple rehearsals.
> *Sight-read:* Accurately reproducing music from notation that has not been previously seen or heard.
> *Play from memory:* Providing a faithful reproduction of a pre-existing piece of music that was learned from notation but performed without notation.
> *Play by ear:* Reproducing a pre-existing piece of music that was learned aurally without the aid of notation.
> *Improvise:* Creating music aurally without the aid of notation.

Most music educators would agree that for children to become competent musicians, they need to be able to develop their capacity to 'think in sound' by being able to aurally represent in their minds what they see, hear, or wish to create on their instrument (McPherson, 1995a,b). One way to test whether children are developing these capacities is to examine how well they are able to perform in the five ways detailed above, so that different dimensions of their abilities to coordinate their eyes and ears with the fingerings necessary to perform on their instrument can be assessed.

Focusing on the above visual (perform rehearsed music, sight-read), aural (play from memory, play by ear), and creative (improvise) aspects of performance ability, robust techniques for assessing performance skills were developed from the studies cited above and used to measure these skills across the initial years of our beginning students' learning. Many of these findings are discussed in Chapter 3, but, as we shall see later, the limitations of this conceptualisation of musical talent and ability soon became apparent. Our cohort would have depleted very quickly had we written off as musical dropouts or failures those with low scores in these measures, or who quit at very early stages of the project. We would never have known the diversity of musical lives that emerges from a sample of ordinary children unless we had determinedly kept in touch with as many as possible over the past 14 years. Had the study stuck to a narrow brief of looking only at skill development on the instruments children were learning in the primary school instrumental programme, the title *Music in Our Lives* would have been a misnomer indeed.

In addition, the technological revolution that has accompanied these young people's developing lives and our tracking of them has forced us to ask questions about how the participants listen to, and use, music. In the renewal of the classroom music curriculum in England during the 1980s there was a noticeable shift away from music listening and appreciation towards active participation and even composition. These trends were formalised in the National Curriculum for England when the teaching of music in primary schools became a statutory requirement in 1992, following high-profile lobbying from musicians such as Sir Simon Rattle and Pierre Boulez. In Australia, where music teaching is still not a general entitlement for primary school children, music education in recent decades has focused either on choral singing or the type of band programmes our cohort were engaged in, following a North American model on performance achievement outcomes (e.g. school, regional, state competitions; see Pitts & Davidson, 2000). We were curious about the ways in which new technologies had given the young people in our study unprecedented autonomy over their listening behaviour and how this related to their music education, if indeed it did. With DeNora's (2000) seminal research about music in everyday life in mind and acknowledging Bull's comprehensive work in the field of the iPod and personal sound systems (Bull, 2007), we discovered that as our participants grew up they used extraordinary amounts of music to regulate their mood and behaviour, and to create and present personal and social identities. In some cases such usage represented a high level of sophistication, in terms of both psychological application and the playlists themselves. In just about all cases, participants' levels of consciously targeted listening would have been unimaginable just a decade earlier. We were struck too by an implication from this that musical development is no more ahistorical than it is acultural. Such a hypothesis resounds with research where teenagers in the USA were asked to sing well-known popular songs from memory. Levitin (1994) found that over two-thirds of the unselected college student sample demonstrated good pitch memory, suggesting that exposure to recorded music on its own (rather than structured stimuli) could lead to the development of pitch memory.

In terms of translational approaches to our study, several key bodies of research have stood out from our extensive search of literature on the psychology of education, motivation, learning, and development. It is only in the last few years that researchers have begun to synthesize literature across and within domains that enable us to develop frameworks that might help us understand the key characteristics and attributes that impact on young musicians' development and achievement.

Sameroff (2009) has recently formulated a theory emerging from his and his collaborators' earlier research that tackles the seemingly perennial debate we touched on at the very beginning of this chapter. He attempts a dialectical integration of nature and nurture in child development by examining how contextual promotive and risk factors, and transactional regulation (as opposed to 'self-' and/or 'other' regulation) impact personal change—whether change is conceptualised as trait, growth, or development. In particular, his discussion of parents' representations of their children and children's representations of their parents resonates strongly with our attempt to understand the impact of those relationships on musical development.

It is premature to give a thorough account of Sameroff's theory. To do so here might also imply that we had imposed this theory upon our study *a priori*. That is not the case. It was in searching for ways to explain our study in holistic senses that we encountered Sameroff's work, not in a literature search that preceded our enquiries. The interplay of self and other regulation, which is central to Sameroff's theory, and its impact on musical development is a theme that runs through our data at all levels. It leads us to postulate an emergent theoretical framework in the final chapters of this book that owes much to a synthesis of Sameroff's theory with research from several other key areas of research. First, as the study progressed, we found psychological needs theories (Deci & Ryan, 2002) especially helpful in explaining our participants' motivation to engage in music. Second, in thinking about how those needs were met through musical engagement, we found ourselves examining music's expressive and communicative power, and the rules that appear to govern the use of expression in musical performance (Sloboda & Davidson, 1996). A more detailed review of these three frameworks will be developed later as they emerge from stories about music in our lives and as we integrate them into emergent theory about musical development.

An exploration of theories from sport psychology research has also proved particularly interesting in our attempts to understand better musical development. We acknowledge, of course, that music is no more the same as athletics, than playing the trombone is the same as throwing the javelin, but we believe that there are useful analogies to be made about motivation and engagement across these domains. Notions of motivation, talent, training, and practice in sport and music, along with parental and societal beliefs about their status and their relative values as serious, useful, vocational or recreational subjects, make comparisons and contrasts between them enlightening.

In particular, the work of sports psychologists Abbott and Collins (2004) provided us with a model of development that proved relevant for our own study in a translated and adapted form. We shall discuss this model in Chapter 6, when we examine the musical lives of two of our participants and look at how, for more than a decade, they consistently maintained high levels of interest to develop high levels of musical expertise.

In the scientific literature on motivation, interest is defined as 'the psychological state of engaging or the predisposition to re-engage with particular classes of objects, events, or ideas over time' (Hidi & Renninger, 2006, p. 112). As a psychological state, higher levels of interest have been shown to promote attention, persistence' and learning, with two prominent lines of research on interest evident (Xu, 2008). The first focuses on a 'person–object' explanation to explain how one's goals and valuing of an activity act in concert with an emotional component as individuals regulate their own actions. Within this perspective, researchers attempt to study how greater interest can be fostered in an activity and how tasks can be made more interesting for learners. A second perspective seeks to provide better explanations of the role of others such as parents and teachers in enhancing children's interest through support and ongoing feedback. Together, these lines of research have demonstrated the need for more detailed accounts and analysis of the thoughts, feelings, and reflections learners have while engaged in an activity, and how others may support these learners to develop an interest or even maintain their interest over time. In all areas of learning, and particularly in an area as complex and potentially fraught with frustrations and difficulties as music, teachers often struggle when teaching students they consider to be disinterested in what they are teaching them. Teachers may also lack an understanding of the positive role they can bring to the development of their students' level of motivation.

For all these reasons, a great deal of the educational psychology literature has focused on the role teachers and significant others play in regulating learners' interest in ways similar to Sameroff's transactional model cited above. Our study has enabled us to examine the complex social networks through which musical development winds its way. The basic premise of much of this recent research is that interest is not fixed or unchangeable, but something that can change over time.

Hidi and Renninger (2006) have recently proposed a four-phase model of interest development based on a number of propositions, including one that suggests interest is always content specific rather than a predisposition. This means that even children who appear to be highly motivated have a discrete set of areas in which they are most interested and others in which they display no interest whatsoever. The model outlines two basic types of interest—situational and individual interest—each of which involve two sub-phases. Situational interest consists of a relatively short-term 'triggered situational interest' that is typically externally supported, followed by a 'maintained situational interest' where learners may display focused attention and persistence over a longer time period. Individual interest is a more enduring predisposition based upon an emotional, psychological, and intellectual engagement with the activity, first as an 'emerging individual interest' and then, in the right conditions and with the right support, a 'well-developed individual interest' (see Figure 1.3).

As shown in Figure 1.3, situational interest might be triggered in music when a child goes to a concert and becomes fixated on either the music or how the music is being played, just as many children in our study were at various times in their musical journeys. In exceptional examples these may even be the kind of intense peak aesthetic experiences that are seen as having a potentially epiphany-like impact upon musical motivation (Whaley *et al.*, 2009). We certainly found this with some of our young learners, who reported becoming interested in certain instruments or the role of a musician when seeing and hearing their school band perform in the years before they began lessons themselves. Lily, whose case study we will examine later, is just one example of many. Some of the other learners reported older sisters or brothers who played in the band and the experience they had, which then triggered younger siblings' initial interest in learning themselves.

We found many children who said they experienced a surge of excitement in the days before and also during the first week of learning their new instrument. In some cases, their individual interest in learning the instrument was complemented by positive situational interest such as going home to perform for their parents or grandparents, where they experienced the thrill of having them applaud and praise their efforts.

Unfortunately, however, some of the children had parents who appeared to lack interest in their own child's learning. Initial experiences reinforced children's perceptions

Interest

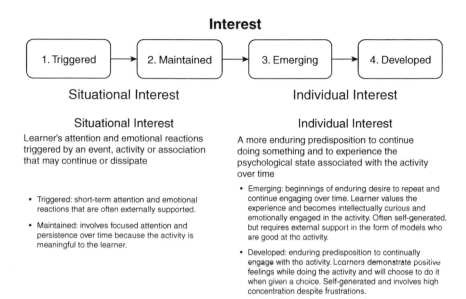

| 1. Triggered | 2. Maintained | 3. Emerging | 4. Developed |

Situational Interest · Individual Interest

Situational Interest

Learner's attention and emotional reactions triggered by an event, activity or association that may continue or dissipate

- Triggered: short-term attention and emotional reactions that are often externally supported.

- Maintained: involves focused attention and persistence over time because the activity is meaningful to the learner.

Individual Interest

A more enduring predisposition to continue doing something and to experience the psychological state associated with the activity over time

- Emerging: beginnings of enduring desire to repeat and continue engaging over time. Learner values the experience and becomes intellectually curious and emotionally engaged in the activity. Often self-generated, but requires external support in the form of models who are good at the activity.

- Developed: enduring predisposition to continually engage with the activity. Learners demonstrate positive feelings while doing the activity and will choose to do it when given a choice. Self-generated and involves high concentration despite frustrations.

Figure 1.3: Summary of Hidi and Renniger's (2006) interest model.

that their first attempts to play music were not something that parents appreciated or that would lead to a sense of feeling special as a result of being able to play the instrument. Examples of parents complaining about the 'noise' of their children practising reminded one of the authors of a parent who had earnestly asked what could be done to stop her 4-year-old son from 'consistently singing "nonsense" songs that he just makes up all the time': what chance for musical talent?

It is obvious then that key 'others' play very significant roles in both triggering—often, although not exclusively, teachers and near peers—and maintaining 'situational' interest. It is in the area of maintaining 'situational' interest that parents in particular appear to play such an important role along with teachers and peers. In thinking about the significance of the home environment, two other key bodies of research have helped us develop some understanding about how its complex practices impact musical development. Both focus on questions of homework in general: in the USA, research (Pomerantz *et al.*, 2005, 2007) has revealed how the emotional climate in the home impacts personal change, whilst in Germany very extensive work by Trautwein and his colleagues (Trautwein & Koller, 2003; Trautwein *et al.*, 2006a,b; Trautwein & Lüdtke, 2007; Trautwein et al., 2009a,b) demands that we rethink what kinds of behaviours from parents and children might constitute effective homework. This has been a particular challenge for us given how we had originally implicated parental support in early outcomes for students' instrumental learning.

We now believe that we are in a position to be able to clarify some of the interpretations we made about that support and unravel a few more of the intricacies of these networks. The significance of effective instrumental music practice and the arrangements made for it by teachers, parents, and students is hardly surprising. The issues around homework are complex for compulsory subjects like literacy and numeracy, for whose importance there is, we can reasonably assume, a pretty much universal consensus. Typically, such homework is a good deal more structured in terms of task than instrumental music practice. How much more complex then are the processes around the latter? One of the aims of this book is to attempt to increase our understanding of what kinds of teaching and practice strategies and support mechanisms might deepen interest, increase commitment, and sustain musical growth.

What much of the literature cited above illustrates is that we may not have looked in enough detail at what Sameroff (2010) calls 'transactional regulation' and at the complex entanglement of interactions that configure human development in general and no less so in musical development. Much of that work only surfaced some way into our project and some very recently indeed. It informed neither initial research design nor publications from the first years of the project. As is so often the case, we have found that hindsight affords a fuller view of things. This book represents a revised view of some of this earlier work and a fuller view in the sense that we have now been following our participants' music lives for well over a decade and are able to interpret earlier findings in the light of much later developments.

In turning to the next chapters then, we wish to return to the early years of the project, to the children's initial instrumental learning and to our initial research and results. This book would make little sense without that kind of recapitulation, even though some readers may be familiar with some of the themes and findings in it from various publications that McPherson and Davidson, along with numerous other researchers engaged in the project, have already contributed to the literature from this study. None of those publications provide the comprehensive overview of the early years of this project upon which we shall now embark.

Chapter 2

Initial music learning and practice

In this chapter we introduce the reader to the cohort of students whose musical lives we trace from the age of 7 until their early 20s. We begin in 1997 at the outset of the project, when we first came into contact with young learners through their primary school instrumental programme. Initially, the aim was to map progress in the instrumental programme over the next 3 years. Obviously, this point does not mark the beginning of our learners' musical lives, owing to the broad range of environmental stimuli that they had already experienced. Indeed, many had already had formal instrumental lessons, some were singing in weekend choirs, participating in musical theatre groups, or taking dance lessons. Other participants had already had some limited instruction on the recorder through classroom music. Our first encounter with the students and their parents was in interviews several weeks before the students began in instrumental programmes. We recruited from eight primary schools in the metropolitan area of Sydney. Following these interviews, a set of protocols outlined in the previous chapter was established to provide as comprehensive a view as possible of subsequent musical development and of past musical experiences.

The significance of the school instrumental programme in terms of shaping the child's musical future cannot be underestimated. The schools regarded the engagement as serious, with parent–child evenings being organized by all participating schools where an ensemble performed for parents and their children, staff explained how the instrumental programme was organized, and children were encouraged to sign up for learning an instrument the following year. Nevertheless, each of the eight schools had slightly different ways of allocating instruments to students. In three schools all students in the preceding year learned the recorder as part of their classroom music lessons. Such teaching was seen as providing crucial developmental stepping stones; a way of introducing students to what was perceived as an 'easy' instrument in order that they gain a preliminary grounding for wider instrumental learning opportunities the following year. Preliminary grounding was seen, mainly, as learning basic traditional clef notation. Most of the schools also had concerts for the younger students, again as a way of introducing the instrumental opportunities that would be available to them in subsequent years and as a means to trigger their initial interest in learning an instrument.

Music in the home in early childhood

Initial interviews with parents provided extensive evidence about children's early exposure to music in the environment. Unsurprisingly, nearly all children were reported as engaging with a range of sound objects and instruments as babies and infants. Activities ranged from hitting pots and pans, playing with cot mobiles, toy pianos and drum kits, or infant music activity centres to glockenspiels, xylophones, and flutes. While one parent mentioned a 'hideous melody train that made a dreadful noise, musical carousels, and mobiles', several others recalled long lists of instruments that their children engaged with: 'chimes with a pull string, xylophone, toy guitar, drum, tambourine, cymbals' or 'rattle, then later castanets, flute, tambourine, drums, xylophone and so on'. One parent even commented that her children made their own musical instruments.

Ten per cent of participants claimed that there were no musical instruments apart from toy instruments in the home. Most participants described an extensive range of instruments in the home, including recorders and 'little flutes', and a third of the homes had a piano. Several of the pianos were rarely played family heirlooms, but others were, or at least had been, played by parents themselves. Some 60% of mothers and 45% of fathers had at some stage in their lives learnt to play a musical instrument. At the beginning of our study, only about 10% of mothers and 15% of fathers continued to play to varying degrees, ranging from the 'occasional tinkering' to playing duets with their children, or in several cases belonging to local community groups such as a wind band, symphony orchestra, or a rock 'n' roll band. One father stopped playing altogether immediately following the birth of his first child. In several other cases, our music learners engaged in positive interaction as young infants and children with their parents around instruments that the parents played, so that 'Naomi would sit on Dad's lap and ask to play his guitar' or 'John wanted to climb on Dad's lap and bang the piano.' Another mother taught the piano and the relationship between her and her son will be discussed in detail in a later chapter.

From infancy, we are fascinated by rhythm, pitch, timbre, and melody (Papoušek, 1996). In households where musical instruments are present, the child may be absorbed into the atmosphere so playing can begin informally very early—touching the piano keys and playing games like the examples from our participants above. In spite of the presence of instruments in most of the homes in our study, there is little evidence to suggest that very few families engaged in musical activities on any kind of regular or systematic basis. Between 5 and 10% of parents could not remember if they engaged in any proto-musical behaviours such as clapping games, bouncing, singing, and general musical play.

Songs and singing in the home

Parents were also asked about singing activities in the home. Some parents talked about how their children sang 'all the time', others discussed the invention of songs relating to everyday situations. For some parents, particularly those from non-European backgrounds (including Chinese, Korean, Indonesian, and Lebanese) singing with their children played an important cultural role, so that one mother remarked how she 'always (sang) Brazilian lullabies, never English nursery rhymes'. Nevertheless, some 33% of parents stated that they did not sing their children to sleep even as babies or young children. Several claimed never to have sung at home: 'We never did, we read instead', 'We didn't sing very much, except for the occasional nursery rhyme. Her child-carers did—from 20 months'. Only 46% of parents claimed to sing often with their children as babies, infants, or toddlers. Asked about when children commenced singing themselves, most parents seemed unable to pinpoint an exact age, but between 10 months and 2 years was the most common suggestion.

The actual definition of 'singing' and its gradual emergence from babblings may explain why many parents find it difficult to locate the precise onset of this skill, in contrast, say, to the first recognizable word an infant utters or step it takes. Nevertheless, one parent stated that her son had never sung, another that she was 'unmusical, so [was] unaware of these things'.

The tape recorder was a popular substitute for singing lullabies and, together with the radio, it was widely used in homes where nearly all children are remembered singing along with songs and moving or dancing. In one or two instances, parents used music consciously to regulate mood and affect, as the following example shows: 'I used music to pacify him as he was a distressed baby (he had a traumatic birth). I played relaxing, semi-classical light music and ambient music like Enya and it really worked.'

Early instrumental instruction: age, context, and constraints

Instrumental music teachers tend to agree that the age a child can start a formal engagement with an instrument is when they have sufficient cognitive and physical resources at their disposal to hold and manipulate the instrument with some control and understanding. In the case of strings, for example, specialist teachers for beginners in the Suzuki method (Suzuki, 1983) encourage preschool children to participate, especially because quarter- and half-size instruments are manufactured for tiny hands to hold. Only one of our sample had commenced learning at the age of 3 and she gave up after just one term. In spite of being taught the Suzuki method (specially designed for very young children), her mother insisted 'she was too young to understand that it takes time, she thought she would be able to pick it up and play straight away'. Two other children had tried learning a string instrument, again violin. A girl had played for 3 years since the age of 5 and gave up when starting the school band programme, despite clearly enjoying playing the violin. A boy, whose musical development we will examine in detail in a later chapter, had already discontinued violin lessons in favour of piano lessons, which he initially pursued alongside his school band programme. To play most brass and woodwind instruments children need to have the physical ability (and the teeth) to hold a correct embouchure and move the air through the instrument to produce a characteristic tone. They are unlikely to be successful until the age of 6 or 7.

There are potential benefits from the individual teaching methods that are typical of most studio practice. However, young children may find the interaction of one-to-one lessons confronting. Instrumental teaching programmes with a large-scale group focus like, for example, Suzuki and Kindermusik (http://www.kindermusik.com) build upon the security of group learning to develop general musical skills through singing, moving, dancing, playing, and listening, or to introduce specific instrumental skills like strings or piano. Frequently, such programmes demand parental involvement too. Similar approaches often form the basis of preschool and junior school music programmes, elementary recorder lessons, and even, as in our study, wind band projects that may or may not combine group and individual teaching. Whilst such programmes, like the ones we traced in Sydney, may expect some level of parental involvement, there are fewer opportunities for the kinds of collaboration around musical activities between teacher, parent, and student to support effective learning.

Group teaching makes considerable demands on teachers' abilities to meet individual needs appropriately. In domains like language or numeracy, the spread of developmental levels in any ordinary year group in schools may range as much as up to 7 years. Studies of literacy and attentive–inattentive behaviour in Australian schools suggest that this is probably true of the local context of our study too (Rowe & Rowe, 1999). The ability to match teaching to individual needs, as opposed to taking no account of the spread of achievement or capacities in any particular group, has become a key competency for effective classroom teaching. This differentiated approach is seen as essential to meet diverse needs in core subjects. Teaching and learning strategies are expected to develop the range of students across the developmental spectrum. Support and extension are key words for those students at either end of the developmental range in any specific domain. It is hard to imagine that any contemporary Western education system would accept that the teaching of numeracy or literacy should focus only on those that display a particular aptitude for it.

Music education may be lagging behind in this respect, especially in the school music we studied, where age and developmental appropriateness may be seen as synonymous. In addition, instrumental music teachers may be particularly ill-prepared for, and even suspicious of, group teaching methods, given that they are most likely to have been taught on a one-to-one basis themselves. In contrast to individual instrumental studio teaching, flexibility in schools may also be constricted by systemic curriculum and timetabling needs. Furthermore, teacher decisions may often be focused on what instruments are available for study, and particularly on which instruments need to be assigned in order to maintain a balanced instrumentation in the school's ensembles.

Data from our cohort reveal that 81 (52%) of the students had never learnt an instrument previously, 43 (27%) had learnt another instrument such as piano, but had already ceased instruction by the time they commenced their instrument in the school programmes, and 33 (21%) were continuing on a second instrument (94% piano) as well as their new school ensemble instrument. The majority of the students with former instrumental experience played either piano or electronic keyboard (86%), and a small number played strings (4%) or woodwind instruments (6%), while one student had received formal singing lessons. Very few (4%) had learned more than one other instrument, and for these students it was either recorder, another woodwind instrument such as the flute, or violin, as a second instrument to the piano.

Choice of instruments

Parents often held strong opinions about their child's engagement with music and the choice of instrument. Many were concerned about the speed of learning and commitment: in other words, investment for reward sentiments. Parents questioned whether one choice of instrument might be easier and result in faster competency than another. They often wanted to be confident their child would be able to continue learning the same instrument in high school and wondered about future opportunities to play with a good ensemble. In many cases parents were also concerned about the ongoing costs involved in learning. They worried about the expense of ongoing lessons, maintenance of an instrument, and the eventual cost of purchasing a quality instrument if the child chose to continue playing.

Children wanted to learn an instrument at school because they thought it would be fun, exciting, or enjoyable. For many children, systematic exposure to performances by their school ensembles was the catalyst for what Hidi and Renninger (2006) describe as 'triggered initial situational interest'. When asked to explain why they chose a particular instrument, a third of the children said that they liked the sound of the instrument, a finding that is consistent with a number of other studies (Delzell & Leppla, 1992; Fortney et al., 1993; O'Neill & Boulton, 1996). Choice of instrument was also influenced by perceptions about the physical appearance of the instrument, its size, ease of manipulation and transportation, whether friends were playing the same instrument, and whether it was considered 'easy' to play. More surprisingly, even the youngest children sometimes expressed concerns about the potential cost of buying an instrument, opportunities for future participation, and the nature of that participation in terms of potential musical genre and style.

Close friends powerfully and pervasively influenced children's 'triggered initial situational interest' in a particular musical instrument. This was observed a number of times at information events for children (accompanied by their parents) who were considering joining the music programme. The teachers described the instruments to the audience, and then asked the children to stand up and go to a section of the ensemble of their choice. Often the teacher would suggest that each child take a closer look at the instrument they most liked and asked the band members to demonstrate the instrument to them. Typically, children would get up in small friendship groups and move together to a section of the ensemble. Groups of girls would often walk over to the flutes or clarinets, and groups of boys to the trumpet or trombone sections of the ensemble. We know of at least one instance when this gender peer pressure directly overrode a girl's previously and strongly declared intention to learn the trumpet, an instrument that would have challenged such stereotypes.

Seventy-six per cent of the students participating in the school instrumental programmes started learning on the clarinet, trumpet, flute, or saxophone. Nineteen girls and eight boys started learning on the clarinet and a similar ratio of girls to boys started learning the flute (20:6). Girls and boys were almost equally represented on the trumpet and saxophone. In lower brass (e.g. baritone horn, trombone, and tuba), which accounted for 16% of total students in the study, boys outnumbered girls by a ratio of 4:1. Eight per cent of students started learning on drums, percussion, keyboard, or electric bass. Girls were represented in this group except for bass guitar, which only one student learnt.

The process of selecting an instrument for learning is an unmistakable example of Sameroff's (2010) concept of transactional regulation, which we introduced briefly in the previous chapter. We know that few children make decisions entirely autonomously at this age. Much more normally, as Sameroff suggests, they appear to be strongly influenced by some external regulation, in the form of direct control or command, or as more subtle psychological or environmental influence and pressure. Guidance or affirmation may come from a friend or peer group, or from a parent or teacher. Some of the young people we were studying were more directed than others: some followed and others tended to lead friends. However, peer influence was not always a contributing factor. Indeed, 20% of children in our study were offered no choice at all but were simply allocated an instrument by the teacher. In such cases, instruments were often allocated following aural perception testing or quick testing of children's ability to blow into various wind instruments or mouthpieces. One teacher explained:

> We basically do the same set-up every year. We invite all the Year 2s to do the aural test and then we get a result out of that and then the kids who get full marks for the rhythm section—we tend to recommend them to the percussion section. If they've done very well in the whole test, then we tend to recommend the harder instruments like the oboe or French horn, which are traditionally more difficult to begin with.

Blowing into several mouthpieces or instruments as a diagnostic test for assigning instruments seems to assume that children will have a natural ability to hold an instrument correctly and form good embouchure without any previous instruction. The following response to a question about the allocation of instruments illustrates this assumption:

> So basically I look at it from the way they form their embouchure and it's very much to how they pick an instrument up. You can tell—it's like a child picking up a cricket bat or a tennis racquet—you can tell that if they pick it up with their feet that they're not going to be able to do it. If they try to play the clarinet from the bell instead of the mouthpiece first go, you can tell that. You get an instinct for it, because I've been doing it for a long time.

A third of our participants made a choice following teacher advice, often informed by test results. It is important to highlight the overall influence of others in music learning decisions. From the onset of this key phase in children's musical lives, autonomy and the capacity to self-regulate learning become central issues for motivation. At opposite ends of a continuum are constructs of self-regulation and other regulation—the learner's or somebody else's choice about the terms of engagement. The idea that development in childhood is simply a linear process of moving from other to self-regulation has been challenged by the flexible and dynamic construct of transactional regulation (Sameroff, 2010). Sameroff acknowledges the negotiation of the transfer of regulatory responsibilities from caregivers, parents, and teachers to the child in general developmental terms. This may be a helpful model also for understanding children's development, interest, and motivation in music. In particular it may enable more sensitive theoretical modelling of the many and complex interactions that surround music learning and its regulation by others and by learners themselves.

Settling on an instrument

Among the music programmes we studied, fixing the choice of instrument from the start was common practice. We wondered whether learners could be given a number of opportunities to learn two or three differing instruments, in consultation with their teachers and parents, before choosing the one that they feel is most appropriate. Instrumental music programmes that recognize the need for careful negotiation for the learner to settle on a suitable musical instrument would place greater emphasis on a preliminary trial period like this. Even though such approaches are not uncommon in sports in schools, this type of sampling opportunity is not typical in most forms of music learning, and was not characteristic of any of the schools in which our study was undertaken.

Some students, however, did negotiate other ways of moving to another instrument in kinds of transactional regulation with parents and teachers. At least 10% of our young learners swapped instruments within the first couple of years of learning. Typically, this occurred during the transition from one year to the next, rather than within the year. The downside was that the student might then lag behind the peer group, and be downgraded to a lower status ensemble than their peers. For other students, learning an additional instrument meant that they progressed from learning the clarinet, for example, to adding a doubling instrument such as the saxophone, so that they could perform in different types of ensembles. This was, nevertheless, far less common and was only evident for students who had reached relatively high skill levels and who wanted to join jazz ensembles at high school several years later. Typically, adding another instrument demanded that parents were financially able to accommodate their child's desire to become more musically involved.

Significantly, students who swapped instruments during the first 2 years of learning were not typically those that had expressed serious unhappiness with the instrument originally selected for them. Students who were unhappy with their initial instruments almost invariably quit the programme within the first 2 years. These students did not try formal instrumental music lessons again during the period of the research study, whether at primary or high school. No student was converted to the teacher's cause, regardless of the quality of teaching that these learners received. Parents and students sometimes realized that teacher decisions about the allocation of instruments were motivated by the needs of the ensemble rather than the needs of individual students.

The ebb and flow—keeping the students learning

Apart from weekly band rehearsals and, in most cases, individual lessons, almost all of the schools held yearly music camps. Camps provided opportunities for the students to be involved in specialized activities over a few days, culminating in a final concert for their family and friends. In at least half of the schools there was strong parental involvement in music-related activities. Committees undertook volunteer activities to raise funds to purchase music and new instruments. Parents assisted through rotational systems with the supervision and organization of ensemble rehearsals. For example, one of the schools had a system where parents had to attend and assist at two rehearsals over the course of the school year, whilst others received relatively little support from the rest of the school or parents. Two-thirds of the schools participated in ensemble competitions and Eisteddfods, with two of them having distinguished records over many years, being placed among the highest achieving ensembles in the state.

There is a strong competitive Eisteddfod culture throughout Australian music education. Many schools in our study saw success in these competitions as important motivators for high-level ensemble performance. Success provided external validation of achievement and the musical capital acquired was highly valued by teachers, the wider school community, and the learners themselves. It is probably no coincidence that the schools who engaged with these competitive festivals were also likely to encourage students to follow formal examinations with their emphasis on technical proficiency and notation. In such schools, many of the students who were receiving individual lessons were also encouraged to take Australian Music Examinations Board (AMEB) grades, an externally assessed examinations system similar to the Associated Board and Trinity College examination systems based in the UK. These involve the performance of a repertoire of prepared pieces with piano accompaniment, technical exercises (i.e. scales, arpeggios), studies, and orchestral excerpts. As teachers commented:

> Oh yes. They must do them. We can't force them, but we strongly recommend it. With the brass, I start my kids on Third Grade—I don't worry about First or Second Grade.

> We do an audition at the end of each year, where they have to do—I base it on the AMEB. If you're in Concert Band 2, you have to do scales up to three sharps and flats— major and harmonic minors—a solo and a difficult sight-reading test. If they come in from Training Band, they only have to do the major scales up to three sharps and flats. Still that's not bad after 9 months.

Nevertheless, there were some strongly dissenting voices among music teachers about the importance of these examinations relative to the ensemble programme. One teacher claimed 'AMEB exams just don't fit into the picture'.

Within schools both classroom and specialist music teachers taught the students instruments and directed the ensembles. Most of the teachers had formal music and or teaching qualifications and considerable professional experience as musicians themselves. Some teachers were seen to be very strict with the students, while others much more relaxed, not least in terms of what they aimed to achieve with their ensemble programmes. Nevertheless, the status of the ensemble itself was often seen as a high priority, offering important cultural and social capital. Such kudos and the opportunities and privileges that accompanied it—concert appearances and trips—may be significant factors in triggering or maintaining interest and motivating students to practise (Hidi & Renninger, 2006). There could be a risk, however, that students' interests remain firmly in the situations—the events, festivals, competitions, tours, and accolade—rather than developing a personalized interest in music-making itself, in spite of the many hours of dedicated practice required to obtain a position in prestige bands. Such bands were often seen as affording high status and, even before they started learning themselves, some of our young learners, having heard them in performance, declared aspirations to play in them.

Practice: time, effort, and content

Previous research into musical performance has shown that a balance between the quantity and style of practice is essential if high-level musical skills are to be acquired.

Sloboda *et al.* (1996) quantified the duration of over 250 children's practical music activities, examining two kinds of individual practice. They distinguished between 'formal' practice (scales, pieces, and technical exercises set by the teacher) and 'informal' practice (playing not for specific teacher-set tasks). Overall, they found that there were large differences in the quantity of practice by students from different kinds of musical performance interest groups. Those who were high achievers undertook significantly greater amounts of 'formal' practice than the other study groups. The amount of time is similar to that reported by Ericsson *et al.* (1993), who collected retrospective data from professional violinists and found that they had accumulated approximately 10,000 hours of practice by the age of 20. Sloboda *et al.* (1996) examined cumulative 'formal' practice over the entire learning period and revealed that the high achievers had amassed approximately twice as much practice time as the children who achieved only moderate levels of musical performance success, four times as much as the children who persisted with lessons but who were not even moderate achievers, and up to eight times as much as that done by the students who gave up lessons. Crucially, high-achieving players also amassed significant quantities of informal practice, playing favourite tunes by ear or from music books, improvising with friends etc. This informal work distinguished the extremely high achievers from high achievers when hours of formal practice were often equivalent.

As part of our project, extensive video evidence about students' practice habits was also collected and analysed. Earlier papers provide keen insights into our learners' practice conditions and strategies (McPherson & Renwick, 2000; Pitts *et al.*, 2000). From early stages of the project, practice was often undertaken in the student's bedroom or the family lounge, usually after school or immediately before going to bed. Instrument cases regularly made impromptu music stands and posture was often inappropriate. Distractions were multiple and often bizarre—such as a young trumpet player who practised with his pet bird flying around the room and perching on his head!

The content of students' practice itself was highly standardized across schools, teachers, parents, and instruments. In all cases, students played through a small number of scales or other technical exercises, some simple solo repertoire, and selected band pieces, although not necessarily in that order. Interviews with the instrumental music teachers revealed that standard advice to our learners about practice was that it should consist of repeating pieces and exercises until a degree of fluency was reached. There is little evidence to suggest that 'fluency' here meant more than playing the right notes at the right time.

Analyses of the students' practice videos reveal that they typically had no practice strategies other than simply playing pieces through from start to finish (McPherson & Renwick, 2000; Pitts *et al.*, 2000). In fact, some 90% of practice time was spent playing through a piece or an exercise once before moving on to the next assigned work (McPherson & Renwick, 2000). At this early stage, if the play-through is the overwhelmingly dominant practice style, it could be a critical determinant of a lack of progress, as Sloboda *et al.* (1996) have suggested.

The play-through strategy had little or nothing to do with 'play' in itself. From the videos of the students' home practice, it was extremely rare to observe children experimenting with their piece or monitoring expression—a theme to which we return later. Indeed, the dominance of notation-based learning appeared to exclude other forms of music performance almost entirely. With the exception of a programme that included some work on improvisation (12-bar blues) as part of its warm-ups, nearly all teachers seemed to think that from notation or learning scales and technical exercises of practice, progress, and achievement.

At the time of commencing their instrument, students were encouraged by their instrumental tutors to practise about five times a week, for about 20 minutes for each practice session. Individual daily practice averages ranged from no practice up to 30 or more minutes every day, with a typical description reported by the mother as: 'Fifteen minutes four times a week'. The students averaged 7.5 minutes average daily practice across their first nine months of learning although there were wide differences among the sample. After 1 month of learning they were typically practising 4.5 days a week for about 15 minutes each session. By the end of their third month of learning the students averaged 3.5 days of practice per week in sessions that averaged 16 minutes. Nine months after commencing they were averaging 3 days per week in sessions that lasted approximately 17 minutes. Overall, most of the students were doing between 15 and 20 minutes of practice per session, and the number of days each week that they practised decreased over the first year.

Typically the young learners all engaged in twice-weekly instrumental sessions in school—normally a band rehearsal and an instrumental lesson (either one-to-one or small group). These sessions were either before or during school activities. Band lasted normally for 1–2 hours, small group lessons from 30 minutes to 1 hour, and one-to-one lessons around 30 minutes. Again, despite some differences in conductor style, the content of the band practice was generally consistent, as would be expected of the 'band method book': playing through sections of music with some small, phrase level repetition and intensive rehearsal, plus brief comments made by the conductor about the coordination of timing and dynamics. Even where some improvisatory activities were included, their status as warm-up activities diminished their musical and educational value to the players. There is no evidence that any of the programmes differed in terms of overall content. Nevertheless, this is not to say that group rehearsals were all the same. Transactions, expectations, and ethos varied considerably in ways that had direct impact on learners' levels of motivation. Nevertheless, our results from patterns of individual practice—viewed from the mothers' and children's perspectives—suggest that individual practice in itself was viewed as a critically important variable.

Most of the instrumental practice research cited in these opening two chapters focused on the practice either of people who went on to become professional musicians or children who attended specialist music schools. In such cases there is a high level of motivation and interest. In examining a large and widely representative sample like our own, we hoped to glean insights into how early practice promotes or puts at risk the kind of interest and motivation that might support development and even lead to high levels of musical expertise. Hallam (1997) alerts us to the Oxford Dictionary definition of the word 'practice' as 'a repeated exercise in an activity requiring the development of skill' (Hallam, 1997, p. 180). As Hallam explains, this limited use of the word 'practice', stressing the repetitive aspect of training, is far from suited to music:

> Musical practice is multi-faceted. The musician not only needs to consider the development of technical skills but must also develop musical interpretation, may have to play from memory, perform in co-operation with other musicians and contend with stage fright. These elements require technical, cognitive and performance skills. These complex skills cannot be acquired, improved and maintained by repetition alone. (Hallam, 1997, p. 180)

Hallam (1997) compared beginner and expert performers' practice with regard to their approaches to interpretation, practice, memorization, and performance. She revealed that beginners' (aged between 6 and 18) practice did not engage in any activity that could be interpreted as indicating that they were considering interpretation. Very few (8%) of the players in Hallam's study made any identifiable attempt to observe the dynamic markings and none seemed to be concerned about other musical aspects of performance and practice. The aim of practice appeared to be restricted to playing the music correctly.

Generally speaking, our study supports Hallam's (1997) findings. However, there is a sense in which many students in our study could not even be said to have aimed to play the music correctly. Instead, we would argue that the aim for a significant number of students was to give the appearance of practice. They would play through the piece once and, however unsuccessful they may have been, tick the box and move on to the next piece, exercise, or a different activity altogether. They had acquiesced to the idea that practice was something to be 'done' because it was good for them. Data from our videos of early practice sessions, learner accounts of practice strategies, and parents' comments support this view of common practice behaviour. Parents were often heard shouting from another room, advising the children to, 'Just keep going for another five minutes and then your practice will be done.' We were struck by an analogy that 'as long as you keep taking the medicine, you'll get better' or that 'the pain will be over in a few minutes'.

Treating practice in this way is an attitude unwittingly perpetuated by teachers and parents, and one that fails to connect with children's intrinsic motivation or to provide them with goals that are attainable. Practising, especially alone, becomes a condition upon which they are permitted to keep their instrument, remain in the ensemble, call themselves a musician. Practice is not expected to be pleasurable and, as a result, it rarely is pleasurable.

It is evident that whatever the shortcomings of the home practice we observed, regular practice is essential for children to make good musical progress. Studies of how parents help their children at home through encouragement and support were lacking when we first started the research in 1997. This was in contrast to an emerging body of literature available in educational and developmental psychology that detailed how parents influence their children's achievement. Creech and Hallam (2003) have since discussed the dynamic relationship between the parent, teacher, and student. These researchers proposed a model to examine these interactions from the perspective of a systems approach. Their model provides a framework for understanding certain types of human behaviour and communication between teachers, parents, and students that work together in the context of instrumental music lessons. Our approach was to examine the complementary literature on how parents help their children with homework and other areas of learning such as sports and consider whether any of that research evidence could be helpful in framing the interpretation of our data.

We now know that students are motivated to devote more time to completing their homework and are most effective with their self-directed learning when they do not experience negative emotions while engaged in it (Trautwein & Koller, 2003; Trautwein *et al.*, 2009a). Trautwein and his colleagues (Trautwein & Koller, 2003; Trautwein *et al.*, 2006a,b; Marsh *et al.*, 2007; Trautwein & Lüdtke, 2007; Tsai *et al.*, 2008; Trautwein *et al.*, 2009a,b) have undertaken extensive research on homework and many of their findings and interpretations seem directly applicable to furthering our understanding of young learners' music practice habits and ongoing commitment. Trautwein *et al.* (2006a,b) refer to research by Cooper, who has suggested that 'homework probably involves the complex interaction of more influences than any other instructional device' (Trautwein *et al.*, 2006b, p. 89). In Cooper's view the homework process includes six key factors: given factors, assignment characteristics, initial classroom facilitators, home-community factors, classroom follow-up, and outcome effects.

In our view, music practice contains identical or corresponding factors that may be even more complex than routine homework. First, interactive processes around music practice may be more complicated because values and beliefs towards music tend to be far more controversial than, say, those towards literacy and numeracy in primary school settings. Second, some parents reported feelings of total incompetency around music learning from the outset of the programme and were unable to provide any form of support for their children. Other parents felt a growing sense of frustration about their own limited musical confidence or skills just as their children began to run into instrumental and music learning difficulties themselves. Third, relationships with and between individual instrumental teachers, band directors, general class teachers, peers, parents, and pupils have the potential to configure extremely complex networks with contested expectations.

Analysis of our learners' practice videos shows that during the first 9 months of the study parents were in close proximity about 65% of the time when their child was practising, and that 81% of this time was spent listening, 12% guiding (e.g. asking what piece the child would play next), and only 6% in an active teaching role (1% of the time was spent distracting the child from his/her practice). Nevertheless we have found that unpacking the range of potential dynamics that constitute the emotional climate around music practice involves many factors. The emotional climate related to distinctions between parental proximity and distance, encouragement and enforcement, reward and punishment, support and supervision, interference and apathy, complaints and compliments, listening, valuing, and enjoying. The dimensions of many instrumental practice sessions are, we suggest, a good deal more complex than, say, the completion of a mathematical problem or comprehension exercise. Tasks like the solving of a mathematical problem or the identification of a synonym in a text are more self-contained and clearly defined than many of the open-ended, relatively long-term assignments that regularly make up instrumental practice.

Practice and performance strategies and measures

A large part of our research between 1997 and 2001 focused on trying to understand how, and in which ways, students developed skill on their instrument. Two key issues concerned us: what type of musical skills needed to be acquired for students to have successful or personally satisfying experiences learning their instrument, and how did students acquire these skills. We examined practice habits, the range of developing cognitive abilities and mental strategies, and assessed learners' abilities and progress across a range of music skills. In doing so, we gained insights into issues identified previously and also identified new themes.

We examined students' practice through direct observation of video footage. Recordings were made in the students' homes at 4–6-week intervals, usually by the parents. Students were encouraged to have as 'normal' a practice session as possible while they were being recorded. Inevitably, some were more easily distracted by the video camera than others. However, the practice strategies employed, even when the students were aware they were being observed, reveal much about the way these students work. Our insights have implications for instrumental teaching and learning.

Three students were selected for case study because each displayed relatively consistent practice behaviour over the time they were being recorded, establishing a personal routine within which changes in attitude and motivation can be detected. Whilst the data generated cannot give a complete picture of practising strategies used by this age group, there are implications for teachers, parents, and pupils.

Case study 1: David, trumpeter, male, aged 10

David, a young trumpeter, is the most independent of the learners considered here. He begins his first practice session sitting on the floor in his pyjamas, with his music propped up on the floor in front of him. David's mother is in the room, and he says, 'So what shall I play?', before starting with technical exercises, in which he plays repeated notes, counting aloud the rests between them. He plays one short piece after another, making no attempt at self-correction, and stopping to chat with his mum occasionally. After about 10 minutes, David is distracted by a sticky valve on his trumpet, and spends some time oiling the key, explaining the process as he does it. When David has finished oiling the valves, he continues playing for a few more minutes, but the sound is poor and his first finger often ends up on the second valve as he pauses to think between each note. He stops again to fiddle with the mouthpiece, and begins to pack away, chatting all the while. This has been a long first session, in which David has demonstrated considerable pleasure in the instrument he has just acquired, succeeding in playing through a number of pieces, if not very fluently.

In his second observed session, a couple of weeks later, David sits comfortably on a chair, with the music on another chair in front of him. He displays greater confidence, announcing the titles of pieces and playing them through, although without any strategies for self-correction. He still chats to his parents between pieces, but is playing for longer periods, with considerable levels of concentration. David is aware of difficulties to the extent that one piece causes him to struggle, shrug, and say 'That's all I know of number 22'. Having recognized failure at that point, he looks rather dispirited and begins to oil his trumpet again, very messily. David is surely displaying classic avoidance strategies, renouncing all responsibility for his learning to his teacher, and becoming preoccupied with the maintenance of his instrument to demonstrate a skill that he has only recently acquired and with seeming confidence. David begins playing again after a few minutes, returning to an earlier piece despite saying, 'I've got oil all over my hands'. He is now pressing the valves with the wrong hand, wriggling in his chair, and making a dismal sound. The second session disintegrates as he packs up with a disgusted expression.

An observation of David 3 months later shows a cheerful, independent practice session. His parents have left him alone in a different room, accompanied only by the video camera and his pet bird. He plays more fluently and confidently, although not expressively. He continues to announce titles and play through pieces, occasionally re-starting or repeating large sections. From the earliest sessions, where his mental strategies limited him to considering each note before he played it, he is now processing several notes, even phrases (although there is no attempt at phrasing) and counting rests. The distractions are plentiful, as after around 10 minutes the bird begins flying around the room, a fact David ignores until intervals between pieces. At these points, he looks around the room to find the bird, and once calls, 'Stay in one place, or I'll ground you for a day'. He clearly likes an audience, saying 'Did you like that?', and then to the camera, 'My bird loves music'.

David hums to himself as he changes his music books around, then finds his warm-up tune; 'I should have played this ages ago'. Neither the water bubbling in his trumpet nor the progress of his bird around the room are excuses to stop work. Even when the bird lands on his head, singing loudly, David continues playing, although he is struggling with a more difficult piece and meeting with little success. Shaking the bird off his head at the end of the piece, he returns to an earlier tune, but he is running out of energy after playing for approximately 35 minutes, and the session is ended as his father comes in to ask if he has finished.

In spite of the remarkable persistence that David shows here and a relatively long practice session when compared to the average of other learners, progress during the session is negligible. Even after 3 months of learning he possesses few helpful practising strategies and never stops playing before he has completed a 'performance'. This idea of practising to an audience is not encouraging him to develop new approaches, as, in his search for fluency he relies on playing pieces through, rather than working on short sections. This is a problem that can be unwittingly reinforced by parents, who will typically praise recognizable melodies that make easier listening, rather than detailed working. Whilst it could be the case that the camera has had some impacts on this 'performance' mentality, other evidence suggests that this is not an atypical practice routine for him. More guidance on effective use of his long practice sessions might sustain his enthusiasm and development.

Case study 2: Maureen, saxophonist, female, aged 10

Maureen is more aware of the camera's presence than David in the previous case study. She pulls faces into it and even waves at the end of her first practice session.

Each session begins with her getting her saxophone and music out of their cases, a process that becomes increasingly protracted over the several months of sessions observed. Maureen's practice usually begins with scales, which are played through without correction, despite a struggle with the high notes, lack of fluency, and poor intonation. The second session introduces what is meant to be a minor scale, which is played inaccurately and improves little over the next few weeks. Scales are clearly a focus of the girl's lessons and something that her mother is aware of when she checks her practice at the end of each session. The exchange between mother and daughter at the end of the second session is revealing:

Mother: Have you done your new scale?
Maureen: Yes.
Mother: Have you done it twice?

Maureen: Yes.
Mother: And you've done all your pieces?
Maureen: Yes—twice.

Throughout this conversation, Maureen has been shuffling uncomfortably with her back to the camera. Her behaviour is not surprising as her description of her practice bears little resemblance to the reality. She has been taught (as has her mother) some superficial strategies for effective practice—starting with scales and playing things twice. However, Maureen seems to have little understanding of why these strategies could be effective, using them instead to fill in time on a task she obviously sees as a chore. Her practice tends to be disjointed and laborious. Although the length of time spent practising increases over the sessions observed, much of the increase is due to time-wasting behaviour.

Maureen's pieces also receive cursory treatment, although there are moments of intense concentration and fluency. Sometimes she announces the title of the piece, although in the case of 'Good King Wenceslas' (in May) she adds, 'I hate that one'. It is rare for the girl to go back over her pieces to identify and correct any problems. In the fourth session she plays 'Yankee Doodle' repeatedly, but its fluency decreases and she makes no attempt to rectify this. Her cognitive strategies for processing the music are limited, although she makes increasing use of singing and fingering each piece before she plays it. Singing is an important feature of her practice sessions. After playing a piece in the second session, Maureen begins to sing more fluently than she is able to play it, moving her saxophone with a jazzy swing and pretending to play at the same time. She appears to take pleasure from this and it seems that her image of playing the saxophone is conflicting with the immediate difficulties of making a sound and reading notation. This adds to her frustration with the task of practising.

As well as singing to herself, Maureen talks between pieces, with comments to the camera such as, 'Why do I have to do this stupid stuff?' Her exchanges with her mother support these private comments and at the end of her second session there is a brief conversation about the pieces being 'really boring'. Although the mother sounds surprised, she decides not to pursue the subject. The mother's role in Maureen's practice is significant, not least because it shows that the disrespectful speech Maureen shows to the camera is not moderated, or checked, when she speaks to her mother. From the first session, the mother is established as a monitor of practice: she leaves the room, but is within calling distance when Maureen shouts, 'Mum, do I have to keep playing?' The answer, 'Yes, a bit more', is followed by some repetition of earlier pieces and a good deal of shuffling; quantity of practice is apparently being mistaken for quality. A few minutes later, the following exchange ends the session:

Maureen: Now have I done enough, Mum?
Mother: Well do you think you've done enough?
Maureen: Yes, I think I'm pretty good at it.
Mother: Okay, that was great.

More effusive praise comes at the end of the third session, when after some dispute about the unsuccessful use of a backing-track tape, the mother says 'Well it sounded great—I couldn't believe it'. Although both parents play the piano, Maureen has evidently established a position as a musical 'expert' in the family, and uses the paraphernalia of changing reeds, selecting music, and packing her instrument away to reinforce the 'superiority' of her knowledge.

Over the sessions observed, Maureen's fingering and notation-reading skills show some signs of improvement, but her playing overall becomes no more musical or fluent. She is clearly practising under duress. Although her parents are supportive, their exaggerated praise and attempts at monitoring do little to lift the gloomy mood that pervades the practice sessions. It is not surprising to learn that Maureen stopped playing the saxophone after 2 years. Whilst she employs a number of potentially helpful strategies in her practice, such as singing and fingering before playing, she does these with such reluctance that the experience of practising becomes increasingly arduous. Maureen is apparently following the instructions of her teacher, in starting her practice with scales, for example, and reluctantly accepts the length of session that is controlled by her mother. Intrinsic motivation, however, seems to be entirely lacking, and positive feedback comes from the mother, rather than any self-awareness of successful, if rare, playing.

There are methodological difficulties in having any observer present for what is usually a private activity, but this case reveals much about the girl's general attitude: the camera appears to be an authority figure to her, against which she wants to rebel, in the same way she challenges her parents in some of the observed exchanges. Her negative comments about the music she is playing need to be taken in this context, but her frustration with the instrument comes across in her actions as well as her speech. It is possible that her concentration would have been poor without the distraction of the recording. On the other hand, it may be that the presence of an observer, albeit an inanimate one, kept her on task longer than might otherwise have been the case.

Case study 3: Julia, flautist, female, aged 9

Julia illustrates even more clearly than the other two that personality and environment are significant factors in students' approaches to practice. Julia is unusual in that she uses a music stand rather than propping up her music on the case. She does her practice first on a small chair, then a larger one, and then the larger one with her feet propped on telephone directories. This is indicative of the importance that practice sessions appear to have for the whole family: Julia herself is unsmiling. Everything is done with great deliberation, so that preparing to play can take anything up to 10 minutes. She is not a 'time filler' in the same way as the saxophonist. Every movement is protracted, and the resulting discontinuity when she plays indicates that her practice is unrewarding. In her early sessions, Julia is struggling at the most basic level, looking intently at the music and often removing the flute from her lips to check where her fingers should go. She displays no outward signs of frustration; it is her father who yawns from behind the video camera and says, 'What are you doing now?' as she changes books and prepares to continue.

Julia's parents become increasingly involved in her practice, with the father beginning the second session with a reminder about posture, and the mother intervening in the third session to offer help when she is struggling. They have been present from the beginning, however, with the first video including an argument between the parents about what instructions they had been given and whether the father's videoing technique was adequate. This is clearly a high-pressure household and Julia's incredible passivity in the face of repeated failure adds to a sombre atmosphere. The parents adopt a variety of teaching roles, with the father refusing, or unable, to intervene when the music stand is still a bent-metal sculpture after 5 minutes of struggling, merely saying, 'Well it didn't work that way, so fold it up and try another one'. The mother, on the other hand, takes the first opportunity to give assistance:

Julia: No, that's wrong.
Mother: Well you still don't know where your notes are, with your fingers. Is that the problem?
Julia: It's just that D is quite hard.
Mother: Well look here, you came down like a scale, and then you did the same note three times, and then you just had to go up again.

[Julia shuffles]
Mother: So what page are you up to now?
[They look for the music together]

Several months later, Julia still seems to be getting little pleasure from her practice, and the same slow and serious approach is evident. Practising has clearly become a night-time ritual, with Julia sitting in her pyjamas in the lounge, presumably before going to bed. She is still looking at her fingers and peering at the music, relying on visual memory rather than doing any aural evaluation of the sounds she hears. Despite the presence of her father there is no discussion, and even when she announces, 'That's all of my practice', he only says, 'Okay, good girl. You can pack up then', continuing to video the lengthy process as she puts her flute away. She seems to be deriving little pleasure from playing: it is another task to be accomplished, rather than an activity with any real enjoyment. Unlike the saxophonist, she is not obviously resentful of her new task, but accepts it passively, submitting to the pressure with which her parents are surrounding her practice sessions. Over the observed sessions, Julia makes very little progress. Despite the quantities of time she spends with her flute, not much real practice takes place.

In musical and cognitive terms, the students in these video case studies displayed few significant changes over time. However, those who began with very hesitant note-level processing became slightly more fluent and able to process longer phrases as their familiarity with their instrument and notation grew. Their practising strategies were negligible, supporting established findings (Gruson, 1988; Hallam, 1997) that the majority of children play pieces through without any attempt at self-correction, rather than identifying difficult sections and working on those. The children we observed did not seem to have a sense of why they were playing through their repertoire, although all had good recollection of what they had been asked to do. They were sometimes aware that a particular piece had not gone very well, but were only conscious of difficulties when they struggled or stopped, rarely picking out small-scale or even global errors such as inaccurate rhythm or pitch, poor tuning, or unpleasant tone.

In contrast to advanced or expert players (Ericsson, 1997; Nielsen, 1997), young beginners seem either to ignore the auditory feedback from their playing, persisting despite unrewarding results, or to become discouraged when their efforts appeared to be getting them nowhere. Either way, they do not appear to have the strategies to identify and correct problems that arise. Teachers, it seems, have an important role to play in fostering skills of self-criticism and evaluation. More worryingly, it is hard to detect in any of these visual diaries, or in the vast majority of the practice diaries we analysed, anything that indicated that music learners were regularly engaged in meaningful musical activity. On the contrary, the disconnection between the practice and the purpose of music at personal, expressive, and communicative levels, so evident in participants' other everyday musical experiences, seems unlikely to encourage investment or commitment for future formal music learning.

Applying Trautwein's model of homework to music practice

Trautwein *et al.*'s (2006a,b) model cited earlier may be helpful in attempting to understand the complex interactions around music practice that these case studies illustrate.

We now attempt an application of the model for this purpose. In our adapted model (Figure 2.1), student, teacher, and parental characteristics, expectations, and values interact to configure practice behaviours and, in turn, produce different musical outcomes. Expectancy value—a function of the value of the goal to which actions are directed and expectations about achieving them—and self-determination motivational theories that account for the extent to which actions are self-motivated and regulated, can be seen as coinciding in a parallel motion with theories of learning and instruction to provide the theoretical framework underpinning the flow of influences in the model.

Teacher's aspirations for pupils often emerged during the first term of study and sometimes within a few lessons. The group/band and individual music teachers in our study all assigned their students specific repertoire and technical work to learn each week, but each had different goals and aspirations for their students. In some cases children were quickly categorized as potential high achievers and others as unmusical, whilst a couple of teachers insisted on keeping a much more open mind:

> I try not to presuppose their ability and assume they have so much potential and this is all they're going to ever achieve. All of a sudden a child will just go through something in their life and they'll just turn around. Something good will happen to them or something bad will happen to them—I think it's just really open.

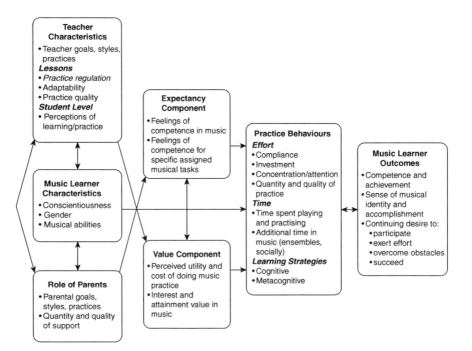

Figure 2.1: Schematic depiction of practice process factors. Adapted from (Trautwein et al., 2006b).

Sometimes pupils formed clear ideas about their teacher's views of their musical potential from the very first lesson. Where pupils were categorized as potential high achievers or as having little potential, there is evidence that these expectations impacted on the quality and quantity of practice routines that teachers' recommended each time they worked with their students.

In the general homework literature, students in classes where teachers assign higher amounts of meaningful homework tend to learn more, but there are also important differences among students within any class that also need to be taken into account (Trautwein *et al.*, 2006b). For this reason much of the homework literature, as with much of the expertise literature in music and other domains, has focused on time spent doing the activity and its relationship with achievement. The relationship, however, is complex, and more sophisticated models are needed to understand the relationship between time spent and time needed to learn each newly assigned task. In music as with other learning activities, a multitude of distractions can have a detrimental effect on students' behaviour so the total time spent practising does not necessarily predict future achievement. In the homework literature, as well as in our study, some students reported consistent and substantial amounts of practice, but these students were not always the most conscientious. Some, for example, wasted much of their time because of problems of motivation or concentration. David, the trumpeter case study cited above, illustrates this dilemma. Relatively large amounts of 'practice' time turn out to be a poor predictor for short-term progress or achievement.

According to Trautwein *et al.* (2006a,b), 'At the class level, a higher number of homework tasks . . . and higher homework frequency. . . have proved to be associated with higher achievement gains, but more time spent on homework has not' (Trautwein *et al.*, 2006b, p. 439). This may have important implications for the kind of tasks that are set for instrumental practice too, especially when, as was often the case in our study, a limited number of pieces were frequently set over long periods of time because of the demands of preparing an ambitious repertoire to a high standard for concerts and Eisteddfods. At the other end of the scale, however, early practice regimes seemed to have too many tasks, or at least too many of the same kind of task—normally playing through (once each) a large number of tunes.

Thus, the left-hand columns in our modified version of Trautwein's homework model (see Figure 2.1) list some of the more important relationships between what each teacher aspires to teach his or her students, what styles of teaching she or he will adopt, and the behaviours or practices she or he will implement during each lesson, especially in terms of the quantity and quality of practice assignments and directions given to students.

Students also differ in many personal qualities and psychological traits, including their conscientiousness and their overall musical abilities. Their parents, like the teachers, exhibit goals, styles, and practices that impact on the quantity and quality of support they give to their child's musical learning. Trautwein (2006a,b) draws out conscientiousness from the other 'big five' personality traits (extraversion, neuroticism, openness to experience, and agreeableness) to develop a strong theoretical basis for defining the homework behaviour of students. Our belief also is that this trait, involving elements of self-discipline, carefulness, organization, and deliberate intention, is an important way of understanding why some of the students in our sample tended to work hard to develop their instrumental skills while others were more 'laid back', less goal oriented, and less driven.

There is a contradiction here though: whilst conscientiousness may enable individuals to develop high skill levels, it is clear that other traits (extraversion, neuroticism, openness to experience) are extremely important for the development of the ability to creatively and expressively apply those skills in personally meaningful ways that sustain motivation and that are essential, for example, to expressive high-level performance. This balance between 'conscientiousness', which in turn predicts deliberate and systematic practice, and 'openness to experience', which predicts creative and expressive experimentation, turns out to be a key dynamic in our participants' musical lives to which we will return later in this book.

A recent analysis of our early data suggests that there is also a link in our study between gender and conscientiousness: girls are more likely than boys to carry on with instrumental studies even though they are not enjoying them (Faulkner et al., 2010). This finding leads us to speculate whether there might be a tendency for young girls to be more influenced than young boys by their parents' or teachers' goals and views about music learning.

Linked to these gendered responses to 'enjoyable' versus 'boring' activities is the value that is ascribed to music as an optional leisure and recreation activity versus its perceived value as an important and useful one. So, whilst parents and learners did value music as an important and useful activity, views of its importance were heavily weighted towards music's potential as a recreational activity. Such a view may make it difficult for parents to see virtue in their children's musical engagement for long periods of time when this engagement is maintained by a sense of duty and obligation alone, rather than by enjoyment.

Transactional regulation of practice

Good teachers carefully choose appropriate learning tasks for their students, diagnose their students' learning and monitor the difficulties they encounter along the way, and provide remedial instruction to help their students (Weinert, 1995). However, this does not necessarily mean that teachers or parents are most effective when they exert too much control on a child's learning. This is where Sameroff and Fiese's (2000) model of transactional regulation is helpful. Controlling environments, such as when teachers set strict practice schedules for their students or when parents are over involved, have been shown to undermine students' feelings of autonomy and competence (Deci & Ryan, 2002). As a result, students may become compliant, invest less energy, concentration, and attention during their practice, and feel less motivated to continue their learning.

A transactional regulation model provides a sophisticated way of understanding effective interaction around practice. A recent decision tree generated from a data-mining analysis of our data illustrates the point (Faulkner, et al., 2010). Counter-intuitively, the model predicts that students in our study who continued into the second year did not practise at the same time every day—a habit that is often anecdotally positively associated with a conscientious approach to instrumental practice. We interpret this to mean that children practising at the same time of day were often doing so under parental or teacher regulation (such as reminders and external encouragement or even coercion), rather than their own internalized self-regulation.

In the same analysis, children's reporting of parental use of rewards to encourage practice was similarly predictive of shorter-term engagement than those students who reported that parents did not use rewards. Regular parental reminders in the first year of study, on the other hand, emerges as one of the strongest predictors for students continuing study into the second year. This could be interpreted as parents not only supporting their child's desire to continue learning—the kind of autonomy support of which Pomerantz and her colleagues speak (Pomerantz *et al.*, 2005)—but also as reflecting parents' own desires for their child to learn music. One parent in our study who gave regular reminders to practise was motivated by the desire that their child should learn:

> to enjoy [it] and feel the benefits of music. It will add beauty to his life and be a source of relaxation, and a point of social contact.

Such views create an emotional climate within the home that enhances perceptions of the usefulness and importance of learning music. In the case of this parent, as we will see later, these kinds of views do seem to support long-term engagement.

Interviews with music teachers, with evidence from practice observation, reveal how some teachers were conscientious and deliberate with the type of repertoire and exercises they assigned to their students, in ways consistent with Trautwein's (Trautwein *et al.*, 2006a) model of good practice. Some teachers drew on a range of examples from various publications to meet each student's learning needs, particularly when they were having problems or needed to be challenged. This is in contrast to other teachers who focused on one method book at a time, and where within-student differences seemed to be less catered for, if at all, within the learning cycle.

Overall, students in the schools who were given tailored repertoire to learn did seem, as a group, to exert more effort into their practice. Nevertheless, the highly teacher-regulated environment, however well intentioned, left some of the children feeling pressured by the continual demands for improvement. There is a sense that high-quality practice assignments were those that had been well prepared by the teacher in consultation with the student. Well-prepared assignments include material that students find intellectually and emotionally satisfying. These assignments vary in difficulty. Students are clear about why they are being assigned tasks and how the tasks aid their progress. In other words, these assignments balanced high levels of transregulation because they were carefully negotiated between teacher and learner, and of self-determination because learners retained a strong sense of autonomy. In addition, a reasonable percentage of tasks had to be manageable in relatively short timeframes. Repeated setting of the same task over a long timeframe was often detrimental to highquality practice. However, benefits accrue when the teacher explains the aims of practice assignments or pieces that are about to be learned in the ensemble and activates student autonomy. Explanations of practice aims enhance the students' sense of control of their own learning, encourage the formation of goals for themselves and their ensemble, and increase understanding of the learning process.

Whilst relationships between practice time and achievement need the kind of extensive qualification attempted above and cannot be interpreted simplistically as 'more is best', the relationship between effort and achievement in learning is less complicated in its positive association (Trautwein & Lüdtke, 2007). There is not always a relationship between effort and time. In our study, as in others (McPherson, 1993), students who had little time to practise every day often seemed to practise at levels of high concentration. These students were often engaged in many and various activities in and out of school. Our findings suggest, however, that the adage 'more is better' is still probably true in the very early stages of learning when students struggle to master a new instrument. As capabilities increase, within-student differences probably become more pronounced, such that some students—particularly those with highly developed self-regulatory skills—might be better able to achieve more in less time than it takes other students. As we will see in the next section, this might simply be because these students are able to put more effort into the limited time they had available to practice, with the result that their practice is more efficient.

Learner autonomy and choice in practice

Our discussion opens up an important question that drives much of the literature in educational psychology: why would one student exert more effort, attention, and concentration than another student during a practice session or over longer periods of time? In addition to conscientiousness traits, another possible answer, hinted at above in discussion about the setting of practice tasks and repertoire, was found in a case study we undertook with a 12-year-old clarinettist. Clarissa was practising pieces that had been assigned to her by her teacher and a piece that she had asked her teacher to learn (Renwick & McPherson, 2000; McPherson & Renwick, 2011). In one practice session Clarissa spent on average 1 second practising per note in the score for her teacher-assigned repertoire. With the piece that she wanted to learn, this increased to 10 seconds per note: an 11-fold increase. A number of other important differences were also observed: when playing teacher-assigned repertoire, Clarissa practised almost exclusively using her 'default' play-through approach, by correcting errors on route as she worked her way through the piece. In contrast to her efforts on the teacher-assigned repertoire, Clarissa's self-regulatory approach to the work she wished to learn scaffolded her to the types of behaviours that Gruson (1988), Miklaszewski (1989), and Nielsen (1999) suggest typify the deliberate practice strategies employed by experts. Clarissa increased her use of silent fingering and silent thinking. She sang phrases, deliberately altered the tempo when repeating sections, and practised longer sections.

Clarissa might have engaged in such high-level practice on the self-selected repertoire because of two critical aspects: her will more generally to improve her playing and her determination to fully master this specific piece. This is in contrast to her practise of the teacher-assigned pieces where she demonstrated some commitment to improving her playing, but less focus and determination to master each piece she was practising. Close examination of the videotaped practice sessions shows that this focus in concentration and determination to master the self-selected piece was critical in propelling her to a more sophisticated level of self-regulation (De Bruin, Rikers, & Schmidt, 2007).

The significance attached to personal autonomy over repertoire is consistent with findings from other disciplines. Research shows that allowing students choice about what to work on and which method to use can increase intrinsic motivation and task involvement (Pintrich & Schunk, 1996; Stipek, 1998). Whilst the example of the clarinettist above was not unique in our study, derogative comments about 'boring' repertoire from students and parents were common, especially after initial situational interest had waned. Music teachers may need to offer students choices between materials and methods, not to mention instruments, if a personal interest in music is the aim of learning.

From our study, a key component of effective instrumental music teaching appears to be the sensitive and flexible negotiation of transpersonal regulation to develop individual interest and musical autonomy as the basis for sustainable musical development. The strategy for doing so may be found in appropriate teacher support for self-regulation at every opportunity, in every lesson—from playing the correct notes, monitoring tone and expression, to the choice of instrument and repertoire.

High levels of interest, and increased effort, attention, and concentration, come, as Trautwein and Lüdtke (2007, p. 433) suggest, because of the learner's expectations for, and valuing of, the activity. Expectations help us understand the learner's belief about being able to reach personal or teacher goals for what is being learned. Valuing, on the other hand, involves understanding the importance that the learner places on doing well at the activity and meeting personal goals. Is it intrinsically enjoyable? Will it be satisfying now and in the future? Alternatively, might the learner feel that the challenge required to master the material is not worth the effort or that learning is too stressful?

Research about homework indicates a relationship between these expectancy value components of learning and the effort that students put into their learning while studying, but not between expectancy values and time devoted to studying and doing homework. It appears that children from homes where musical engagement, even everyday practice routines, were viewed as meaningful—regardless of parents' musical abilities—were much more likely to value the activity and have higher expectations of their ability to tackle musical challenges than children from homes where this was not the case. As Trautwein and Lüdtke (2007) explain:

> . . . drawing on self-determination theory and empirical findings, the homework model predicts that parent–child communication and parental valuation of school subjects are positively related to homework effort, whereas the quantity of direct parental engagement in the homework process is unrelated or negatively related to homework effort. (p. 433)

Our data about learners' early practice strategies also point to a counter-intuitive hypothesis. Levels of parental supervision or pupil practice time in themselves are not associated with high-level outcomes and progress. Instead, first, it seems that it is the quality of these phenomena, when defined as how parents, learners, and teachers value the activity and what expectations they have for engagement and achievement that matters. Second, it appears that it is how learners spend their time practising, rather than how much time they spend practising, that is associated with higher levels of achievement. The adaptation of Trautwein's model appears, at this stage of our study at least, to be a helpful framework for thinking about our learners' practice, engagement, and musical development thus far.

The extent to which the young instrumental music learners in our study had the capacity to engage in the self-regulative processes that unsupervised home practice demanded is controversial. In the following chapters we will examine this 'self-regulative crisis'. Table 2.1 illustrates the dimensions of musical self-regulation from typical self-regulation theory perspectives. In it, socialization processes are seen as essential prerequisites to self-regulative ones. It is these socialization processes in musical engagement that come under the spotlight in our study. Single dimensional linear views of this developmental pathway help researchers focus on particular attributes and how they might develop over time but do not provide a complete picture of the many varied ways in which these typically interact. This is where Sameroff's model of transactional regulation may provide a useful way for us to expand on this conception as we think about alternative pathways to the self-regulation of musical behaviour and development. Such pathways may help us to better understand students' early achievements and development in music, to which we turn in the next chapter.

Table 2.1: Dimensions of musical self-regulation (McPherson & Zimmerman, in press)

Scientific question	Psychological dimensions	Socialization processes		Self-regulation processes
Why?	Motive	Vicarious or direct reinforcement by others	→	Self-set goals, self-reinforcement, and self-efficacy
How?	Method	Task strategies are modelled or guided socially	→	Self-initiated covert images and verbal strategies
When?	Time	Time use is socially planned and managed	→	Time use is self-planned and managed
What?	Behaviour	Performance is socially monitored and evaluated	→	Performance is self-monitored and evaluated
Where?	Physical environment	Environments are structured by others	→	Environments are structured by self
With whom?	Social	Help is provided by others	→	Help is sought personally

Reproduced from *Self-regulation of Musical Learning: A Social Cognitive Perspective*, McPherson, G. E. & Zimmerman, B. J., in *The New Handbook of Research on Music Teaching and Learning*, R. Colwell & C. Richardson (eds), pp. 327–347, (c) 2002 with permission from Oxford University Press. For more information please see McPherson and Zimmerman, in press.

Measuring musical development and achievement, like the measurement of any artistic competence, is complex. The chapter that follows describes our early attempts to plot learners' progress during the first years of their instrumental lessons. How could we assess participants across the five ways of performing that were highlighted in Chapter 1? What were the students thinking when they were performing music in any of these modes? What thinking-about-thinking strategies did they adopt to monitor their own performance and practice? What did musical progress over these first few years look or sound like? Which of our participants succeeded in the primary school ensemble programmes and which ones did not, and what impact did all or any of this have on the development of these young musical lives?

Chapter 3

Early progress in music performance

In addition to the video observation discussed in Chapter 2, another analysis was undertaken to define ways in which we could try to assess what the students were thinking while engaged in each of the five ways of performing music: *performing rehearsed music, sight-reading, playing by ear, playing by memory*, and *improvising*. We were interested in tracing the development of meta-cognitive processing strategies as our learners acquired instrumental skills over the first few years of the study. The expectation that students would exercise significant levels of self-regulation, in what were frequently and increasingly unsupervised practice sessions, assumes the ability to apply some kind of self-monitoring process. We therefore attempted to understand these monitoring processes and especially the extent to which students engaged in conscious, reflective strategies that made instrumental practice and learning more effective. What kind of practice repertoires did they possess and were they able to select and apply them to solve particular learning challenges?

It soon became clear how rarely learners were asked to engage in any form of improvising activities as beginners, a fact in itself that illustrates the limits of the teaching to which they were exposed and its strong framing within traditional music literacy-based parameters. Given how difficult it would be to analyse reliable data on the use of improvisational strategies, it was decided not to ask the students about the strategies they used when improvising, as almost no one was improvising.

We sought to assess participants' ability across these five ways of performing (including improvising), using a battery of tests that was developed or adapted from previous work by McPherson (1994a,b). Students' performances on each of the five measures were analysed in ways that ensured that the same performance standards in years 1, 2, and 3 were allocated identical scores (see McPherson, 2005). The terms year 1, 2, or 3 are used here to mean years 1, 2, or 3 of learning the instrument, and should not be confused with the school year group. Participants in year 1 were in school years 3 or 4, aged between 7 and 9 years.

Performing rehearsed music

Well before annual individual research sessions, parents were asked to help their child choose a piece of music that the child liked and could perform 'best' from the music he or she was learning at the time. Performances were then recorded and assessed. Scoring in the first year used a 21-point scale from 0 to 10. Assessors were asked to give a mark for the overall impression of the performance, taking into account the difficulty of the piece, accuracy (melodic and rhythmic), technical accomplishment, tone and intonation, articulation, dynamic, and expression. Similar procedures were followed for second and third year performances except that marking scales were incrementally increased (In year 2 from 1 to 17, and in year 3 from 2 to 23) to establish ceilings for years 2 and 3 that adequately reflected the increasing skill of the students across the 3 years of the study.

On the basis of a review of wider literature and discussions with colleagues, four distinct organizational and improvement strategies were identified as being potentially important to the development of a student's ability to perform rehearsed music. Participants' employment of these strategies was then examined, looking for relationships with levels of practice and/or the assessment of performances of rehearsed music outlined above.

Organizational strategies

Keeping track of what is to be learned

Self-regulated learners are more likely to monitor and control their learning (Zimmerman, 1994, 1998, 2000), especially through the use of notes and diary entries (Hong & Milgram, 2000). We investigated the extent to which the students actively used a practice diary to take notes about what needed to be practised and how to practise. Responses to questions about how students kept track of learning and practice, and observation of students' music diaries (where they were kept) were coded in two separate categories. The first related to students who had a practice diary and conscientiously used this diary to keep track of what they were learning. The second category related to whether the student had a diary but did not normally take notes about what needed to be practised or did not use a diary at all. As shown in Figure 3.1 students who actively kept track of their learning assignments in their practice diary, by noting

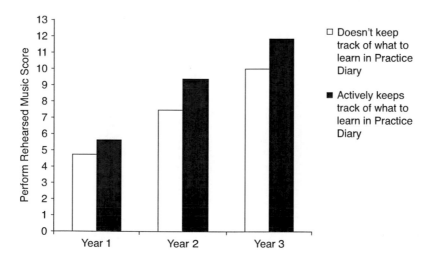

Figure 3.1: Perform rehearsed music scores according to the use of a practice diary.

comments from their teacher and reflecting on their own progress, or keeping track of issues to ask their teacher about, scored significantly higher on the performance of rehearsed music measure across each of the three initial years of learning than their peers who did not have a practice diary or who did not use it conscientiously.

Order of practice

The order in which students complete their homework is influenced by their personal interests and individualized working styles (Hong & Milgram, 2000). Analysis of students' responses to questions about order of practice resulted in the identification of two basic tendencies according to whether the students tended to start their practice by focusing on the pieces they were asked to learn for the next lesson before moving on to pieces they enjoy playing, or started with literature they enjoyed playing before moving on to pieces they needed to learn. Across all 3 years, students who practised to improve before playing for enjoyment scored significantly higher than their peers who played for enjoyment before practising to improve (Figure 3.2). Further questioning suggests that the more strategic group were deliberately more conscientious by focusing their efforts on what had been assigned and then rewarding themselves in the last part of their practice by playing the pieces that they enjoyed most. In contrast, the other group of students claimed to doodle and 'muck' around during the first part of their practice, which meant that many devoted far less time to practising the pieces that might have challenged them to improve.

Practising to improve

The students were asked how often they play a piece through that they could not yet play and were having difficulty learning. This question of persistence in the face of difficulties might be one of the more important indicators of long-term achievement. Its potential significance was reaffirmed subsequently in case study video analyses of the students' home practice habits described in the previous chapter (Pitts *et al.*, 2000; McPherson & Renwick, 2001; McPherson & Zimmerman, 2002). Coding involved

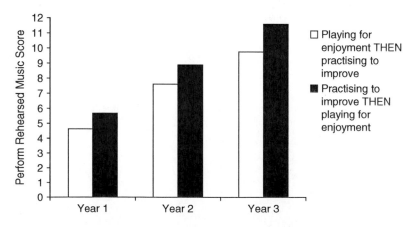

Figure 3.2: Perform rehearsed music scores according to order of practice.

four distinct categories. The first category was an orientation to play hard pieces just once during each practice session (e.g. 'I play my pieces through just once. I want to get them over with.'; 'If I'm going really well I play it a few times. If it's bad then I only play it once, except I know it should be the other way around.'); the second category involved playing the piece a couple of times with little evidence of any concentrated effort (e.g. 'I do each piece about twice, out of habit.'); in the third category students played the piece a few times until it had improved (e.g. 'I try to make it better by playing it over and over.'); in the final category students displayed a more concentrated ability to refine their playing (e.g. 'First I play it once and see how good I am, then I practise it again and again until it's at a standard that I can take to my tutor.').

Self-correction strategies

A final series of questions sought to determine what the students reported doing when they made a mistake. The students were asked a series of closed and open-ended questions that enabled coding into four categories. The first was defined by students who displayed a sense of hopelessness or lack of persistence (e.g. 'I usually give up and keep going.'; 'I don't try to fix it, I go through everything once.'); the second, superficial attention to mistakes (e.g. 'If I get it right I move on, otherwise I'll play the mistake over once or twice.'); the third, a more concerted effort to correct the problem (e.g. 'I go through the section and find the trouble spots, and I go over them really slow and then speed them up.'); and the final category, showing evidence of a more developed meta-cognitive capacity to think strategically and reflectively together with a more deliberate attempt to refine the playing (e.g. 'I try to think about how my teacher played it, then go back over it slowly and then speed it up.'; 'I play slowly, play the section with different rhythms and think about it before I play it again.').

Sight-reading

The *Watkins–Farnum Performance Scale* (WFPS) (Watkins & Farnum, 1954) standardized measure was used to assess sight-reading ability. An important reason for choosing the WFPS was that the scoring method focuses the evaluator's attention on the accuracy of reading ability to the exclusion of other factors (such as those used to assess the students' ability to perform rehearsed music). Previous work with young intermediate and advanced level musicians has identified basic strategies that help distinguish between their sight-reading abilities (McPherson, 1994b). For example, good sight-readers tend to seek information relevant to an accurate interpretation prior to commencing their performance, by actively checking the time- and key-signatures and scanning the music to maximize comprehension and identify possible obstacles (see McPherson, 1994b). As a result of this work, similar techniques were used with the students involved in the current study. After completing the last item on the WFPS that students appeared capable of playing, participants were shown the next example on this measure. This piece was then unexpectedly hidden from sight immediately before participants began playing so that they could be asked to describe what they were thinking in the seconds before they commenced their performance. A content analyses of the students' comments resulted in the identification of five strategies

Table 3.1: Sight-reading strategies across the first three years represented in percentages

	Year 1	Year 2	Year 3
Studying first measure	25	49	60
Identifying key signature	23	36	56
Identifying time signature	45	50	53
Establishing an appropriate tempo before commencing performance	17	40	26
Scanning music to identify obstacles	5	14	20

that were deemed important for efficient sight-reading. These included studying the first measure of the music to gain a sense of how the piece commenced, actively searching to find the key and time signatures, establishing an appropriate tempo by thinking about how the piece should sound, and scanning the entire work to identify possible obstacles, so that the piece could be played in an appropriate style and tempo that would help facilitate an accurate performance.

Table 3.1 shows the percentage of students across the 3 years who reported each of the five strategies. With the exception of establishing an appropriate tempo between years 2 and 3, all percentages increase. This may suggest that this strategy becomes more automatic as students gain proficiency on their instrument. Surprisingly though, the strategy of identifying time signatures only increases slightly between years and even after 3 years is only reported as being used by 53% of learners.

Playing from memory

The measure for assessing students' ability to play from memory consisted of five tasks in which the students were asked to study the musical notation of a melody they had not seen before for 30 seconds and then perform the piece twice after the notation had been removed. This measure attempted to examine how well the students could form a mental representation of the score in their minds as they studied the notation, and then transfer this information into the instrumental fingerings needed to perform the melody back from memory.

The students were asked immediately after their performance of their last item on the playing from memory measure: 'Can you tell me exactly how you memorized that melody; what did you do in your mind as you studied the notation?' Content analysis of the responses to this question identified five distinct strategies that the beginners used to memorize music from notation. For the purpose of this analysis, the five strategies were identified as representing a conceptual, kinaesthetic, or musical approach to the task, as follows:

Conceptual

Mental strategy 1: Independent of the instrument and how the melody would sound. Students in this category tended to think about the contour of the melody and whether it went up or down, or the letter names of individual notes. For some students this involved trying to 'take a photograph' of the musical score. Indicative comments include:

> I was trying to write the notes in my mind but it didn't work so I tried each bar separately.
> I was just looking at it to see what notes were where. I was saying things like, 'The bars are different, there are two that are not crotchets.'
> I picture them in my mind. I take a photograph and keep it in my mind. That's what my mum told me to do with phone numbers.

Mental strategy 2: Independent of the instrument but involving the chanting of rhythm or letter names of the notes. A typical response was for the child to demonstrate what he or she was doing by chanting out loud the approximate rhythm of the piece. Alternatively, the child might read or say the notes to him or herself, for example:

> I was trying to say it and get it stuck in my mind. I keep looking at it and saying the names of the notes over and over.

Mental strategy 3: Trying to sing the melody but not explicitly linking this with instrumental fingerings. Often this involved chanting the rhythm or pitch with a rough contour and breaking the music down into individual segments (often as a single measure rather than a phrase). For example:

> I was humming it to myself and trying to remember the notes. My singing wasn't very accurate.

Kinaesthetic

Mental strategy 4: Trying to chant the rhythm or pitch with rough contour while fingering the melody through on the instrument, either in sections or from beginning to end. This strategy became obvious each time a student demonstrated to the researcher what she or he was doing. For example, one boy said:

> I was just going through it like this [then chanted the rhythm of the melody while demonstrating how it would be fingered on the instrument].

Musical

Mental strategy 5: These students demonstrated their ability to link the sound of the melody to instrumental fingerings by mentally rehearsing as they studied the example in addition to processing the notation holistically by working from the beginning to the end of the piece in the way it would be performed. As might be expected, students who reported this strategy displayed the best-developed capacity to coordinate their eyes, ears, and hands.

> I was singing it through while I was playing it on my instrument. Like this. [The student demonstrated mental rehearsal of the music by singing the melody out aloud while fingering it through on the instrument]. I kept doing this over and over until you covered the music and asked me to play it back.

Playing by ear

For the four playing-by-ear tasks, the students were told the starting note of a melody they heard performed four times from a CD recording, after which they were asked to perform the piece twice exactly as it sounded on the recording. This task examined the students' ability to transfer the mental image of the melody they had just heard into the instrumental fingerings necessary to perform this back by ear. As for the previous measure, the scoring method for the four test items included separate scores for consistency and accuracy of pitch and rhythm, scored from 0 to 10, which were then combined to provide a total score for each task.

As for the play from memory strategies, and based on previous research (McPherson, 1993; McPherson *et al.*, 1997) a content analysis of the students' responses to the question, 'Can you tell me exactly how you prepared to play that melody; what did you do in your mind as you listened to the recording?' after they had performed the last task on the measure resulted in five strategies for playing by ear that could be grouped accordingly into three categories: conceptual, kinaesthetic, and musical.

Conceptual

Mental strategy 1: Students in this category employed a visual approach by thinking independently of their instrument and how the melody would sound. Often this involved them thinking about the contour of the melody and whether it went up or down, or even how it might look if it was notated on the page. Examples of students' comments include:

> I was thinking how many notes up and down it goes and saying to myself, it goes up, then up again, then down.
>
> I was listening to the notes and trying to work out the names of the notes as they look in music.
>
> I was trying to think what notes they were and thinking how they go up and down and how they would look in music.

Mental strategy 2: Independent of the instrument but involving the chanting of the rhythm, or singing while trying to decide what notes these pitches might be. For example:

> In the gap I was doing this [then chants the rhythm of the melody with very rough melodic contour].

Kinaesthetic

Mental strategy 3: Trying to think about how the notes might be related to fingerings on the instrument. This was often not fluent fingering but either working in sections or groups of notes and, if there was time, piecing these together. One child remarked:

> I tried to play the first part of the piece in the gap and when I heard it again I tried to add the next part. I was thinking about how the notes would be fingered on my clarinet.

Mental strategy 4: Fingering through the melody while chanting the rhythm or pitch with a rough contour of the actual sound of the melody. Often the student tried to finger the piece through while listening to the tape, as indicated in this comment:

> I was listening to the player and fingering it like this [child demonstrated fingering with out of tune singing]. I also played along with the recording and did it by myself during the gaps.

Musical

Mental strategy 5: These students had a sense of how the notes could be reproduced on their instrument and could demonstrate how they mentally rehearsed the music either by playing along with the recording or in the gaps between performances. They displayed the most highly developed capacity to coordinate ear and hand, as evidenced by comments such as:

> I was singing and playing it on my instrument like this [student demonstrated accurate singing while showing how she fingered it on her flute]. I did it over and over.

Improvising

Students were asked to play the opening of a given phrase and to continue by making up a complete melody (i.e. motif item), and also to improvise a piece that had a beginning, a middle, and an end (i.e. complete piece item). The directions for each task were that the ending of the piece they improvised should sound finished.

In the first year, improvisational ability was assessed using a global 21-point scale (from 0 to 10 with 0.5 intervals) for each of the two tasks that were then summed and, as for the perform rehearsed music scores, establishing ceilings for years 2 and 3 that adequately reflected the increasing skill of the student. The scores of 0 in year 1 were given to two students who stated that they could not think of anything to play. Evaluations were based on an analysis of the instrumental fluency, creativity, and overall musical quality of each improvisation as shown in Figure 3.3 (see also McPherson, 1993, 1995b).

Progress on the five performance skills

As can be seen in Tables 3.2 to 3.6, the abilities of the students on each of the five aspects of performance differed substantially within each year and across the first 3 years of their development. Some students had made very little progress by the end of years 2 and 3, and failed even to achieve scores close to those received by some of their peers at the end of their first 9 months of learning. As an indication, 4 (4%) of the year 3 students had not reached the mean score of the year 1 sample for performing rehearsed music. For the other skills it was 18 (19%) for sight-reading, 8 (8%) for playing from memory, 11 (11%) for playing by ear, and 19 (20%) for improvising. Further comparative analyses between the top and bottom 50% of scores on each of the measures showed that the students who scored in the bottom half of the sample in

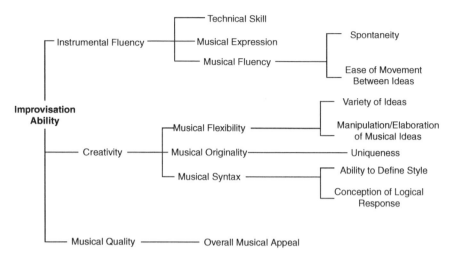

Figure 3.3: McPherson's (1993, 1995b) evaluative criteria used to assess children's improvisations.

Table 3.2: Descriptive statistics for the measure 'performing rehearsed music' in years 1, 2, and 3

	N	Mean	SD	Minimum	Maximum
Perform rehearsed music					
Year 1	124	5.28	2.04	0.5	10
Year 2	101	8.51	2.67	1	17
Year 3	97	10.88	4.05	2	23

Table 3.3: Descriptive statistics for the measure 'sight reading' in years 1, 2, and 3

	N	Mean	SD	Minimum	Maximum
Sight-read					
Year 1	124	14.74	10.55	0	50
Year 2	101	23.95	12.55	1	63
Year 3	97	29.49	14.42	0	65

year 1 for the skills of sight-reading and playing by ear were significantly more likely to cease instruction (see McPherson, 2005).

Even though a majority of students improved across the 3 years on each of the performance assessments, it had become apparent that some had not been able to keep up with their peers. Consequently, to provide information on individual differences over

Table 3.4: Descriptive statistics for the measure 'playing from memory' in years 1, 2, and 3

	N	Mean	SD	Minimum	Maximum
Play from memory					
Year 1	124	82.56	36.47	0	159
Year 2	101	115.29	33.34	2	172
Year 3	97	130.49	33.74	6	199

Table 3.5: Descriptive statistics for the measure 'play by ear' in years 1, 2, and 3

	N	Mean	SD	Minimum	Maximum
Play by ear					
Year 1	124	82.99	33.99	0	153
Year 2	101	106.24	26.73	0	156
Year 3	97	117.25	28.40	10	160

Table 3.6: Descriptive statistics for the measure 'improvise' in years 1, 2, and 3

	N	Mean	SD	Minimum	Maximum
Improvise					
Year 1	124	4.99	3.44	0	16
Year 2	101	8.91	5.71	0	33
Year 3	97	10.01	6.77	1	40

time (i.e. rates of improvement or deterioration) the students' scores were converted to a percentage based on the range from the lowest to highest score across the 3 years on each of the measures. To gauge the extent of these differences, year 1 results for each skill were subtracted from year 2, and year 2 from year 3 results, so that the mean percentage change between years could be calculated.

As can be seen in Tables 3.7 and 3.8, the mean percentage increase from years 1 to 2 ranged from 9.4% to 14.88%, and for years 2 to 3 from 2.63% to 10.78%. The mean differences between the five skills was significant for both year groups, with the greatest improvements occurring for the skill of playing from memory across years 1 to 2, and playing rehearsed music across years 2 to 3, and the least improvement occurring in both year groups for the skill of improvising.

Tables 3.7 and 3.8 also indicate the percentage of students whose scores increased, remained the same, or deteriorated from years 1 to 2 and years 2 to 3. The most marked improvement occurred for the skill of performing rehearsed music, where only 1% of the sample in year 2 received the same scores as in year 1, and only 1% of the students

Table 3.7: Differences in performance scores from year 1 to year 2

	Differences between year 2 minus year 1		Largest decrease (%)	Largest increase (%)	Decreased (%)	Same (%)	Increased (%)
	Mean	**SD**					
Perform rehearsed music	12.95	7.22	0	36.96	0	1	99
Sight-read	13.24	10.83	−7.69	41.54	8	5	87
Play from memory	14.88	13.63	−23.62	60.30	11	0	89
Play by ear	12.76	15.64	−43.75	49.38	16	1	83
Improvise	9.40	11.99	−18.75	60.00	13	7	80

Table 3.8: Differences in performance scores from year 2 to year 3

	Differences between year 3 minus year 2		Largest decrease (%)	Largest increase (%)	Decreased (%)	Same (%)	Increased (%)
	Mean	**SD**					
Perform rehearsed music	10.78	8.62	−2.17	36.96	1	6	93
Sight-read	8.74	11.88	−20.00	43.08	20	2	78
Play from memory	8.76	14.33	−24.62	76.38	23	4	73
Play by ear	8.33	15.97	−42.50	73.13	21	1	78
Improvise	2.63	14.01	−35.00	55.00	38	8	54

deteriorated in skill from years 2 to 3. This result is in contrast to the other four skills, where the pattern of improvement was distinctly different. For example, 8% of the students in year 2 actually received lower sight-reading scores than their year 1 results, and this increased to 20% of the sample in year 3. Eleven per cent and 23%, respectively, deteriorated in their playing from memory abilities in years 2 and 3. The most marked results were for the skills of playing by ear and improvising, where a sizeable percentage of the students either received the same or a lower score in year 2 (as compared to year 1) and year 3 (as compared to year 2). Considering the importance that all the programmes clearly attach to musical literacy, the falling sight-reading scores in particular are extremely disturbing. It is hard to imagine that individual skill development trajectories like this would be acceptable in any other curriculum learning area, and certainly not in numeracy and literacy. More worrying still, if performing rehearsed music is the only skill that made marked improvement through the programme, what impact does this kind of music education have on sustainable, self-regulated musical development and ongoing musical lives?

Table 3.9: Pearson correlations between scores across the 3 years

	Years 1 and 2	Years 1 and 3	Years 2 and 3
Perform rehearsed music	0.79*	0.71*	0.92*
Sight-read	0.83*	0.74*	0.87*
Play from memory	0.67*	0.62*	0.75*
Play by ear	0.67*	0.62*	0.70*
Improvise	0.56*	0.46*	0.61*

*$P < 0.01$

As shown in Table 3.9, Pearson Product Moment correlations between scores across the years ranged from very high levels (0.92 for years 2 and 3) for performing rehearsed music down to 0.46 (years 1 and 3) for improvising. Comparing the year 1 and 2, and year 2 and 3 correlations shows that students who performed poorly or well relative to their peers in year 1 tended to perform similarly in years 2 and 3. The stronger pattern of correlations suggests that this trend was most evident for the visual skills of performing rehearsed music and sight-reading, followed by the aural skills of playing from memory, playing by ear, and finally the creative skill of improvising.

Summarizing early results about initial progress

Taken as a whole, this early research into students' initial performance progress shows that progression was in many ways smooth, with most learners improving, however gradually, across the initial years of their learning. This result was consistent for all five skills from years 1 to 2, and for all skills except improvising from years 2 to 3. The levelling off on the skill of improvising was not unexpected since the students were not normally being taught to improvise at all during their lessons. This finding reflects the kind of privileged position that playing by notation still enjoyed in instrumental music teaching a decade ago. We have no evidence to suggest that there has been any fundamental change since then. Nevertheless, in spite of the exclusion of improvisation and playing by ear in these programmes, many of the students were still able to create interesting melodies, with a small number reporting doodling and improvising during their daily practice. In marked contrast, there were also learners who found it difficult to improvise even a simple response for the two tasks of completing a phrase and creating a long extended melody.

It might be expected that students who had previous experience learning another instrument and who therefore had been exposed to more musical training would progress more rapidly on their new instrument as compared with novice learners. However, this was not the case for the skills of performing rehearsed music, sight-reading, and improvising. For the aural skills of playing from memory and playing by ear, students who were continuing to learn another instrument such as piano in addition to their new school wind instrument were significantly better at these skills when compared to novice learners. This finding, consistent with other evidence

(Elliott, 1982a,b; McPherson, 1993), suggests that having lessons on two instruments enhances a student's development on the aspect of learning where the two instruments overlap; that is, aural skill development.

In spite of the impression that students overall were making a smooth progression and steady progress, the results also show that by the end of year 3 some of the students had not attained the standard of the average of the sample's year 1 results: around 4% on the skill of performing rehearsed music to a high of 20% of the students for the skill of improvising. Thus, significant incremental improvement in attainment was evident from one year to the next, but this was accompanied by large within-group differences on each of the five performance skills. Consequently, by the end of the first 3 years there were extremely wide differences between the students' performance abilities across the five performance skills—a finding that is even more alarming given that a significant number of low-achieving students had already ceased instruction by this stage. Nevertheless, this finding only endorses evidence about the spread of abilities within other domains in any year group that we cited in the previous chapter. It is our contention that it is the failure to recognize this fact that condemns so many young people to frustrating and often futile journeys that may even sour their taste for certain kinds of musical experience for the rest of their lives.

Music programmes, however prestigious or well-intentioned, that fail to recognize and take account of individual 'readiness' for instrumental music learning at cognitive, emotional, physiological and environmental levels are unlikely to enable children to fulfill their musical potential. Importantly, early difficulties in learning to read notation, as evaluated by the student's sight-reading results, and their ear-to-hand coordination skills as demonstrated by their ability at playing by ear, were associated with students who ceased tuition. Students who scored in the bottom half of the sample on these two measures in year 1 were more likely to cease instruction.

Such wide individual differences provide indications of how challenging learning an instrument can be for some young people, and how this results in a 'survival of the fittest'. Most importantly, these results reinforce the need for all concerned—teachers, parents, and researchers—to understand better the problems encountered when commencing music instruction, and what we can do to help young students learn more efficiently and with less frustration, especially when they are experiencing difficulties or problems.

While it is true that the students' accumulated practice partly explained their scores on the performing rehearsed music measure, mental strategies was consistently a more powerful predictor for explaining their ability to sight-read, play from memory, and play by ear. These results are not unexpected given that much of the students' home practice would have been concentrated on learning repertoire for the next lesson and it could be reasonably assumed therefore that practice would exert most impact on the skill of performing rehearsed music. However, the results suggest that understanding students' musical progress involves much more than simply examining the relationship between the amount of practice they have accumulated and their achievement on their instrument, as discussed in the previous chapter.

Watching the young students develop across these first 3 years of engagement and analysing their responses revealed that better players possessed more sophisticated strategies for playing their instrument from very early in their development. Importantly, these were the players who knew when and how to apply their strategies (especially when asked to complete the more challenging musical tasks), possessed the general understanding that their performance was tied to the quality of their effort (particularly effort expended in employing appropriate strategies to complete individual tasks), and were able to coordinate these actions to control their own playing. In this sense, the high achievers on the sight-reading, playing from memory, and playing by ear measures were those students who were in the beginning stages of developing their abilities to image, monitor, and control their playing in the manner suggested by Ericsson *et al.* (1993) and the deliberate practice literature.

In the two clearest examples of this link between skills and strategies, Figures 3.4 and 3.5 depict the relationship between scores on the sight-reading and playing by ear measures, according to the year level and hierarchy of strategies the students employed to complete each task. As can be seen in both representations, there is a strong link between the performance scores and the cognitive strategy employed, such that it did not matter whether the child was in year 1, 2, or 3; if they were employing the wrong cognitive strategy, then they were unlikely to show progress or achievement on the measure (see McPherson, 2005).

One of the major conclusions of the McPherson (2005; McPherson & Renwick, 2011) analyses was that students who applied musically appropriate mental strategies very early in their learning were more likely to succeed in comparison with their peers. This trend was evident for all skills but slightly less so for the skill of performing rehearsed music, suggesting that the student's home practice varied greatly across the sample and that the strategies chosen for analysis were not sufficient to explain how quickly the students developed. A problem with studying such young, inexperienced players is that proper practice habits take years to develop. This has been confirmed in the videotape analyses of our participants' home practice cited in the previous chapter

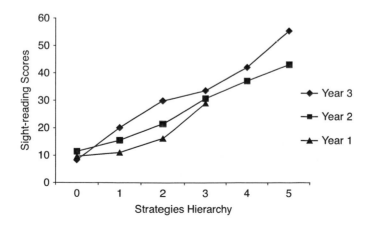

Figures 3.4: Relationship between sight-reading performance scores and strategy hierarchy, according to year level.

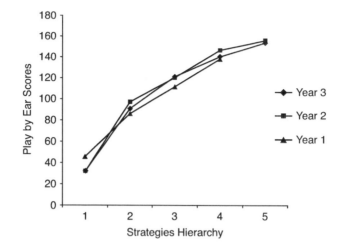

Figures 3.5: Relationship between play by ear performance scores and strategy hierarchy, according to year level.

(McPherson & Renwick, 2001) where over 90% of practice time was spent simply playing through a piece from beginning to end, without adopting a specific strategy to improve the performance. Barry and Hallam (2002) suggest that this is because beginners are not always aware of where they are going wrong, and have not developed appropriate internal aural schemata to identify and correct their own mistakes.

One of the implications of research such as this is that music teachers need to recognize the importance of reacting perceptively to students' performance errors by analysing why they might occur and trying to understand what the student is thinking about mentally, especially when introducing a new skill. In our view, helping children to adopt regulatory strategies that encourage them to reflect on what they are doing, how they are doing it, and to consider alternative approaches to performing would go a long way to improving instrumental music instruction.

Additionally, it is clear that learners who commence group instrumental teaching projects on the basis of age alone are likely to cover an extensive range of achievement and states of readiness. Such a spread places a very large burden on teachers to match individual abilities immediately and consistently. The consequence of not doing so will be an ever-increasing gulf in the range of musical skills and abilities, and subsequent frustration and disengagement. These issues have very serious implications for the kinds of projects that we have been following because they demand a differentiated, student-centred approach to music learning and development rather than an ensemble-based approach that sees fall-out as an inevitable by-product. The following chapter looks in detail at the incidence of fall-out from the band programmes in our study, looking at when, how, and why individuals gave up on this particular episode of their musical lives.

Chapter 4

'For how long can you expect a child to blow into a French horn?'

The title to this chapter was originally a question asked by the mother of one of our participants in an interview during the first year of study. She had serious doubts about her daughter's commitment to playing the French horn and seemed torn between the knowledge that her daughter had been allocated the instrument because she had scored high in a music perception test and the realization that her daughter was not particularly happy with the instrument. Initially, we assumed that the question was a straightforward one about the suitable length of practice time. In revisiting the data, we found ourselves asking if it was actually a rhetorical question, targeted, with an element of sarcasm, not just at the issue of the length of practice time, but of long-term commitment to learning a musical instrument in the absence of genuine motivation.

The previous two chapters have raised doubts about how long the majority of young students could be expected to commit to ongoing instrumental learning in the face of a range of *demotive* factors: serious short-comings about the quality of practice sessions, lack of parental support and even significant antagonism around practice sites, boredom, an absence of personal musical engagement, limited learner autonomy over nearly all areas of learning, restrictive forms of music making and learning (i.e. the dominance of performance from notation and absence of other forms of performance like playing by ear and improvising), and, for many, very limited progress in terms of musical skill development in both instrumental/technical and notational/literacy areas. If there is one concept that might encapsulate the key deficit that was created by these shortcomings it might be *meaningful musical fluency*. In its repeated absence, many students' initial triggered situational motivation turned to frustration because experiences were not matching expectations for musical outcomes.

This chapter examines the fall-out from the programmes and learners' disengagement with formal instrumental music learning, which in some cases began at the end of the very first term of the programme. The decision to quit the school programme might have also meant the end of participation in our research study. As far as our original view of things as researchers was concerned, musical lives might have been seen as coming to an end here. Fortunately, this is not the case: young people are not likely to give up on music even when they might feel, as some of our learners did, that formal music education has given up on them. Later on in this book we will hear accounts of the rich musical lives that some of these relatively early 'quitters' went on to lead, not just by virtue of their listening habits and regulation of everyday life through listening, but as expert performers too. For now, it is important to get a sense of the scale and range of disillusionment, frustration, and disengagement, and attempt to understand in more detail some of the factors that contributed to decisions to give up.

Parental expectations and representations

With a few exceptions, it seems that mothers took primary responsibility for the supervision of students' practice in our study and for issues around music learning. This is not to say that fathers had no impact on their children's musical development. On the contrary, depending upon children's representation of them, and consequently the weight children attached to their approval or disapproval, fathers had considerable influence on many of the musical lives in our study. Nevertheless, nearly all of our interviews with parents ended up being interviews with mothers.

An earlier paper (McPherson & Davidson, 2002) explored mother and child interaction during the first 9 months of instrumental learning. It noted that mothers seemed to make an assessment of their child's ability to cope with practice within weeks of their beginning in the instrumental programme. Whilst some mothers continued to remind their children to practice in spite of decreased motivation, others withdrew such reminders. Reasons for this were wide-ranging: simply to prevent arguments over progress, because they believed the child was not coping emotionally, or because they believed that if their child was genuinely interested he or she would practise without reminders. Perhaps linked to parents' assessment of music as an optional and recreational activity, some parents were unwilling to invest the time and effort to help regulate this activity, even if they did so for other kinds of homework. Finally, parents sometimes steered their child into other activities in an attempt to anticipate an inevitable defeat on the child's part in music or because they thought that their child would be more successful in a different kind of activity.

Given that there is strong evidence to suggest that mothers are far less good judges of their own children's temperament than they are of other peoples' (Sameroff, 2010), there is good reason to be suspicious of mothers' assessments of their children's ability to cope with the challenges that learning a new instrument presented. Unfortunately though, there is also a serious risk that parental doubts about their own children's resilience, buoyancy, conscientiousness, or any other trait actually become self-fulfilling prophecies. As Sameroff (2010) points out, 'documenting such differences in parent representation would be of no more than intellectual interest, if there were not consequences for later development of the child'. In our study, mothers who were worried that their child would not do enough practice before they began instruction were indeed mothers of children who were more likely to cease within the first year of learning. Similarly, the children of these mothers did turn out to practise less than children whose mothers had not expressed such concerns (McPherson & Davidson, 2002).

Assigning an instrument

The French horn, typically, was one of the instruments most regularly assigned to, rather than selected by, students. Twenty per cent of participants were allocated instruments in this manner and this assignment of instruments was a large cause of early discontent, demotivation, and disengagement.

Lewis was assigned the baritone horn and his mother noted how he was 'not given a choice of instrument. He did not like the baritone.' After several months, mother and son asked to change instrument. That Lewis wished to change instrument rather than simply quit surely reflects some level of motivation towards instrumental music learning. Lewis was then assigned another instrument, as his mother explained: '*He was then given the keyboard. In both instances he did not like being the only player of each instrument.*' Being the sole player of any instrument in an ensemble is a significant responsibility. It is also more isolating socially and this, according to Lewis's mother, was the heart of the problem:

> Lewis came to the school in Grade 3 and he had not established friends, he didn't seem to cope, perhaps, with all the changes in his life, but didn't know how to explain. Perhaps it was unfortunate timing. They (the school) could have been more aware of a child who is feeling apprehensive but still would like to learn how!

Neither were there any other support mechanisms available to Lewis. Lewis's school did all instrumental teaching in groups through the wind band and small group tuition. Although many parents bought private instrumental tuition, Lewis's mother, not surprisingly, was 'not inclined (to pay for a private teacher) because he didn't like his instrument.' Lewis quit the band programme completely within the year.

The assignment of particular kinds of (less popular) instruments also brought other issues about the role these instruments typically play in ensembles to the fore of motivational concerns. Typically, the instruments that were assigned were relatively unusual instruments like the French horn or bass line instruments. Even where learners showed some initial commitment to practising the instrument that was assigned to them, both children and parents expressed concerns about the music or 'part' they played in ensemble pieces. Usually these parts were of little interest melodically and would in all probability have made little if any musical sense to beginners when practised in isolation. The meaningful musical fluency we spoke of above was, in such cases, a future and even distant aim. Whilst tutor books offered some melodic compensation for those students that played instruments like the baritone horn, trombone, French horn, or even second and third parts on more popular instruments (flute, clarinet, trumpet, saxophone), this was not always the case. It is clear that the issue of practising band parts that made little musical sense was significant for some learners.

Responding to special needs

Other mothers were disappointed about what they saw as a failure to take adequate account of individual needs, even when their children were recognized as having 'special needs'. Tim has an attention deficiency disorder, asthma, and a speech disorder. He has problems with fine motor co-ordination and has regular sessions with an occupational therapist. In spite of these very significant disabilities, Tim enjoyed his first year in the 'beginner band, where he was very happy'. His mother felt Tim had made good progress and that the experience had been very beneficial for him. At the end of the first year all students in his year group were expected to progress to the junior band, but Tim's mother was opposed to her son moving up to the next level:

> I didn't think he was ready for it. The bandmaster and band committee ignored me when I said he couldn't cope, so they put him up and he couldn't cope. He was demoralised. He just gave up, everyone knew. I regret the politics involved. I was just ignored when I said he had problems. If I could do something different I would be far more outspoken earlier. I would make someone listen.

Tim quit the junior band half way through the school year, 18 months after commencing. This was in spite of the benefits that his mother had seen from the programme during the first year and the enjoyment that Tim had experienced in it.

The examples of Lewis and Tim above are two of the clearest cases where provision failed to meet individual needs and made demands that students were not yet able to meet. The standardization of programmes and teaching methods, and a lack of differentiation did mean that in many cases prior biological, social, and psychological experiences appeared poorly matched with present teaching provision and learning expectations. If objectives existed at all in any explicit form, they were certainly inappropriate for the two individuals discussed above and also for many other students. In a wider context, parents often saw the value of instrumental lessons as relating to the possibility of increasing children's self-esteem, to potential therapeutic benefit, and to ideas of recreation and relaxation. Significant numbers of parents came to believe that outcomes like these were not forthcoming from the instrumental ensemble programmes on offer. Having come to this belief, parents tended to withdraw their own commitment if they perceived that their child was struggling or simply becoming disinterested.

Children's unrealistic expectations

Children can make unrealistic objectives too and nowhere was this more evident than in our participants' tendency to over-estimate the amount of time that they would practise their instrument for before they actually started learning. This might not be seen as a matter for serious concern except that, as shown in Figure 4.1, children who ceased learning within the first 3 years of the project had grossly over-estimated the amount of time that they would practise when compared to those who continued beyond the first 3 years.

Within 1 month the students who had made such ambitious estimations were actually practicing significantly less than those who continued beyond the first 3 years. They continued to do so until they ceased participation. Taken with other evidence, we believe that the unrealistic predictions made by some of the participants are symptomatic of a more general lack of readiness, not least in psychological maturity, to embark on this particular phase of musical development.

Of the 24 children who gave up in the first year, 15 (62%) were children who were learning an instrument for the first time, 4 (17%) were children who had learned a previous instrument but ceased playing that instrument by the time they commenced learning the band instrument, and 5 (21%) were continuing to learn another instrument in addition to their new band instrument. Our analyses show that children

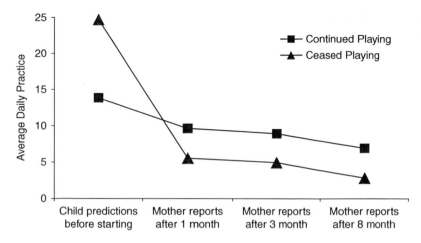

Figure 4.1: Average daily practice across the first 9 months of learning: child predictions before starting versus mother's reports of actual practice.

without former experience were not more likely to cease instruction at early stages of the project than children with prior experience (McPherson & Davidson, 2002). Children who had made some significant progress on the piano prior to beginning in the wind band were a particular case in point, as the following quotes indicate:

> I love the piano and I am considered talented at it, but I got sick of the practice for the horn. When I announced I was giving up my parents were upset.
> Clarinet is her second instrument and piano is her first instrument. She soon realized that it was too much for her to practise two instruments.

First-time learners and their mothers gave explanations for giving up like the following:

> He enjoyed practising when it was easy at first but as soon as his pieces got hard he refused.
> It was good at first. But I wasn't good enough to tour with the school band so I couldn't be bothered to try.
> She only did it for 9 months—there was no real problem, she just couldn't sustain the dedication.
> I loved being able to play, but I hated practising.
> Fitting in the time's so difficult (to practise) as I get older.
> She didn't want to get out of bed early enough to go to the band rehearsal before school. She had a lot of things on and she needed to make a decision on what she wanted to devote some time to.

By the end of the first school year, 131 (84%) of the students were continuing to learn their instrument, and this declined to 109 (69%) by the end of the second school year and to 107 (68%) by the end of the third school year. By the end of the fifth year of the study, following transition to high school, less than half or 65 (41%) of the original sample were still playing (see Table 4.1).

Table 4.1: Participants from the first 5 years of the study

	Year 1		Year 2		Year 3		Year 5	
	N	%	N	%	N	%	N	%
Continued playing	131	84	109	69	107	68	65	41
Ceased playing*	24	15	42	27	44	28	82	52
Left study**	2	1	6	4	6	4	6	4

*'Ceased playing' refers to students who chose not to continue learning their instrument in their school ensemble program.

**'Left study' refers to students who had moved to different schools, interstate, or overseas and were no longer contactable.

Significant family issues

Whatever the risks that schools and teachers may present to children's ongoing musical engagement and development, it is clear that the home setting is the site of significant high-risk factors too. Issues surrounding practice itself are often symptoms of far more complex social and psychological factors. During the first 3 years of our study, at least nine parents (6%) separated that we know of, while many other children experienced serious family or personal problems that disrupted their progress. In most cases of separation, instrumental teachers (and classroom teachers) had reported that the child had been unsettled in lessons, often for months before and after the actual separation took place. However, at the time of reporting these concerns, most teachers were unaware that the child's parents had separated. Subsequently they were unable to provide any kind of support to help their child through this difficult period and often misinterpreted a sudden loss of motivation or increased disorganization on the part of the child. Normally the genuine cause of such changes in practice only came to light after the child had made a decision to stop learning.

Figure 4.2 depicts the practice patterns of nine children whose parents separated. Roslyn, Sally, Katie, Adam, and Neil all ceased playing within days of the father moving out of the house. In three of these cases, the instrument was brought back to the school within a week of the separation, with the explanation from either the remaining parent or the child that music was no longer a priority or that it was just too difficult to make lessons or commit to practise. Even Katie, whose average daily practice had previously far exceeded the average for the entire sample, ceased practising and then playing within days of her father leaving the home.

Paul and Connie continued learning their instrument for another 6 to 12 months after their parents' separation. In both cases, previous above-average practice times (compared to the sample) dropped dramatically so that they did very little practice immediately after mother and father had separated. Megan and Peter saw reductions in their practice averages, but remained active as players. In both cases, the remaining parent provided continuing support and proactively endeavoured to make sure that

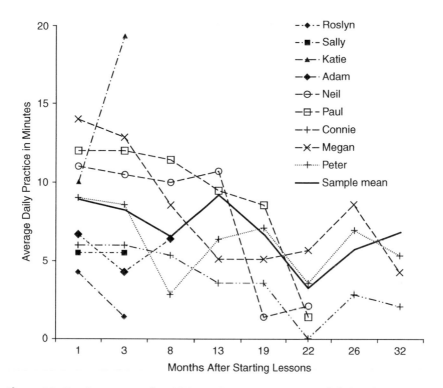

Figure 4.2: Practice averages for children whose parents separated during the first 3 years of learning.

their child's education, including the child's musical education, was affected as little as possible. In all cases except Peter's, the father had left the home. Peter's father, like Connie's and Megan's mothers, expressed a determination that his son would not miss out on any opportunities available to his son's peers at school. This father, who had previous experience playing the guitar, even took up the clarinet so that he could practise with his son. As can be seen in the line plot for this boy, his average daily practice was about the average for the sample up until 3 months of learning, at which time his parents separated. Interestingly, even with this support, it was not until around 16 months after the separation that Peter's practice schedule returned to the average daily practice time for the sample.

We are aware of many other traumatic events in the student's lives. Close family members or student themselves had periods of illness or faced other medically related issues (e.g. broken arm, asthma, dental braces), and there were deaths in families too. In almost every case, the student's motivation to practise and to participate diminished suddenly, often to the extent that there were periods of weeks or even months where no or little practice was accomplished, even if a more consistent practice schedule was re-established later. In some cases, these events triggered a serious deterioration in interest for music, with the result that the child eventually ceased learning music altogether. But this was not always the case, and in some instances potentially demotivating events, like children having dental braces fitted, were turned to an advantage as one of our case studies in Chapter 6 shows. Less dramatically, but not necessarily any less significantly, parents also reported how the arrival of a new baby, a change of work, or an increase in demands at work and the need to work long and late hours, moving house or house renovations all impacted domestic transactions around their children's instrumental practice routines and the progress they made. Nevertheless, identical events, like the fitting of braces, represented a threat to musical development for some students, but an important opportunity for others. Understanding why this is the case, and explaining how and why children are able to respond with resilience or buoyancy in the face of events that are critical setbacks for others is crucial. We shall attempt to cast further light on this question later in the book, when we refine theory about promotive or demotive factors for instrumental music learning.

Negative feedback to the child

However resilience and buoyancy emerge and interest is triggered and maintained, it is clear that parents have very significant roles to play in their children's musical learning that have little to do with musical expertise. These roles relate to the attachment of meaning to musical activity in the home and to the support of children's musical endeavours, however limited they may be, especially in the face of challenge. There were many instances in our conversations with parents where it was evident they had little idea of the challenges that are a normal part of learning a musical instrument.

One father, interviewed about his daughter's practice routine soon after she started learning, reported that, 'The noises are getting better, but we still ask her to play with the door closed because we can't stand it'. It is hard to imagine why any child of this age would feel motivated to practise against such a negative background, especially given that music is often valued within society because it is a lived, shared experience. A hypothetical analogy with an infant learning to talk seems appropriate here: 'Shut the baby in the other room until it stops making those noises and learns to speak properly!'. The analogy is not as ridiculous as it might appear because it reminds us of the essentially social function of music making, like language, and that this communicative and expressive purpose is a very significant part of music's function and meaning. A child might be able to share and experience music socially in a school ensemble, but as the example above shows, the very essence of music as a social activity may not be evident within many home environments. A failure to recognize this, especially at early stages when a young person is attempting to acquire either verbal or musical technique, vocabulary, and repertoire, may very well explain why the activity becomes demotivating. If an infant's motivation to communicate in pre-verbal forms is stifled when there is no social context, what motivation could there be for those large numbers of our young students with little prior musical experience, who were consistently banished to their bedrooms, when their aspiration was surely to make meaning with musical forms.

Playing for a while or for life?

As part of initial interviews taken before the instrumental programme began, the students were asked a number of open-ended questions about how long they thought they would continue playing their new instrument. Unlike their predictions of future practice commitment, student's responses here turned out to have strong predictive power in relation both to subsequent levels of achievement and ongoing engagement. Most of the students expressed clear intentions, such as the following:

> I'll play one or two years and then change instruments.
> I don't want to be a musician when I grow up. I think I'll quit when I'm about 13 because when you're a teenager you've got lots of other stuff to do.
> If there's a band in high school then I'll keep learning, if there's not then I won't.

Students were also asked to identify whether they thought they would play their instrument 'just this year', 'all through primary school', 'until the end of high school', 'until I'm an adult', or 'all my life'. Information gathered from both the open-ended and circled responses was condensed into three categories. Thirty-five children (26%) expressed short-term commitment for learning their instrument up until the end of primary school (i.e. grade 6), 60 (45%) for medium-term commitment that included high school, and 38 (29%) for long-term commitment into adult life.

During the next 9 months the students' parents were interviewed at regular intervals and from these interviews an overall indication of each child's average weekly practice over the year was computed, based on how many home practice sessions there were each week and for how long the students were practising across the year. Scores were collapsed into three categories according to the bottom 20%, middle 60%, and upper 20% of reported practice. In the bottom 20%, 27 students reported average levels of weekly practice of less than 20 minutes (mean 19.84, standard deviation (SD) 7.58), 79 (60%) averaged just less than 50 minutes a week (mean 47.83, SD 9.95), and 27 reported average levels of practice that were nearly twice as high as the middle group and five times higher than the lowest group (mean 93.97, SD 27.08). A pattern seemed to be emerging that is remarkably similar to the findings of Sloboda *et al.* (1996), cited in Chapter 2, about the ratio between practice levels across the range of achievement.

In assessing the relationship between a student's commitment to continue playing an instrument and their average weekly practice time with scores on the WFPS (discussed in Chapter 3 and in McPherson (2001), it became clear that students who expressed a short-term commitment to learning their instrument scored lowest on the performance measure. This was true irrespective of whether they were undertaking low, moderate, or high levels of musical practice. Students who expressed medium-term commitment achieved higher average scores that increased according to the amount they practised during the period studied. The highest achieving students were those who displayed long-term commitment to playing, coupled with high levels of practice (see Figure 4.3).

An analysis of the initial student comments according to results on the performance measure 9 months later was used to substantiate the statistical analyses. The eight lowest-scoring students stated that they only intended learning for a couple of years,

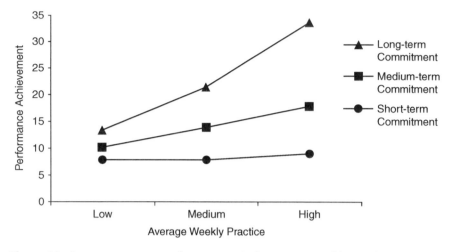

Figure 4.3: Average scores on performance scale for average weekly practice (over 9 months) and commitment to playing instrument.

or until the end of primary school. Of this group, five (63%) had ceased instruction within the following 12 months. The contrast between these students and the eight highest-scoring students on the performance measure was striking. All high-scoring students were continuing to learn their instrument 12 months later and all expected to be playing as adults. Of these eight highest-scoring students we know that five are still playing musical instruments as young adults.

Early drop-out

As shown in Table 4.2, the 24 (15%) students who ceased instruction during their first 9 months practised an average of 3.49 (SD 0.90) minutes a day as compared to those who continued to learn, who practised for 8.02 (SD 4.52) minutes. Examining these data for significance, and looking at students who persisted in their learning and those who gave up during the first 9 months, analysis revealed a significant interaction between quantity of practice done and whether the student persisted or gave up. So, across the first 9 months of learning, the students who gave up were undertaking less than half the individual practice of their peers who persisted. At around the time they gave up, their daily average drops even further. By contrast, the students who continue to play were far more consistent with their practice over the 9-month period investigated, beginning with 9.59 (SD 4.90) minutes of practice, then 8.91 (SD 5.26) minutes and ending the school year with 6.90 (SD 6.12) minutes of average daily practice.

A similar pattern emerged over the early years of the project, with strong correlations between low or dramatically declining levels of practice and ceasing to play. The following quotes were indicative of explanations about declining levels of practice:

> Learning the instrument was hard. I didn't have enough time to practise, so I couldn't read the notes.

Table 4.2: Average practice per day across the first 9 months of learning

Average daily practice	Ceased playing N = 24		Continued playing N = 133		
	Mean	SD	Mean	SD	Significant difference?
Child report: predicted before commencing instrument	24.72	39.96	13.80	10.46	Yes
Mother report: After 1 month of learning	5.50	4.51	9.59	4.90	Yes
Mother report: After 3 months of learning	4.91	5.61	8.91	5.26	Yes
Mother report: After 8–9 months of learning	2.82	3.23	6.90	6.12	Yes
Mother report: Average over year based on reports at 1, 3 and 8–9 months of learning	3.49	4.52	8.02	4.52	Yes

$P < 0.05$

> He wasn't practising and he was complaining about having to go to practices at school.
>
> He lost interest and didn't pick it up unless it was to take to school. He just didn't like it.
>
> His teacher told him to practise, but he didn't practise. I told the teacher what was going on, and he told him that if he didn't practise they would take his instrument away from him. He didn't practise so in the end his teacher said that he would give it to someone who would practise.

As early as the end of the first 9 months of learning, mothers reminded their child less often to practise (down to 48% after 9 months), suggesting that mothers tended to be reactive to their child's practice. If their child began with enthusiasm, she or he was left to get on with the practice alone. Much of the qualitative reporting supports these assertions:

> She didn't need me because she just loved doing it.
>
> At the beginning when she started to learn I did support her by listening, but not anymore. She gets on with it now.
>
> Sometimes I played teacher and played duets with her but she didn't always want me there.
>
> I'd wander in and out when she wanted me to.
>
> I always go in when she's doing a new piece—she'd ask me to listen.
>
> She doesn't like to be monitored so we leave her alone.

From the data above, mothers in the first 5 years of the study generally made some conscious assessment of what needed to be done in order to get their child to practise, but in many cases this seems to have been based on how the child felt about having the mother around. Indeed, by the point at which students gave up lessons and ceased involvement in the band, many were not practising at all. Typically, mothers could already see no value in attempting to regulate children's practice. Alternatively, they were unable to bring any influence to bear that might help to positively motivate their children to do so themselves:

> By the time she stopped she was not bothering. Right over the vacation she didn't get her instrument out once. I wasn't going to nag her. I thought: It's her decision, and so I'll respect that.
> It was clear she wasn't interested. It's a shame, but there's no use in forcing the issue.
> Initially I was trying to help her, but as she lost interest I didn't force her to do it. When she lost interest I just went along with it.
> I wasn't very effective at all. She didn't always remember to practise and I figured that if you loved something you'd do it anyway.

Even David, the trumpeter from the video case study that we reviewed in Chapter 3, did not manage to sustain motivation. His initial eager—'When I first got it I would play until my mouth got sore'—if ineffective practice strategies were replaced by a decline in practice towards the end of primary school. The long summer holiday followed and there was no strategy or arrangement in place for the subsequent transfer of musical experience to secondary school. Disturbingly, this was almost always the case for all participants when transitioning from primary to high school. As he moved on to a new environment, his trumpet and musical engagement were left behind in a previous life. In a very real sense, like so many of the participants, interest was still very much at the level of the historic and situational, i.e. the primary school. Insufficient momentum and individual interest had been generated for the learner to take responsibility for his journey to continue and other regulators had failed, as they often did, 'to mind the gap' during major transitions that might have helped relocate interest. This conflict between situational interest–playing in the school band, social capital, opportunities to go on tour and perform in concerts–versus individual interest has continued throughout our young people's lives to date.

In all of the themes highlighted above as being significant factors in young learners' frustration, disillusionment, and disengagement, alternative scenarios are imaginable and were often evident. It is not difficult, for example, to predict potential outcomes for motivation and learning on the basis of the following student perceptions of their music teachers and their teaching styles.

> I like him a lot, he is funny and talks to you, and he expects your best from you.
> She's alright, but I don't like it when she screams at me for not practising.
> I dislike it when he gets angry at the trumpets.
> We have three music teachers. They yell a lot.
> She is good because she goes through the tricky pieces a lot and pays attention to see what we're playing wrong.
> Yells at us all the time, goes off at us. Before we go on a performance she brags about us, which makes us more nervous because we have to play harder. After the concert she yells at us.
> He provides a challenge because he pushes us to play harder pieces.
> He is very mean and gets angry easily.
> She is really nice, she will always help you, never put you down and funny.
> Strict and unfair—yells a lot.
> He's really nice, he helps us with pieces and if someone is having trouble he'll help them. He's very encouraging.
> Dislike mean-ness, like niceness. Don't like him.

When you have a bad time and then improve for the next lesson she gives me nice compliments. She's very encouraging.

He gets angry when someone does a wrong note.

She's very nice and she's been playing a lot. We start a lesson by talking about what we did though the week, she tells me about her music. She's funny and likes jokes. The last teacher we had was more interested in herself rather than us. Our new teacher is more interested in us and what we want to learn. I like my new teacher because she's genuinely interested in what I want to learn to play.

I dislike her saying that all the trumpets have made a mistake when I know I haven't.

He teaches well with children. He helps me improve my technique and pieces.

She sometimes just says to practise at home when we can't get the part of the piece in the lesson, so we don't learn much.

She's nice, when we're stuck on something or we can't play a note or something, she's good, she helps us.

He's ok—he mucks around and tells silly jokes and he picks up on absolutely every little mistake. He knows exactly when I play wrong—he's really fussy.

She doesn't get too mad if I haven't done practice and she gets really happy if I've done a lot.

He gives us hard pieces sometimes and picks on me because I'm the only tenor sax.

She's really nice. She gives me the right kind of pieces, the right standard and level, she's always in a nice mood, she's not frustrated.

Amongst the many models of leadership, teaching, and parenting styles, Scott and Dinham (2005) developed Baumrind's (1991) earlier work on effective parenting to produce four prototypes of leadership or teachership. As can be seen in Figure 4.4, these four prototypes are categorized along two dimensions (Dinham, 2008). The first

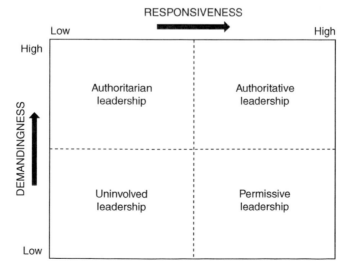

Figure 4.4: Four prototypes of leadership (Dinham & Scott (2005), after Baumrind). Reproduced from Journal of Early Adolescence, 11 (2), Diana Baumrind, The Influence of Parenting Style on Adolescent Competence and Substance Use, page 62, copyright © 1991 by Sage Publications. Reprinted by Permission of SAGE Publications.

is the degree to which the teacher is responsive to being able to deal emotionally and intellectually with students' needs or those of the teaching environment. The second concerns demandingness, or the way the teacher might insist on adopting a certain way of working, irrespective of how students might feel or wish to work themselves.

Uninvolved teachers are low in 'responsiveness' and 'demandingness'. Under such leadership students are simply left to their own devices with their teacher having little if any positive impact on their education. Obviously, this style of teaching would rarely be seen in schools. *Authoritarian teachers* are high in demandingness and low on responsiveness, meaning that they expect compliance from their students and are unwilling to negotiate or consult. Authoritarian teachers also tend to rely heavily on rewards and rules, and whilst achievements may be high, there is often an ethos of fear or coercion that can be stressful for the student.

Permissive teachers are high in 'responsiveness' and low in 'demandingness'. They may allow a considerable amount of freedom, have high interpersonal skills, and value consensus. Cultures or systems led by them are often happy places but there is a risk of underachievement and lack of direction, especially for those individuals with low levels of self-regulation themselves. Other highly motivated individuals may excel. Finally, *authoritative teachers* have high levels of both 'responsiveness' and 'demandingness'. According to Dinham (2007), such leaders 'always seek ways for every student to experience success and to achieve' (p. 36).

We will return to these constructs of leadership in teaching and parenting later in the book. In the meantime, we invite the reader to think for themselves about the kinds of teacher/leadership styles that the quotations from students cited above are indicative of. Using Figure 4.4, we can plot these quotations to provide a scatter chart of students' perceptions of teacher/leadership styles.

One of the most useful implications of Sameroff's (2010) work on transactional regulation is that it challenges the notion that younger learners are simplistically in charge of their own learning environments. As this chapter shows, they frequently are not! Sameroff's ideas demand that we pay very careful attention to transactional regulation of development. A brief glance over the themes of this chapter illustrates how persuasive 'others' are in developmental processes and how any understanding of those processes needs to unpack transactions around development very carefully indeed. This is a task that we shall embark upon later. For now it should be clear that, in the first few years of this programme at least, and in so far as many learners actually had very limited opportunity to self-regulate their own learning because of external environmental factors and demands, we will need to revisit the role that teachers and parents play in transactional regulation. If we are serious about fulfilling the high aspirations with which nearly all parents, children, and teachers set off on this developmental journey, we cannot assume that young students will be able to adopt high levels of self-regulation.

Even at this level, doing music for the 'love of it', which we discussed in Chapter 1 (Booth, 2000), may be crucial to both the motivation and capacity to self-regulate. When few of the tasks set seem likely in the short term to enable the learner to demonstrate meaningful musical fluency that 'the love of it' demands, self-regulation may become too hard for many young music learners. The results of the consequent crisis of self-regulation, where doing music practice becomes an arduous long-term invest-ment 'for the good' of some future, quality musical experience, are all too clear for many of our participants.

As young people grow up, move through adolescence, and arrive in young adult-hood, they are clearly able to take increasingly greater responsibility for their learning and development. Transactions with 'others' will, nevertheless, continue to influence and mould the course that is taken. It is to these phases in the musical lives of our participants as young adults that we now turn.

Chapter 5

From childhood participation to adulthood involvement and experiences

In many senses this chapter is a watershed in the story told thus far. That is, we have left behind the results from the original study and arrive at the present day and so are able, with contemporary knowledge, to reflect upon the young musicians initially surveyed and the research evidence we have discussed along the way. We can now examine these early theorizations and predictions in light of the current lives of these participants as we have longitudinal data that has permitted us to trace them, some 11–14 years after their first interviews, depending on individual participants and the number of follow-up interviews after a survey that was administered in 2008. We hope that the reader is as curious as we were to discover what pathways the young people are following in their lives, musical and otherwise. Since the start of our project, the participants have finished school and are walking into a new phase of their lives: the transition to adulthood.

Through a survey, interviews, and some observations, we were able to develop a descriptive profile of the participants' musical lives: the length of time they were or are still engaged in music activities, the reasons why they ceased or continued playing, the nature of their ongoing musical experiences, what they had taken from their previous music learning experiences and their beliefs about music and music education. In some cases we had not been in touch with participants since the first year of the project, when they had been among the first to quit the primary instrumental learning programmes. Others had been followed across the transition into the first year of high school. Beyond that, we had lost touch with participants as they progressed through high school.

For the original 157, we used family contact address records, phone directories, electoral roles, social networking websites and snowballing, and were able to find 104 of the original participants to help us examine how their musical lives had developed in the time since our last encounters. Data from previous years of our studies were used to compare those re-contacted with the non-respondents based on several variables: music performance ability measures, reported average daily practice, the participants' need for reminders to practise, and the length of time the participants thought they would continue playing an instrument (this is explained in detail in Evans *et al.* (in preparation)). Comparing those re-contacted with those not contacted, no significant differences could be found between them on a range of measures we had for the first 5 years of study, indicating that the 66% who were re-contacted as adults were representative of the original sample as a whole.

To begin discussion of these data, it is necessary to explain that both a quantitative survey and qualitative interview schedule were developed in association with Paul Evans, who was a higher degree candidate for the project, and we express our deepest gratitude to him for the data collected and the analyses and insights offered on many of the results that appear in this chapter. We refer readers to his PhD thesis (completed at University of Illinois Urbana-Champaign), which was based on the survey, and his Masters thesis, which was based on qualitative aspects of the project (completed at University of Western Australia; see Evans, 2009, 2011). The survey questionnaire, delivered some 11 years after initial contact with the students, was conceptualized to examine the motivations for learning and ongoing commitment to both reflect upon the earliest years of engagement and also to consider current activity. It also attempted to fill as many gaps as possible about participants' musical experiences in high school. Many of the questions asked during the initial 5 years of engagement were repeated, but some seemed less relevant to the young adult, so offering a straightforward replication of the original survey was not a viable option.

Profile information about the cohort is now presented to gain a sense of the overall musical activities and interests pursued by the cohort from primary school age to adulthood.

Profiles of the young adults surveyed 11 years after initial contact

Table 5.1 summarizes the numbers of participants engaged in music activities through each year of high school. From it we see that although numbers diminished slightly between years 7 and 8, more than 80% of respondents were still playing. This figure dropped dramatically, however, in years 9–10 and even further in years 11–12.

The figure of 23% of the cohort still playing at the end of their school careers does not represent the percentage of participants playing at the time we were finishing this manuscript—some 14 years after having started their first school band programme—since we know that a small number of participants took up instruments again after leaving school. There is perhaps between 23–25% of all those we initially surveyed currently playing music in some form. Although this is not a majority, it is a

Table 5.1: School years in which music was studied (*N* = 84) (Taken from Evans, 2009, p. 86).

Year	*N*	%
7	74	88
8	69	82
9–10	31	37
11–12	19	23

sizable minority. Consider how many of the same students will have studied football, art, geography, drama, physics etc., and how many of them have continued with these activities after their school careers terminated. The reality is that not very many of them will have persisted with any of those subjects. In this context, as a whole cohort, it seems that the musical investment these individuals made in primary school was positive: a quarter of them are using some of the musical skills acquired in primary school in an active manner in their adult lives.

Having established who played during the formal years of schooling, it is important to note that there were many activities pursued, comprising a range of ensembles and instruments, that occurred both inside and outside of the school context. Table 5.2 reveals that the types of musical engagement in high school were diverse. In his thesis, Evans notes that in some individual cases the most engaged of these musical participants were involved in 14 out of a possible 17 categories of musical activities. There were no patterns to the combinations of these activities, although the formal school associations of the band, music lessons, choirs, and examinations make up the main proportion of activities. Also, looking at the list in Table 5.2, we see the emergence of out-of-school peer-motivated interest in musical forms associated strongly with rock bands and musicals, and general just hanging out and playing with friends. There are

Table 5.2: Frequency of participation in each music activity throughout high school (N = 84) (taken from Evans, 2009, p. 87)

Activity	N	%
School and (concert band) or orchestra	63	75
Stage or jazz band at school	33	39
Stage or jazz band outside school	4	5
Rock or pop band/group at school	10	12
Rock or pop band/group outside school	13	15
Community concert band or orchestra	7	8
Folk, ethnic, or traditional music group	1	1
Church band	2	2
Private lessons on primary school band instrument	2	51
Private lessons on another instrument	28	33
Performance exams (e.g. AMEB, Trinity)	26	31
Competitions or eisteddfods (as a soloist)	8	10
Rock band competition or festival	6	7
Choir	28	33
Musicals	26	31
Playing for fun on my own	48	57
Playing music with friends	35	42

also activities more probably associated with an adult or other role model figure who has inspired the participation, such as folk, ethnic, and traditional music, which the young people are less likely to have been exposed to in their school or peer experiences.

Another crucial category of activity in this list is playing for self-satisfaction: 'I just played my own tunes for my own enjoyment.' This use of music for self-regulation and emotional expression and satisfaction is something that was not articulated when the participants were younger. Whilst children and parents had articulated 'playing for fun' as a key motivation for beginning to learn to play an instrument, accounts from both children and parents suggest that this was rarely an outcome, in domestic contexts at least. As we noted in the last chapter, playing at home was more normally associated with onerous practice tasks than with the celebration of meaningful musical fluency that allows music to work at the personal regulative levels. Clearly, the younger the child, the more dependent they will be on social support, especially through parents, but in these older children, this notion of using music as a technology for self-regulation is striking. In other words, these data point to three specific functions of musical participation:

i.   formal, competitive, skills-based for external incentives

ii. creative, peer-based and social for both external and internal (self) satisfaction

iii. personal, self-regulating function (changing mood, relaxing, being in one's own company).

The results suggest, therefore, that for these participants at least, there are several interacting layers of experience that relate to their stage of development and the social and institutional frameworks in which they are moving and obtaining opportunity.

Formal learning achievements were assessed through questions about examinations taken, and it was found that the majority (57%) did not take any examinations in music at all and only a small, but steady, stream of between six and eight students (around 5% of the cohort studied) took exams up to Grade 8 AMEB standard—the standard typically associated with university entrance (see Evans, 2009, p. 89). The majority of students who kept on playing were doing an average of two to four practice sessions a week, rarely for more than 40 minutes in duration. Practice time itself was split between new and familiar pieces, with restricted attention being paid to warming up, improvisation, and sight-reading. So, in fact, practice habits, even amongst the highest achievers, had not changed significantly since primary school, although as we see, the extra school band rehearsals, orchestras, choirs, etc. that some engaged with were adding many hours to their overall musical experience.

Most of the students were still taking recommendations on practice and repertoire from their teachers, but in about a quarter of cases the students were taking only partial advice from their teachers and selecting a good proportion of the music themselves. Thus, the overall picture is one of increasing independence for the highly motivated learners. That independence is facilitated by what often appear to be less authoritarian kinds of leadership from teachers and directors. Indeed, as we shall see with the boys in the Hulme family in Chapter 8, the camaraderie encouraged by the teacher/director of Benjamin's Big Band was both inspirational in terms of motivation for participation and also offered a role model of conduct and love of music.

Participants in secondary/high-school music activities were typically participating in a performance opportunity every 2–6 months, this being coincident with school timetables: at the end of semester, before a major national celebration, and so on. But, in a small number of cases there were opportunities monthly, if not more frequently. Performance built different types of experience to lessons and rehearsals and each performance required dedicated practice and commitment.

As Rebecca comments:

> I love playing and I did enjoy performing with the clarinet group. One time we got into the end-of-school music festival at the Opera House. It was nerve-wracking.

Interviewer:

> I think I was there.

Rebecca:

> Oh really; that was me blowing away on that thing there! ...[Memories] just snatches of being on stage in the concert band and everything. And the main thing was getting ready for those. It was such a buzz of excitement, and I remember everyone shushing the kids because you were so excited to go on the stage and being able to perform in front of all these people, mum and dad. I think it's more of a proud moment, being able to say that you actually got up there and had done it.

Overall, and somewhat strikingly, these data mirror some of the results obtained by Davidson and colleagues in their study of the five groups of learners in the UK. The average profile of the 104 students is generally rather like group 3, that is, students who played music as one of many other activities in their lives (Davidson *et al.*, 1997). Here is a view from one of these players, Cathy, which shows where music was situated in her life:

> I've still got my clarinet and I do play it every now and then . . . It was during school that it was pretty much one of the main things I did. Apart from that, I did karate. If there was a clash I went to music, right, because [of other people], but I went to whatever I could with both of them. They were very close in importance but music was maybe a bit more fun, throwing jokes around.

The above quote shows a sense of commitment, but also split loyalties that hindered Cathy's motivation to invest fully in the music.

Of the 20% plus who are still actively playing musical instruments, a number had achieved Grade 8 AMEB[1] and in two of these cases the individuals were following trajectories similar to the young people in Davidson *et al.*'s original group 1. That is, they were in pursuit of tertiary-level music training. Anthony was studying for a degree in engineering, but even during his studies he was taking on professional orchestral and band jobs. We will find out much more about this national championship soloist trombonist in Chapter 6. A young woman, Martha, was playing flute and reading for a music and arts degree, had studied all her AMEB grades, and was

---

[1] Based on an Australian Music Examinations Board performance assessment

continuing to play in a range of other ensembles as well as in rock bands, where she wrote songs and instrumental compositions. Martha provides us with some interview data here and assesses the overall influence of musical experiences on the passion she developed for music, including a band tour to the United States:

> It was the only thing I've kept doing and kept being good at [practice], and kept going forward and forward . . . It's a sense of pride in something . . . It's great to come together and play with others . . . Playing at Carnegie Hall with the band was incredible, wow! . . . And I think it would be a huge waste if I stopped playing because it is years and years and years of work and lots of money down the drain . . . I do set personal goals for myself and just continue in playing. There are so many things you can do with music . . . play, you can listen too, you can write, you can compose, and you can change things around. And I just love it, and so it's just kept me going.

Martha's final perceptions and interpretation of her experiences of music are quite different to Cathy. It seems that Martha invests highly in her music, her whole identity being expressed through her musical encounters, whereas Cathy's is not. Cathy is still sampling the experiences, rather than investing highly in them: music is placed as a low-key and background status, like karate. It is perhaps too simplistic a parallel to draw comparison between our young adult cohort who had just finished school and those participants in Burland and Davidson's work (2004) because, of those 119 highly successful school-based musicians (group 1) who had taken part in the original Davidson *et al.* study cited above, the research did not establish what proportion went on to become professional musicians. Burland and Davidson were able to trace only 20 of the original 119, the majority being in their mid-twenties when interviewed, so their professions were still not determined. Like the early studies by Davidson *et al.*, Burland and Davidson asked the young adults about the influence of other people, the role of motivation, and the impact of educational institutions on their careers. Examples of their results are described below and are used as points of comparison with data from our own study.

The types of family support had shifted from sitting in and reminding to practice to becoming a base. As one of their interviewees put it:

> They are my sort of base on the planet as it were, they are my feet on the ground. (Burland & Davidson, 2004, p. 232)

The parental support was offering security as a base from which the young musician could develop.

As a representative of our own successful continuing learners, Martha can be compared with Burland and Davidson's interviewees. Martha acknowledged supportive parental behaviours:

> Your parents support you and—especially when you are learning—say to practice every day, or else you're not going to get anywhere . . . Dad's never played an instrument or anything, he had kind of introduced me to the Beatles, Elton John, Rolling Stones, David Bowie. He wasn't big on music, but he was the first person to say, 'Here listen to this record'. I guess my Dad has had a part in all this.

So, while parental roles in the other regulation of musical development may have changed dramatically from explicit support during the early years of learning, parents still often provided important transactions in musical development during the high-school years. Indeed parents, teachers, and peers all remain key agents in transactional regulation of musical development throughout teenage years.

Burland and Davidson also found that teachers had a similar positive impact, influencing how the participants developed their musical lives. This young professional singer commented of his teacher:

> She's influenced me not to focus completely on singing, not to focus only on music . . . and she felt strongly that if you had a brain then you should go to university. (Burland & Davidson, 2004, p. 232)

In our study, Martha felt that her teachers were even more of a positive influence on her than her parents:

> I got a different teacher who also taught me musicianship, which was good and helping me a lot. And then I, in my last couple of years, switched to another teacher who was like amazing, and so was really good for me . . . She showed me a lot of different styles of music as well, like other pieces that I could play . . . Yeah, she was really influential and it ended up becoming like one of the best things that I could do.

Burland and Davidson (2004, p. 232) also found peers often inspired and were close allies:

> You're just drawing on each other's imaginations all the time, and in that sense it often gets the very best out of me.

Martha was also acutely aware of the benefits of peers:

> I've got lots of friends who come over and we just get a couple of my guitars and we'll have a jam. I used to do this more when I was still at school. Yeah, it's not like get the music out and, no, no, no. We just do whatever. Yeah, I always like friends through music.

The follow-up research by Burland and Davidson (2004) showed that the young adults they had pursued had found the institutions they had attended to be hugely influential, especially the high-powered music school:

> It had become a rat race of who you know, and who you last spoke to, and . . . it did not necessarily depend on how good you were. (p. 233)

Martha did not refer to any negative associations with school or university, but rather saw them as places that provided positive opportunities to try out different musical experiences. She was looking forward to the potential of joining a range of new ensembles and meeting new friends at university in the next semester.

For Burland and Davidson (2004), it was a love of music that seemed to motivate their learners to persist, through thick and thin:

> There is a physical response, a necessary response to do it.
> [Music has brought] unbelievable amounts of pleasure. (p. 233)

The single most striking outcome of the research by Burland and Davidson was their observation that those they had interviewed who went on into high-level music making (professional or advanced study) had devised very significant psychological strategies for coping with the pressures of the musician lifestyle. One student, for instance, had been a pianist, but changed to harpsichord to facilitate a niche:

> I was on my own as a harpsichordist, so I got to do everything. I got to play things, I got to organise groups . . . So, I made some huge mistakes, but I had some great successes. (Burland & Davidson, 2004, p. 237)

Music became the central means of communication and a strong determinant in self-concept:

> [Music is] a great comforter. It is always something that's there, always be there, and that's nice in a way. (Burland & Davidson, 2004, p. 240)

These elements were all part of Martha's beliefs:

> Music's kind of the centre of everything. As soon as I started to play the flute and then as I started listening to music as well, yeah I just realized that it was pretty much my favourite thing. Music is my social life. This new guy's just moved into our house and brought is guitar so we just sit there and do whatever. Music's just wherever everybody can do together . . . [Listening to music] it's like I'll put on something to sleep, something to wake up, something if we feel like dancing. I'll play it in the car as well . . . It sets you apart from other people . . . .Well, I've spent more time listening than playing but I don't think that's important. I think generally like as a broad idea the most important thing when it comes to music is just the appreciation of it in whatever way you can.

To account for these kinds of influences, Burland and Davidson proposed a tripartite model of experiences and beliefs that is necessary to sustain and nurture successful musical careers: positive interactions with institutions and social networks of family, teachers, and friends; a realistic set of strategies for coping with career challenges put in place for successful learning to continue; and perhaps above all a clear and committed sense of music as being a determinant in the individual's perception of self (see Figure 5.1). The applicability of this model to the data shown so far is useful,

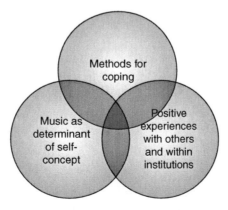

Figure 5.1: Tripartite model of experiences and beliefs (Burland & Davidson, 2004, p. 65). Reprinted by permission of the Publishers from 'Training talented musicians', in The Music Practitioner ed. Jane W. Davidson (Farnham etc.: Ashgate, 2004), pp. 225–250. Copyright © 2004

but it is a simple model and one that does not address the entrances and exits into music-making which we began to see emerge as we interviewed a cross-section of the original sample of participants.

Understanding the complexities of interactions and opportunities, core and crucial relationships with others, and the developing notion of self in relation to music may be easier with the aid of Sameroff's model of development, where social, biological, and psychological experiences 'foster and transform each other' (Sameroff & Fiese, 2000, p. 20). For Sameroff, the notion of 'transactional regulation' accounts for the complex entanglement of interactions that configure the shifting responsibilities of caregivers, parents, teachers, and other social networks and institutions to the learner him/herself.

The significance of these circumstances is found in research by Gutman *et al.* (2003), who tracked children who scored both high and low on IQ tests from 4 years of age through to the termination of high school. The research shows that children who scored low on IQ measures living in low-risk contextual conditions consistently did better in terms of academic achievement than those children who scored highly on IQ measures but lived with high-risk conditions. The transactional model that was developed in light of these results associated family processes (including family climate, parental involvement, support for autonomy, and emotional climate), family management (including social and economic pressures and resources), pro-social and anti-social peer groups, local community, neighbourhood, and school. Other measures were also used to compare psychological adjustment, self-competence, and academic performance with the level of 'risk' conditions.

Some of the individuals we interviewed had persisted, given up, then restarted while others had given up playing completely but were highly active in other forms of musical engagement. Also, some were making music in the most extraordinary and unlikely ways, given their early childhood experiences. Accounting for these multiple entries and exits became an imperative for us in this book, and as we shall see over the next four chapters, many musical lives were extremely complex and rich, and we needed a high-level framework to account for these unbelievably fast shifting series of opportunities, relationships, work ethics, motivators, and overall alignments.

This seems like the right moment to introduce a novel concept to describe the serendipitous alignments of circumstances that enabled some participants to make the progress they did and to sustain it for so long—from primary to high school and beyond, at home, in school, and beyond. The term 'syzygy' has recently been used by Davidson and Faulkner (in press) in a discussion of the multiple determinants of greatness. Used in an astronomical or astrological sense, the term refers to a unity that is created by alignment. If we synthesize this concept with Sameroff's risk factors, we see how syzygistic alignments create consistently positive and supportive conditions which exclude the negative factors that represent risk to development.

The smoothness of some journeys to musical expertise in wider historical contexts and in the lives of several of our participants is often facilitated by repeated syzygies—alignments and realignments of environment and experience, personality and temperament, present skills and challenges, teaching methods and styles, parental support, inspiring musical events, the continued recognition of achievement, and aspirations for even greater ones. Even in times of change and transition, the consistency of supportive and motivating mechanisms across ecological systems at various micro and macro levels is striking. This is true of Martha's journey and it also describes the journeys of two other participants in particular, whose case studies we will report in the next chapter. A unity across the beliefs, conventions, and practices of families, peers, institutions, and the local community towards music for any period of time is unusual enough it seems. What is even more noticeable about these journeys is not just the consistency of attitudes towards musical talent and behaviour across ecological systems, in the dimension of space, but a consistency through time from childhood, across various transitions, and into early adulthood.

What Davidson and Faulkner propose is a model of emerging musical talent in typical Euclidean time and space dimensions. The development of talent is dependent on syzygistic alignments that govern individual trajectories in any particular developmental domain and across them because of the constant and unifying influence these syzygies exert on those pathways. Whilst a whole range of constellations or factors normally forms these alignments, it is their unity that provides a gravitational pull for exceptional development in a given area. Personal syzygies that sustain individual trajectories may still be dominated by key constellations or even by a single force such as an outstanding instrumental teacher, a hugely influential peer model, a community music group, or even a parent. Given the complex lives we live and the multifaceted systems we live them in, there still needs to be a sense of unity that provides a natural sense of continuity and progression across and throughout these developing musical lives.

We shall return to this idea of syzygistic musical development in the next chapter, but we cannot leave the discussion of the survey data from our young adults without commenting on major trends that appeared for those participants where such alignments were thrown into disarray, undermined, or were never really aligned in the first place.

Give-ups, drop-outs, and unhappy experiences

Three-quarters of the 104 surveyed adults had given up musical instrument playing and negative views of their instrumental learning experiences were widely reported. For example, reflecting on school, increasing disillusionment surrounded Emily's music-making opportunities. She experienced poor resources and few opportunities, but above all Emily had a strong feeling that she was not being treated fairly by her teacher in the assessment of tasks for her final qualification, the Higher School Certificate (HSC):

> I gave up the clarinet when I finished the HSC because my teacher wasn't all that great, and she kind of put me off in a way because she'd be pushing me and pushing me and I'd do my best and she'd give me a low grade. I did a composition and I put so much work into it and she gave me . . . there was another girl in the class who she favoured, and she seemed to always want to mark her up whether she did well or not. And she did—like, that morning—she did a four-line piece of music, and I had written like four pages, and I only got like one, maybe two marks above her. She'd pass her for anything, kind of like a best-friends type of thing, rather than a student–teacher relationship. (cited in Evans, 2009, p. 137)

Several interviewees reported this sort of experience with its associated ethical issues. Such incidents clearly led to resentments, the students being extremely sensitive to biases or a lack of positive encouragement. As we noted in Chapter 2, even in primary school teacher behaviours had the capacity to motivate or de-motivate students. If the teacher was 'too pushy', the child's emergent sense of self-determination in learning was undermined; if they were not sufficiently supportive, the child felt left to flounder.

The statements from students that we cited in the previous chapter might give the impression that the representations of teachers were superficial and simplistic: a two-dimensional authoritarian or authoritative option. As we will see in the case study chapters that follow, students like Emily offered detailed and nuanced accounts of teacher styles, and a sense of fairness and equity was a re-emerging theme in them.

We returned to our original survey data and found that parents had also raised similar concerns in the initial surveys when they saw their children failing in their music learning, and though there were more positive comments about teachers than negative ones, sometimes the reason given for quitting was associated with the teacher:

> I actually think she's been discouraged at school. I don't think her flute teacher has been encouraging her. Talia doesn't like playing scales and her teacher doesn't approve of this.
> She's not a good music teacher, she's retiring, she's awful to Leah.
> He gets angry too much, and yells a lot.

We have already seen the positive social influence of peers, but reflecting on their earlier experiences, some respondents commented that a best friend's decision to cease learning could also upset a close circle of friends and throw a negative shadow over a peer group learning experience: 'My friend left, so there was not as much point in me continuing.'

Views about the value of school subjects regulated decisions that were made about continuing with instrumental lessons or about the level of commitment that was desirable or possible. Comments like: 'I had to prioritise my academic subjects' were common, especially where music had been described as a peripheral hobby.

Timing of drop-out

As we have already seen, institutions had a crucial role to play in supporting and developing learning. There was one key piece of evidence that emerged from the new survey that relates directly back to Chapter 4: the link between reasons for quitting and the participant's major transition in schooling. Figure 5.2 highlights how drop-out peaked at the times of school transitions.

Of course, Chapter 4 showed that many of our students surveyed over the initial 5 years had ceased in the transition between primary and secondary school, but Figure 5.2 reveals that the commencement of the senior years of high school (years 10 to 11) and from the end of year 12 leading into post-secondary education or work represents another significant drop-out point. In Australia, as in other countries, these major transitions are periods when students (in consultation with their parents and teachers) reassess their learning priorities. Many started to focus more on their long-term goals

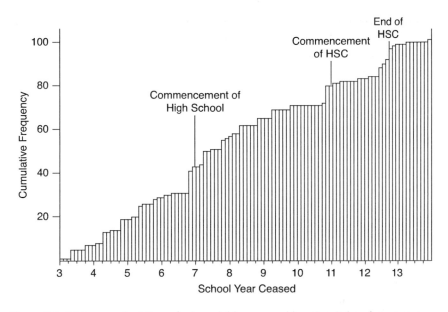

Figure 5.2: Histogram depiction of when children ceased learning (taken from Evans, 2009, p. 94). NB: HSC refers to the Year 11 and 12 Higher School Certificate.

and aspirations. Consider the following indicative samples from the free report section of the survey the young adults completed:

I changed school and just didn't continue playing.

I stopped because I started year 12 but never started again after school finished.

I didn't have enough time when I started high school: priorities.

I had reached a stage where I need to decide where my priorities were. I was at a high level of skill but didn't want to put in the hours of practise that were required to keep on progressing.

I do not attend high school anymore, thus I am not a member of a band/orchestra, and not in an environment that encourages regular practice, etc. I still own my clarinet, but it has sat under my bed for the last 2 years! . . . It was just put under my bed, and literally forgotten about amidst all the new hobbies and interests I have taken up.

Another feature present in Figure 5.2 is that these periods of major transition and significant fall-out are typically preceded by a relatively stable period in the year before the transition actually takes place. The findings are surprisingly consistent with the early evidence that some of the students started their instruments with an attitude that they would probably only play the instrument for a short period of time, typically until the end of primary school.

Some students became less and less interested in their instrument after the novelty of the experience had worn off, but were still encouraged to continue playing by their parents, with the full realization that this may only be until they moved to high school and could pursue other interests. Eistedfodds, significant concerts, competitions, and even at high school level prestigious and hugely ambitious overseas tours gave incentives for students to persevere until the end of term concert or tour.

> We worked for the end of year. We worked hard together. Then I stopped.
> I promised I'd work for the concert and then stop.
> It was easiest just to stick with it until I was leaving school. It was a routine.

These results are consistent with the literature already discussed, but, as music educators as well as researchers, we had a particular interest in asking whether there may have been a more complete theoretical framework to account for such high attrition from formal music learning. Such a framework might provide an explanation for why similar experiences and opportunities could have such different outcomes for different individuals. The work we began to consider was self-determination theory, which proposes that we all employ strategies to maintain and promote psychological health through activities that make us feel competent, vital, and socially integrated. If the activities in which we engage do not fulfil these needs, we are not inclined to pursue them.

In their development of self-determination theory, Deci and Ryan (2002) have proposed three psychological human needs, which they suggest can be linked to people's everyday health and growth:

+ *competence*, the need to feel effective in one's pursuits and successful in the acquisition and execution of skills
+ *relatedness*, the need to feel socially connected and integrated
+ *autonomy*, the need to feel that one's activities or pursuits are self-endorsed and self-governed. (see Evans *et al.*, under review)

In our final survey, we adapted Deci and Ryan's original scale to suit the music learning context. We must remember, of course, that this was a completely retrospective survey, and noting that quitting tended to be associated with major educational transitions, we start this section of the chapter by exploring how constructs of competence, relatedness, and autonomy relate to peak primary school and secondary school experiences and at the time of quitting.

Psychological needs and quitting

Pairwise comparisons of the psychological needs between peak primary school and secondary school experiences and at the time of quitting are shown in Table 5.2, taken from Evans (2009, p. 156). In these quantitative analyses, we see that statistically, levels of perceived competence and relatedness drop at the point of quitting, but autonomy does not. Thus, according to these results it seems that the learner feels far less competent and related at the point of quitting. But what does this mean? Interviews offered detailed qualitative insights. The next group of quotes are taken from Evans *et al.* (in preparation), showing the students' reflections on their decisions to give up:

> I love music but I did not feel as though I had the best skills to perform. I had a good friend who is amazing at the drum kit and I guess that made me feel ashamed of my ability. (competency related: lack of ability)
>
> I didn't enjoy my private lessons as I didn't feel I was any good/progressing. (competency related: lack of ability, not improving)

I have a sister who is extremely musical and was very into it and that made me realize I was not. (competency related: unmusical)

This feeling expressed by the participants of being beneath what was recognized as a benchmark for competence was common. Ironically, it was also the case that some students gave up because they felt more competent than their peers and were frustrated with the school band system:

[High school band was] behind the level that I was at and I found it most boring and frustrating. (competency related: unchallenging)

Competency appears to be a double-edged sword, but whether feeling either under- or over-competent, in the main, it seems that those surveyed did focus motivation to give up or persist in their formal music learning on the basis of their sense of competency being appropriately managed.

The construct of relatedness—the need to feel connected in and endorsed by one's social network—was defined against the backdrop of relationships with teachers and peers, and the authoritative styles that students identified amongst teachers and ensemble directors:

The conductor was pretty much a bastard and I just started to hate it so I stopped. (relatedness related: teacher relationship)
I was not enjoying the musical experience at my primary school, predominantly due to the band conductor. (relatedness related: teacher relationship)
I wasn't playing it often anymore. It didn't seem 'cool' at the time. (relatedness related: impedes social life with peers)
I continued to play the clarinet in high school but felt it isolated me socially. (relatedness related: impedes social life with peers)
I made good long-term friendships, going on international tours. (relatedness related: enhances social life with peers)

Once again, the construct of relatedness was significant, working in both positive and negative ways.

Table 5.3 shows that senses of autonomy were rarely reported. This could be because, on the whole, given reported involvement of others in learning through early childhood, one is simply less autonomous given social and cultural reasons relating to immaturity and social dependence. However, Evans *et al.* (in preparation) offer quotations from the survey that relate to autonomy and, despite the lack of statistical outcome on this dimension, they found many qualitative examples of the participants reporting that they needed to feel that their activities were self-endorsed:

I quit bassoon following the Higher School Certificate. At the time, it was feeling like a chore—not something I was doing for enjoyment. (autonomy related: unenjoyable/chore)
I felt like I was forced to play it in the first place and then forced to practice music that was not of my choosing so I felt restricted and oppressed. (autonomy related: pressure)
My mother only required that I learn up until year 6 so after this I stopped. (autonomy related: parent enforced)

Deci and Ryan (2002) argue that psychological needs are not necessarily experienced singly, and much of the interview data reflected complex interactional reasons

Table 5.3: Pairwise comparisons of psychological needs between time points (Evans, 2009, p. 156)

Measure	Time (a)	Time (b)	Mean difference(a – b)	P
Competence	PS	HS	4.74	< 0.01*
		Quit	7.05	< 0.01*
	HS	PS	−4.74	< 0.01*
		Quit	2.31	0.04*
	Quit	PS	−7.05	< 0.01*
		HS	−2.31	0.04*
Relatedness	PS	HS	3.95	< 0.01*
		Quit	8.16	< 0.01*
	HS	PS	−3.95	< 0.01*
		Quit	4.21	< 0.01*
	Quit	PS	−8.16	< 0.01*
		HS	−4.21	< 0.01*
Autonomy	PS	HS	−1.80	0.07
		Quit	0.84	0.33
	HS	PS	1.82	0.07
		Quit	2.66	< 0.01*
	Quit	PS	−0.84	0.33
		HS	−2.66	< 0.01*

PS, primary school; HS, highest level of engagement during high school; Quit, the time at which the participant ceased learning a musical instrument.
*$P < 0.05$.

for persisting or giving up. Feeling pressurized, for example, may relate both to senses of autonomy and senses of relatedness, rather than just autonomy.

> I was made to learn an instrument for the first two years of high school. My skills deteriorated and the experience tore from me any love that I had left for playing music. (relatedness and competency related: pressure, lack of ability)
>
> I quit playing my instrument because I felt pressured into practising my instrument by my family and my instrument teacher and I felt my teacher was harsh and we didn't get along so I lost all enjoyment. (relatedness and autonomy related: pressure, teacher relationship)
>
> I quit the trombone in year 8 because the music we were playing was not challenging and crap, along with the fact that I wasn't noticed for my skill, didn't have many friends doing it, and the instrument wasn't used in the music I listened to at my leisure. (relatedness, autonomy and competency related: not socially relevant, impedes social life, ability not valued)
>
> See Evans et al. (under review) for more details and examples.

These are very powerful data, giving us an overview of the kinds of memories and experiences the young adults recalled. It seems that if the psychological needs of the learner were not met, they tended to give up engagement with their instrument. The construct of psychological needs seems to account for underlying reasons why participants ceased their musical activity. If we refer back to Martha and her successes we can see that the syzygistic alignments fed into the positive fulfilment of her psychological needs.

In reference to competency, Martha has strong views:

> I can do anything with music, I can go anywhere with it.

From very early, Martha cannot recall any difficulties with music, she always was able to achieve tasks quickly:

> Put something in front of me and I could play it in five minutes like sight-reading, I was great at, something I could just do. I didn't always find improvisation as easy. But for a year I was practising and I got really good at it and it's alright because I can. I loved that I taught myself to do improvisation. I've always wanted to do music, yeah I realized it was pretty much my favourite thing.

Repeatedly, Martha enforced the idea of relatedness as she explained how music acted as a social glue that bonded her to friends and bound important social connections together:

> It's just whatever everybody can do together...Coming together with friends to play these great pieces. And it's not that many people, but they're something that you really miss and you can forget how good that experience was.

As well as these strong beliefs in her competency and in music as having the power to unite, Martha was very certain of herself and the role music had in her sense of independence and control over her own future, thus fulfilling her autonomy needs too:

> I think I was my own best influence. I'm the one, because in the end, no matter how much someone's going to pressure you to do something, if you don't want it, you're not going to do it. I just listen to music for hours. It is just the appreciation of it in whatever way you personally find it best. I think it's kind of a good thing, it's taught me to have my own really good ideas about music and um that's a huge influence on my ideas and I really like this and I will play it and I'm into this.

Martha was incredibly self-possessed and her musical life was an area of clear autonomous decision-making.

As Martha's last quotation indicates, musical participation does not only mean playing an instrument. As Davidson and Faulkner had been engaged in research looking at the functions and uses of music, especially listening and socialising, it seemed both timely and important to know how the young people used music listening in their everyday lives and how this related to other musical elements in those lives (Davidson & Good, 2002; Bailey & Davidson, 2003, 2005; Faulkner & Davidson, 2005, 2006). The survey instruments and the interview revealed rich data that demonstrated that in terms of both relatedness and autonomy and in general self-to-other relationships music listening was perhaps the most significant tool in these young peoples' lives.

Current listening

The survey also collected data about listening habits and revealed an astonishing diversity in the musical styles, lists of favourite radio stations selected, and qualities of the sound of music that attracted individuals. The most popular response to what type of music was preferred was 'many types', with least preferred genres often being cited: 'I don't like rap, but I'm keen on very many other styles.'

The young adults distinguished a range of purposes for which they used music. Popular reasons included 'to help me relax', 'to pass time', 'to have fun', 'to move or dance to', 'to take my mind away from other things', 'to remind me of people, places, or events', and 'to put me in a good mood'. Participants' listening was on the car stereo (73%), MP3 player or computer at home (78%), and 83% of them said that this was with friends. They did this sort of listening much more frequently than playing music on the stereo system at home, or singing or playing the music themselves or attending a live gig. Whilst they all browsed websites and music stores (online and in shops), the most frequent way of learning about new music was through sharing it with friends and their MP3 players, or hearing music on the radio. The young adults reported listening to music in these ways for an average of 2–4 hours a day (Evans, 2009).

The exploration of Martha's specific story shows someone obsessed with listening. She revealed that she regularly listened for 12 hours a day. In her part-time job in a clothes shop, she often put on music to:

> [Help the customers to] walk around faster and they'll be more upbeat. I've noticed that a lot of music sort of really affects the general ambience of the area. I've found a whole bunch of CDs that I take with me to work and they're totally cool with me playing them and it makes the day go by faster and it makes it easier to talk to customers. Yeah.

Also, unlike most of the participants in the young adult study, she only listened to vinyl or CDs, not MP3 files. She enjoyed the aesthetic of the LP and said she preferred the sound quality of the CD. She was a very discerning listener, with a huge CD collection. Of course, on every level, Martha's young adult engagement with music was high.

For Martha, listening was as important as playing, and indeed for all participants, whether they had given up or not, music listening was still a crucial part of identity formation.

Psychological needs were often addressed through the experience and independence found in music listening expertise. In many cases these needs had not been met significantly through formal instrumental music opportunities, although as we shall see later, some participants found their own ways of making informal instrumental skills meet those psychological needs by claiming autonomy for their own musical lives beyond listening. If Martha's musical development bears the hallmarks of a syzygy that supported and directed that development to levels of high expertise, she was not alone. In the chapter that follows we will examine what are two of the most unswerving development trajectories in our entire study.

Current musical lives

Our final section of the survey given out in 2008 asked the young adult participants about their subjective experiences of music, and all our participants indicated that they believed music to be an important, useful, enjoyable, and interesting part of their lives, whether or not they had persisted or given up their practical music learning. Jack, for instance, was someone who had cruised through primary school, hardly aware that he had even learned a band instrument. It seemed that is was a fairly quotidian activity, something that everyone just did. In secondary school, composition lessons were singled out as being unpleasant experiences, being too theoretical and turning his interest away from music.

We had noted the absence of improvisation, composition, or even playing by ear in early instrumental teaching and learning. Processes were dominated by the performance of rehearsed music by notation and even simple improvisation was virtually invisible. It might come as no surprise then that the teaching of composition appears to come from the same notation and theoretically based framework that allowed little opportunity for genuinely creative invention and experimentation. Then, independently, Jack began playing the guitar. During this period, he listened to new music, and through his friends started to play gigs in pubs. His commitment to this musical world of guitar playing and listening sustained him where school music and its formality had failed to capture his interests, and where teachers were regarded as the killers rather than the promoters of interest and understanding.

Mapping individual journeys

Given the overarching results of this survey of our participants as young adults and the indications emerging from the interview data, it seems essential to attempt to understand the routes to musical successes and failures more thoroughly though a deep engagement with the interview data. We are of course limited to a set volume of the text, and so we have decided to spend the rest of the book focusing on nine individuals. In Chapter 6 we look in depth at two participants who have both acquired high levels of expertise in traditional Western classical musicianship along unique syzygistic trajectories. In Chapter 7 we hear how musical development pathways can be defined by far less linear pathways and by exits and entrances around musical engagement. The next case study chapter provides unique insights into family life, investigating family scripts and individual musical identities and experiences among three siblings. Finally, in Chapters 10 and 11 we turn to two highly creative individuals who have come to live and express their musical lives in ways very different from their initial music lessons and who are continually reinventing those musical lives, even as we have been preparing this book. We will see that in addition to fulfilling psychological needs, these cases reveal how circumstances, encounters, and opportunities shape and mould interest and engagement. In addition to the data collection that has been outlined in this chapter, the authors engaged in further qualitative investigation. Extensive interviews, email communication, telephone, and Skype conversations have helped deepen our understanding of the musical lives of 25 young adults from our original participants even further.

Turning to idiographic frameworks

Substantial components of the five case studies that follow in the next three chapters were generated from a theoretical framework that has been gaining recognition in music psychology over the same time span as our longitudinal study itself. It is an approach that would have been almost unthinkable in the discipline before the participants in our study were born. Davidson pioneered the use of interpretative phenomenological analysis (IPA) in music psychology in a series of studies that focused on individual perceptions of lived experiences (Davidson & Smith, 1997; Davidson, 1999, 2002, 2004, 2007; Davidson & Burland, 2006; Davidson & Faulkner, 2010). A qualitative interpretativist method, IPA was developed by Jonathan Smith in idiographic studies that were concerned with identity in areas of health, sexual identity, homelessness, pregnancy, and wellbeing (see Smith, 1996, 1999; Flowers *et al.*, 1998). It is no coincidence that a great deal of the momentum for this and earlier theoretical development came from pioneering grounded theorists who were also working in the areas of health, welfare, and identity (see Charmaz (2000) and Glaser and Strauss (1967) for the origins of grounded theory). More recently, phenomenological psychologists like Smith *et al.* (1995) have challenged the established methodological hierarchy in psychology with calls for a psychology of individual difference based around idiographic investigation. All these methods owe a great deal to the ethnographic approach to social science research that originated in what became known as the Chicago School in the 1920s and 1930s, with their rich studies of the everyday life of the urban homeless, prostitutes, unemployed, and marginalized.

Over the past decade or so, IPA has proved a useful framework for studies of musical identity. Such studies have included young adult expert musicians (Davidson, 1999, 2007; Davidson & Burland, 2006), Icelandic male singers (Faulkner, 2003, 2006; Faulkner & Davidson, 2004), and amateur singers' perceptions of the impact of singing on health and wellbeing (Davidson & Faulkner, 2010). Other researchers have used similar kinds of qualitative methods in, for example, music education (Green, 2001, 2008) and sociological studies of music and everyday life (DeNora, 2000). In ethnomusicology, a very different kind of 'gaze' has enabled researchers like Titon (1994) and Rice (1994) to base whole research projects around the life histories of individual musicians or their families. The discussion in Chapter 8 about the family of one of our participants shares a concern with Rice's study of a family of musicians in Bulgaria (Rice, 1994) and Faulkner's (2006) discussion of Baldur and his Icelandic family, about how music is constructed and practiced in a contextualized domestic settings, even though those accounts come from different sub-disciplines.

In recent phases of this study, extensive data that was collected and analysed using IPA provided a key dimension for the triangulation of wide-ranging data that had been accumulated over the previous decade or so. It is these multiple perspectives that have enabled us to provide detailed accounts of our participants' musical lives so far. The substantial interviews we took with 25 of our participants as young adults provided a lens through which we were able to view and interpret data that we had collected much earlier in the study. In some cases, these participants provided their own views of earlier statistical data regarding practice, testing scores, surveys, videos, student, parent, and teacher interviews, and about some of our analysis and interpretations. The group included young people who we knew were extremely active in music making of various kinds and others that we assumed, from survey responses, were probably not. The chapters that follow reveal that things are not that simple. The musical lives of our participants are complex and dynamic, and even this longitudinal study of them remains an interim report.

Chapter 6

Anthony and Alistair: a smooth progression to talent?

The completion of Grade 8 trombone by the age of 16, the winning of a national open championship by the age of 20, and auditions, albeit unsuccessful, with two of Australia's leading orchestras might be considered reasonable criteria for applying the label 'talented' to describe one of the participants in our study. Anthony is by no means unique among the sample in having completed the advanced performance grades as a teenager, even though those who did complete these examinations represent only a tiny percentage of the original learner group: Martha completed Grade 8 on the flute and Alisha completed Grade 7, also on flute. Others like Tristram (percussion and bassoon) and Chloe (piano and flute) actually completed two advanced level instrumental exams before the age of 18. Another brass player, Alistair, also completed Grade 8, this time on the trumpet. Simultaneously he continued playing the euphonium, on which he obtained third place in the national open championships in his late teens. Typically, these are the kind of expert instrumental skill levels deemed appropriate for entrance into a tertiary music course, with an eye towards a future career in music. However, as will become evident in this chapter, for our trombonist Anthony and for many other participants in our study, achievements such as winning competitions and completing grade examinations represents only one very limited dimension of musical talent.

Defining musical giftedness and talent

It is only in recent decades that education and psychology research have begun to standardize definitions to describe anyone who is good at a particular endeavour. A growing consensus recognizes a basic distinction between *gifts* as innate abilities and *talent* as observable skill, such that these terms are now being used in educational systems around the world (Gagné, 2009; McPherson & Williamon, 2006).[1] A major problem with using these terms in research literature however, has been their often inappropriate use in everyday language to describe the extraordinary achievements of child prodigies, such as in the cases of Mozart, or the countless YouTube videos that

---

[1] Some exceptions to this include England, where the Office of Standards in Education defines 'gifted' as 'those with high ability or potential in the academic subjects' and 'talented' as 'those with high ability or potential in the expressive or creative arts or sports' (Providing for gifted and talented pupils: An evaluation of Excellence in Cities and other grant-funded programmes, 2001, p. 2)

have been uploaded by parents who believe their child to have some extraordinary talent in one particular developmental area.

In terms of the most accentuated upper limits of development—child prodigies—we have moved over many centuries from a theological view, in which gifted children have been regarded as 'heavenly', a gift from God, to a metaphysical phase that stresses individual aptitudes but which also fosters many myths, such as stereotypes of the 'crazed genius', to a more contemporary empirical approach that tends to focus on domain-specific training, the interaction of genetic and environmental factors, educational measures and individual differences, and how these differ among cultures (Stoeger, 2009; see also McPherson & Lehmann, in press; Davidson & Faulkner, in press).

Bearing in mind how definitions and conceptions of giftedness and talent can be problematic across a wide range of human endeavours, this chapter focuses especially on the stories of two brass players in our study, Anthony and Alistair. It explores what, in the context of our study, is their unique achievements. For reasons of space we focus on the musical life of Anthony, recognizing that there are strong similarities and some key differences between these two respective musical journeys. Whilst both these stories are unique in themselves, they are in many ways also indicative of several other participants in the study and probably of many young people all over the world who are considered to be high achievers, talented, or even gifted within the framework of Western classical music education and development.

Gagné (2009) differentiates between early emerging forms of *giftedness* that have biological roots and fully developed forms of *talent*. Gifts, according to Gagné, include a cluster of natural abilities, aptitudes, or potentials in various domains: four related to mental processes (intellectual, creative, social, and perceptual) and two related to physical abilities (muscular and motor control). Physical characteristics are indisputably inheritable, and we know also that 'general cognitive ability', or 'g' as it is widely known, is one of the most inheritable of behaviour traits. Research on over 10,000 twins suggests that genetic effect size accounts for about half of the total variance in 'g' (i.e. intelligence) scores (Plomin *et al.*, 1997). Not surprisingly, 'g' has potential implications for processing information, memory, and learning, and therefore for a skill set associated with learning a musical instrument. To the extent that identifying the genes associated with the heritability of all these abilities is at an early stage, Gagné's theory remains controversial, but predictions by genetic psychologists such as Plomin (1999) that associated genes would be revealed by screening thousands of DNA markers for associations with 'g' through DNA pooling methods are already being confirmed (Burdick *et al.*, 2006). Recent research even suggests that some specific cognitive abilities, like face processing, may be linked to genetic make-up (Zhu *et al.*, 2010) and this raises questions about whether other specific cognitive abilities might be independently heritable too.

Be that as it may, even if specific cognitive abilities linked to sound processing were found to be heritable, the complex nature of a higher function like music will not be explained by such a discovery alone. It needs to be remembered that even if we are able to differentiate between levels of achievement in various domains early in childhood and ascribe the term 'gifted' to the top 15% of achievers in any particular one of them, this does not in any way demonstrate that these abilities are untrained or spontaneously expressed. Given what recent research has revealed in the past two decades about the plasticity of the brain, the impact of in-utero, neo-natal, and infancy trauma on its development, the potential for in-utero music learning, and the implications of initial social interaction—especially from research into infant–mother communicative musicality—it is difficult to see at what stage observable musical or social abilities could be empirically substantiated as 'untrained' or untainted by environmental opportunities. All this illustrates the problems around conceptions of 'gifts' and 'talents'.

Some renowned scholars in the field of intelligence and creativity (e.g. Sternberg & Reis, 2004) would even challenge the appropriateness of measures used in attempts to assess abilities in these domains. We have already highlighted a contradiction between Trautwein's emphasis on the relationship between conscientiousness, homework, and achievement in general academic parameters, which we also recognized as significant in our own study of children's practice in the early years of their learning, with other psychological traits that are seen as predictors of creativity. When we talk about talent in music we may be talking about a great many different things, including technical instrumental expertise and creativity, as Davidson and Faulkner (in press) have recently discussed.

The creative, visual, and aural aspects of music performance and music learning, highlighted in Chapter 1, underline this very point. The pathways to high achievement as performers and composers respectively may be radically different ones: talking about musical talent or giftedness as if there was an empirically based, as opposed to a socially constructed, consensus about how *it* (in the singular) is configured, might be unhelpful if not simply misleading.

What is undeniable is that the abilities Gagné describes are easily observed in young children and develop throughout childhood, into adult life, and some, like creativity, contrary to popular belief, can even flourish in old age (Cohen, 2005). Indisputably, all of the domains of intellectual, creative, social, perceptual, muscular, and motor control abilities are important to developing certain musicalities, but they may not be all equally important to all of them. For example, creativity may not be a key ingredient of some forms of musical expertise such as performing to a high technical level within the Western art music tradition. It is, however, an essential ingredient of the skills needed to compose and improvise. Likewise, certain physical attributes involving muscular speed and endurance, plus motor control mechanisms involving agility, coordination, dexterity, and balance, are essential for instrumentalists but not essential for composers.

So, whilst folk claims that composers like Wagner and Berlioz did not play instruments appear exaggerated, these two 'great' composers did have limited instrumental skills when compared to expert music performers. Nevertheless, both Wagner and Berlioz developed high-level performance skills as conductors (and extraordinary organizational and entrepreneurial skills) in order to disseminate their own compositions. If various abilities, traits, and experiences are required for various forms of musicianship, talk of musical development as if it were a hermetically sealed bag of proverbial tricks or abilities is unlikely to prove helpful in understanding the mechanisms involved or for developing strategies to support whatever it is. As our study of music in people's lives has developed and grown with the young people involved in it, we have come to recognize the need to think of the development of *musicalities* and, at the same time, to resist the temptation of privileging one particular form of musicality above all others, as many arrangements for music education traditionally have and as much of the teaching in our own project initially tended to.

Anthony and Alistair: the journeys

Obviously, we were not able to assess in detail the 'gift'—genetic or environmental—that parents bestowed upon the young people in our study. We have only parents' retrospective accounts of the gifts that they may have imparted in infancy and early childhood through their musical behaviour and the values they demonstrated towards music that we discussed in Chapter 2.

Even leaving the problem of defining 'giftedness' and 'musicality' to one side, Gagné's model (as shown in Figure 6.1 and adapted for music by McPherson and Williamon (2006)) may still prove helpful for understanding the musical lives of some of our participants, like Anthony and Anthony, who from early in our measurement of musical skills (e.g. sight-reading) were already achieving in the top 15% level. Surprisingly though, by whatever mechanisms Anthony had come to develop fluency in sight-reading—and he had already been learning the piano for 2 years—our initial measures of musical aptitude (Gordon, 1982) revealed no exceptional level in terms of aural perception. He scored high on the tonal measure, although not in the top 15%, but more surprisingly, Anthony actually scored in the lowest 15% for rhythmic measures. As Hallam and Shaw (2002) have illustrated, musical ability is most commonly and strongly conceptualized as rhythmic ability and on the basis of this social construction of musicality, Anthony seems an unlikely candidate for high-level achievement.

The home environment, expertise, support, and partnerships

Whatever Anthony's genetic inheritance, we have every reason to believe that Anthony was regularly exposed to musical stimulus from an early age, making the low score on rhythmic measures even more surprising. His mother recalled how, when Anthony was a baby, they would 'sing every day—nappy change time, during tea, and so on' and she claims that Anthony was in fact 'very aurally aware' from infancy:

> Right from birth he's been very aware of sounds and changes in sounds, so, for example, he could tell if the doorbell battery was going flat.

Anthony's mother is a piano teacher, and his first formal instrumental tuition, from the age of about five, was actually from her. It was only a few months after starting the trombone that Anthony stopped having piano lessons with his mother, when, according to her, the burden of practice became too great for him. It appears to have been a trauma-free decision: as Anthony's higher level of motivation for

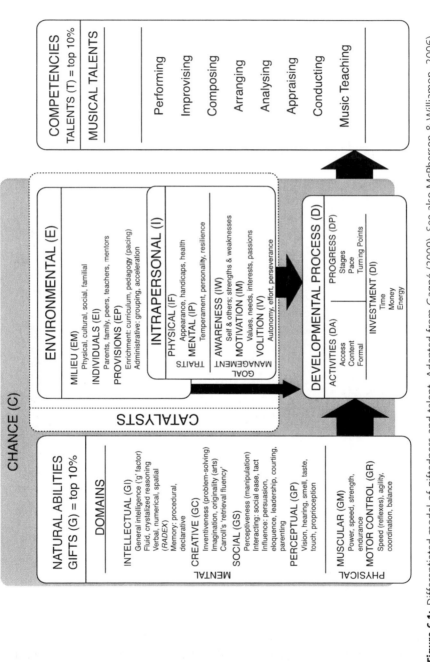

Figure 6.1: Differentiated model of giftedness and talent. Adapted from Gagné (2009). See also McPherson & Williamon, 2006). Adapted here with permission of Prufrock Press Inc. (http://www.prufrock.com) from: Leading Chance in Gifted Education: The Festschrift of Dr. Joyce VanTassel-Baska, B. MacFarlane & T. Stambaugh, pp. 61–80, © 2009.

the trombone emerged, a strategic reviewing of priorities revealed an obvious pathway for a specific kind of musical development. In spite of her being a professional piano teacher, Anthony's mother's aspirations for his instrumental learning are simple:

> To enjoy it and feel the benefits of music. It will add beauty to his life and be a source of relaxation, and a point of social contact. The piano is very much a solo instrument, so band is a good social contact . . . he's a very sociable boy.

When it came to the trombone, his mother claims that they never had to 'tell him anything, because he enjoys it so much'.

In the ways shown above, Anthony's mother has always supported her child's development, although the quality of this engagement has changed as Anthony became more resourceful and skilled on his instrument.

This is a far cry from the emotional climate of some homes in the study where children were coerced into practice, offered rewards, or threatened with the discontinuation of lessons. We discussed earlier how in data-mining analysis of predictors for participants continuing in the instrumental programme, emergent decision trees revealed that regular parental reminders are indeed predictive of ongoing playing (Faulkner *et al.*, 2010). Parents giving rewards for practice, however, and even more surprisingly, children practising at the same time of day during their first year of study are both predictive of later disengagement. We interpret this to mean that practising at the same time of day more often reflected a parent-imposed regime than individual personal commitment. It suggests that ideal conditions for ongoing engagement are a high level of self-regulation, even from a very early stage, supported by parents, but neither enforced by them nor reinforced through extrinsic rewards (Faulkner *et al.*, 2010). This hypothesis resonates strongly with Kohn's warnings about the danger of employing rewards as a motivation strategy even in early stages of learning (Kohn, 1994), and with self-determination theory (Deci & Ryan, 2002).

Anthony is one of the few exceptions to the poor predictive power of same time of day practice, probably because it was his, rather than his parents' or teacher's decision to organize his practice systematically, by practising at the same time on most days. Whereas the following account reveals that his parents encouraged a regular daily routine, there is no suggestion of even the slightest coercion or tension around it:

> I suppose Mum and Dad were extremely encouraging in wanting me to become good, and just encouraging me with my practice every morning before school. I'd get up half an hour before school and try and play, so I think that's why I was quite good from the beginning.

Research has clearly indicated that in homework in general there is a positive relationship between parent communication, parent's valuing of the subject itself, and homework effort (see Cooper *et al.*, 2000; Pomerantz *et al.*, 2005). In contrast, however, there is surprisingly little relationship between the levels of direct parental involvement in the homework itself and the levels of effort that children expend. Many parents in our study felt unqualified to get involved in their child's practice and early publications by two of the present authors highlighted the relationship between the absence of parental support for children's instrumental practice and subsequent achievement. Parent's feelings of musical inadequacy were often accompanied by a tendency for them to give up on their children's musical potential and resort to claims that their child simply did not 'have it in them' (Davidson & Borthwick, 2002; McPherson & Davidson, 2002). Representations of their children as 'unmusical' were quickly formed. Interestingly, however, the issue has crystallized for us as the study has progressed, so that it has become clear that it is not whether parents are *able* to directly help their children practice that matters most. Some parents who would have been able to make very substantial input to their children's practice, like Anthony's mother, did not actually do so. Supporting our finding, Anthony's ensemble director explained when asked what he thought of parental supervision of practice:

> That's a difficult one. I don't think it makes any difference. I think parental supervision makes no difference; I think parental support makes a lot of difference. Sitting there with the child practising is just going to annoy a lot of kids. It annoyed me when I was growing up—I know that.

What seems to matter is not musical expertise itself, or even parental perceptions of competency or incompetency, but the attitudes and beliefs parents hold about the desirability and accessibility of the activity, how these are transmitted, and the emotional climate that is generated around it. Anthony's mum regularly reminded him to practise and her doubts about the suitability of the instrument were quickly dispelled because it was clear that Anthony was not depending on his parents to regulate his practice, only to remind him. In fact, when he first began trombone, Anthony's parents were initially only 'moderately happy' with the allocated instrument:

> We didn't have a say. They had a test at school on four different mouthpieces—and rarely are any changes made. I would have preferred more of a melody-line instrument. It was shocking sound for the first few months, but the tutor is very pleased with his progress.

One of the key reasons for Anthony's immediately high level of self-regulation is found in his very first and highly successful trombone lesson. Anthony was strongly motivated by the experience—even inspired—and his parents were soon encouraging him to play for visitors and relatives. His tone improved rapidly and thereafter it seems that neither his mother nor Anthony ever question the possibility that he could become 'good'. Significant also, in terms of the climate around Anthony's learning, is his mother's genuine enthusiasm for the trombone itself:

> I love the trombone, and I love the sound, a good strength in its sound, I'm curious about the instrument because it is so different from the piano.

This 'difference' may be important for motivation in other ways too because it takes considerable power away from Anthony's mother that was central to the piano teaching/learning relationship. She is not a trombonist, the trombone is *Anthony's* instrument, part of his own personal identity and not simply an extension of hers. It satisfies needs to establish an autonomous personal musical identity that becomes the catalyst for future commitment to the development of that identity and the skills needed to maintain and perform it. Mother and son develop a very significant musical partnership, but it is the power of music itself, the valuing of playing music and a healthy respect for each other's musicalities that maintain it, not the exerting of authoritative parental power-plays.

A similarly supportive environment is typical of Alistair's home, even though there is a good deal less musical expertise in it. Alistair's mother did play the piano as a child:

> ... but I didn't keep it up because I didn't have friends who learned—I felt I was missing out on playing with them when I had to practise.

Whilst Anthony's siblings all play musical instruments, none of Alistair's were playing when he begun the cornet and later changed to the trumpet. His mother comments too how she enjoys the sound of his instrument. In fact, she is one of the few parents that explicitly stated at an early stage of the project that she thought Alistair had a 'gift for music'. She comments how they had 'only sung at bedtime and at playgroup once a week' when Alistair was young and although there was the usual array of children's musical objects in the home, Alistair did not play them very much at all. According to his mum, it seemed that only when Alistair took up the cornet did this 'gift' emerge. Reminders to practise still had to be made, but, interestingly, Alistair's mother never believed that he should have to practise every day, so that early on in the programme he frequently only practised about three times a week for about 30 minutes at a time.

Just as the importance of emotional climate in the home for homework has been highlighted (Pomerantz *et al.*, 2005), our study suggests that this may be even more true of activities like learning a musical instrument. Many musician parents know from their own personal experience how attempts to help their own children with music learning, either through direct instrumental teaching or in efforts at assisting with practice or music work, easily become emotionally charged and quagmired by the interpersonal politics of such close bonds. It takes a very special kind of parent–child relationship to negotiate these boundaries as successfully as Anthony's mother appears to have done. In fact their special musical relationship seems to have been an extremely important nurturing factor in Anthony's musical development. She has been able to use her skills as a pianist to accompany Anthony and they have clearly engaged in many hours of music-making together. She regularly played for his grade examinations until about Grade 7, although more recently when Anthony has had a solo they will do 'a run through together' and then he will get a different accompanist.

The teacher and a flying start

The biggest gift that Anthony may have received from his parents appears to be a mother with a unique range of musical and parenting skills that facilitated and complemented Anthony's own and very individual musical development. Anthony's account of early trombone lessons illustrates how skills beget skills, especially when their acquisition is recognized and celebrated by other key figures. His previous experience on the piano turns out to be far from the cul-de-sac it might appear to have been: from the very first trombone lesson, Anthony was immediately highly motivated by his teacher's recognition of the skill he had already developed. The literacy skills had clearly been transferable from the piano, and, most likely, aural skills too:

> I think it clicked quickly because of the piano, I had already learned the bass clef, so I could read my music, so I think that's why I had an advantage over quite a lot of other kids. I remember my very first lesson on trombone—I learnt the B flat major scale, and my teacher said he'd never done that with anyone before, so I think that excited me a bit, made me want to play a lot. Looking back, I had no idea what that meant on the first day. Teaching students now, I realize that it might take half a year for some to be able to play the high B flat.

Playing the high B flat is less easy to explain in terms of previous experience since it depends on a physical skill related to embouchure, air pressure, and physiological features. This achievement might even be seen as justifying the 'four mouthpiece tests' to which children in this school were subject (although such testing was clearly of little help to the many other learners who gave up instruments that were allocated on a similar basis). Nevertheless, Anthony's previous experience of the major scale and notation skills—not least in the bass or F clef—were surely some of the many components that came into alignment here to facilitate a flying start to learning the trombone at a rate of progress that was clearly fairly exceptional.

Gagné (2009) has proposed that giftedness can be recognized by measuring or categorizing growth within and between developmental stages, such as how quickly an individual is able to learn or refine a new skill, as compared to other skills he or she may wish to acquire, or how quickly the person learns or refines new skills as compared to others of his or her own age and/or ability level. Anthony's teacher appears to have applied this same criteria and, unsurprisingly then, gave Anthony the clear impression that he was special or gifted. This impression turns out to be hugely significant, regardless of any basis that Anthony's achievement might have had in previous experience. Without really problematising the basis upon which such judgements are made, Gagné recognizes the importance of incidents like these within his conception of the developmental process. Accordingly, along any developmental trajectory there will be incidents where talent is recognized by a teacher or significant other, just as we observed with Anthony from his very first trombone lesson. Previous experience and physiological aptitude for blowing combine to give the impression of exceptional progress that is celebrated as talent and sets in motion a very special relationship and developmental trajectory. Anthony's response testifies to the power of these early mastery experiences and feelings of being special that were clearly missing from the experience of many of our learners. Sadly, they were far less well prepared for their early instrumental lessons than he. The initial relationship of Anthony's teachers as helpers and friends, and later as role model 'expert' musicians became absolutely central to Anthony's musical journey, as his mother recognizes in this account of the 'rapport between Anthony and the band director':

> His instrumental teacher has shown a personal interest in him; he is a member of the ballet orchestra, and he invited him and us to an opera in which he was playing, and we got to see it, and got to go backstage and in the pit after the performance and they (teachers

and band directors) have all been strong, and have been able to develop his playing, they are very good at encouraging him.

Whilst Anthony was unsuccessful in his own recent audition for the very same orchestra, there is a sense here in which the audition closes one particular circle of motivation and musical talent more than 10 years after his inspirational visit to the orchestral pit as a child. Anthony and Alistair's stories are littered with incidents that provided opportunities to engage at a continuously higher skill level through access to prestigious musical groups, the winning of music prizes and competitions, performances in high-profile venues, the awarding of high grades in an examination, and the recognition of his achievements by family and friends. During their school years, there was also a particularly close friendship between these two boys and their other friends who were also learning instruments in the instrumental programme that was initially important to stimulating their psychological needs. These strongly promotive environmental factors repeatedly formed positive alignments with psychological traits and needs that motivated both Anthony and Alistair on to impressive skill levels.

The role of music examinations and programme expectations

It is surely no coincidence that the school Anthony and Alistair attended was much more systematic about the use of graded instrumental examinations as part of the teaching and learning sequence than any other in the programme. Even so, our research has not led us to advocate for graded music examinations in instrumental learning programmes in general. Instead, our data demands that careful consideration is given to the relevance and the usefulness of such examinations where potential costs and benefits, and motivating and de-motivating factors are defined at local, cultural, and individual levels.

Seven of the 20 pupils involved in the project who attended the same primary school as Anthony and Alistair had completed at least Grade 3 before the end of their third year of learning. None of the other seven primary schools had such high levels of pupil achievement in terms of graded music examinations. More importantly, attendance at this particular primary school is not just an important predictor of the development of early musical talent as measured by such formal assessment, but also of long-term commitment, even into early adulthood. Interestingly, however, the very first battery of sight-reading tests reported that scores from this school were already higher than any other, suggesting that the preliminary music programme, which included recorder lessons, had created a smooth interface with subsequent instrumental learning in the wind band project.

Practical music examinations and even just music performance itself are not always positive turning points. Whilst self-efficacy has strong predictive power for outcomes from practical music examinations (Davidson & Scutt, 1999), McPherson and McCormick (2006) illustrate how bad experiences in this kind of setting can have a very significant negative impact for ongoing musical development too. In other words, the same musical events have the potential to become huge risk factors as well as promotive ones, so that judging what are appropriate musical events, especially in relation to any kind of public or shared performance, becomes crucial to the paths musical lives follow.

Such turning points, for better or worse, are not always musical events either: our study provided clear examples where the death of someone in the family, a marriage break-up, family illness, or, as we shall see in the next chapter, a whole series of unfortunate events, have very considerable impact on young peoples' desire to continue studying music. The impact of such non-musical events is dramatically under-represented in models of musical development.

Gagné's differentiated model of giftedness and talent adapted for music

All kinds of variables clearly shape the growth of individual talent. Gagné's (2009) model is attractive because of its multi-faceted approach and efforts to give due weight to a wide range of environmental and psychological factors. Amongst these are what Gagné terms *environmental* and *intrapersonal catalysts*. On the one hand, according to Gagné there are a wide range of environmental catalysts that he subcategorizes as milieu, provisions, and individuals. On the other hand, *intrapersonal catalysts* filter this environmental experience at personal levels, so that the same kind of environmental experiences will not necessarily have the same kind of impact on individual development.

Intrapersonal catalysts refer to two types of traits and three types of goal management processes. As explained by Gagné (2009), physical traits help individuals to succeed because of their specific 'build'. They include such characteristics as personal appearance, ethnicity, disability, and illness. The impact of such traits is not widely evident in our study and hardly at all in the stories of Anthony and Alistair. Where it does appear to have some significance, the more important factor for musical development appears to be the way in which these needs, arising from the incidence of specific physical traits or states, are met by other environmental factors like the quality of teaching. We might be tempted to think that Anthony had physical characteristics that were particularly appropriate for good embouchure on the trombone, for example, but bear in mind that Alistair has successfully swapped between cornet and euphonium for a great deal of his musical life, suggesting that the physiological justification for choosing a small or large mouth-pieced brass instrument may often be overstated. Their teachers spent very considerable effort 'teaching' good blowing techniques, and remember too that both Anthony and Alistair had braces on their teeth for several years. The trauma of wearing braces has seen wind instruments and especially brass instruments prematurely rejected from countless young musical lives, but Anthony's teacher had a completely different take on the problem that this potential crisis exposes:

> My teacher said braces were good for me, because it would make me not push hard on my mouth, and it would make me use more air, and we sort of did that as an advantage and it seemed to work perfectly fine.

The teacher helped Anthony to filter out negative elements of this experience so that whilst Anthony's response and management of it may have something to do with personal buoyancy, we are left in no doubt that what happened here is an interpersonal, transactional regulation of experience that recalls Sameroff's (2010) theory where self and other regulation interact in dynamic ways to impact development.

In a very different example, the failure of a wind band programme to match teaching strategies to a specific disability that another of our learners had is resentfully blamed by a parent for her child's frustration and disengagement from what had, for more than a year, been a very meaningful and enjoyable enterprise. It seems that whatever impact physical traits or states have on musical development, their impact is heavily mediated by other factors and especially by teachers' attitudes and their ability to find flexible teaching strategies, like Anthony's teacher did above.

Mental characteristics in Gagné's model (2009) 'cluster around two major constructs: temperament and personality, which represent the nature and nurture poles respectively, or basic tendencies as opposed to behavioural styles' (p. 69). The distinction between temperament and personality is not universally accepted, however, and it might be helpful to think of these two constructs as basic tendencies (extraversion, openness, neuroticism, agreeableness, and conscientiousness) from the big five personality traits on the one hand, and cultural or environmentally characteristic adaptations like values, beliefs, skills, and behaviours on the other (McCrae & Costa, 1996, 1999). Even here though, there is no consensus about whether the environment influences personality traits in any way at all, or whether, as Bouchard and McGue's (2003) study of twins suggests, environment and heredity contribute pretty much equally. Nor is there even full agreement about the validity of the 'big five personality trait' tendencies. We did not engage in psychological measurement or profiling of our participants, so the evidence we offer about psychological make-up is based on parental, teacher, and learner comments, and responses to direct questions about personality and temperament and observation of behaviour, as evident in some of the video analysis discussed in Chapter 2.

However endogenous tendencies may be, young people learn values and behaviours, including how to tackle everyday adversity and major life-traumas. Psychological buoyancy or resilience are key constructs of coping with the new, the challenging, and the unexpected; they have been widely implicated in academic achievement and across contexts of school, play, work, and home, where they are linked to the emotional climate already discussed. Whilst we have no record of major traumas as Anthony and Alistair grew up, they are both described in terms that would suggest a high level of buoyancy and positive orientation. Anthony is described by his teacher and mother as being open and sociable, whilst Alistair's mother described him as a little introvert and sensitive and as much better with concrete things rather than abstract concepts. Both were seen by their mothers and music teacher as being disciplined, highly motivated and ambitious for achievement and recognition. This was also evident in their classroom teachers' reports. For example, in the first year of learning, Anthony was described by his classroom teacher as 'extremely keen to do his best. He is highly literate, articulate and numerate and has an insatiable appetite for work which is always of a high standard' whilst Alistair was described as a 'dedicated and motivated student who gives of his best at all times. He enjoys good relationships with his peers and gives well-prepared class presentations.'

As Gagné illustrates, awareness, motivation, and volition form the basis of the goal-management dimension because being aware of personal strengths and weaknesses enables a person to plan ahead and formulate specific plans of action that are crucial for improving personal skill. Thus, knowing *what* one might wish to achieve and *how* one might go about reaching this goal helps to define the type of motivation that typifies conscientious individuals who strive to achieve at the highest level, as Anthony and Alistair and several other learners in our study clearly illustrate and aspired to from early times in their instrumental learning.

According to Gagné's model, *intrapersonal catalysts* filter *environmental* catalysts. The environmental catalysts 'pass through the sieve of an individual's needs, interests, or personality traits' (intrapersonal catalysts) because along the road to achieving excellence individuals 'continually pick and choose which stimuli will receive their attention' (Gagné, 2009, p. 69). Environmental catalysts, according to Gagné can be of three basic types. Macroscopic (geographical, demographic, sociological) and microscopic (family size, socioeconomic status, neighbourhood services) influences create a general milieu that can facilitate or impede one's development. For example, living close to a music conservatory or, like Anthony and Alistair, a school with a highly developed and well-organized music programme creates opportunities that may not exist for others who do not have access or the opportunity to take advantage of the expert guidance that is available in such institutions. The social environment in which the person lives may also impact significantly on an individual's progress in a certain field, particularly when significant others such as parents, family, peers, teachers, and mentors are willing to devote the time and attention that is needed to scaffold a learner to work at an even higher level. This part of Gagné's model owes much to Bronfenbrenner's widely known ecological model of development, with its layers of micro and macro systems (Bronfenbrenner, 1979).

Anthony and Alistair found support for their musical development at the micro level of family and peers. They were fortunate not only to attend a primary school where the band project and its director were held in high esteem, but whose links with an outstanding local community band ensured that these two musicians frequently found themselves playing with people who had developed and were able to provide excellent models of music expertise. So Alistair's mother talked of the impetus that was generated by a workshop organized by the community band and led by the principal trumpet of the Sydney Symphony Orchestra. His parents, without any special claims to being musical, still noticed and commented on the improvement of breathing and tone. As this and many other examples illustrate, significant others often made available provisions that enriched learning experiences and provided scaffolding that accelerated the ascent to expertise. More broadly, learners may be exposed to enrichment programmes through the influence of key figures who extend far beyond what might normally be offered to other individuals, regardless of gift or talent.

The idea of intrapersonal catalysts filtering environmental catalysts like a sieve is not unattractive, but there is a sense in which it may fail to capture the much more dynamic interactive processes that are involved in human development as the key relationship triangle of Anthony, his mother, and his teacher illustrates. Even if we accept that personality traits remain unchanged by experience and environment, individual needs and interests do not. This is why we believe that Sameroff's (2010) concept of relational transaction provides a strong theoretical framework for understanding development. In such a theory it is not so much that experience is sieved by intrapersonal catalysts—as if the only active elements were environmental catalysts passing through immobile intrapersonal objects—but that environmental experience is blended with the intrapersonal. In such an analogy, traits, rather like primary colours, remain constantly present and may even dominate our responses and colouring of experience, but personal and malleable adaptations make various and changeable shades and hues possible too. These adaptations are clearly influenced in turn by the experiences that they blend with and by the subconscious and conscious responses that are made to them.

Leaving it to chance or making a match

Many of the experiences, events, and circumstances outlined above might fall into what is one of the more controversial aspects of Gagné's model—chance. Chance may have a role in talent development as 'a qualifier of any causal influence' (Gagné, 2009, p. 70), particularly as chance refers to the accidents of birth and background over which we have no control. Our family and the social environment in which we are raised are but two of the important ways in which chance impacts on our development. Our study revealed hundreds of seemingly casual events that shaped musical lives in all kinds of ways, but many of them sit uneasily in our minds with the notion of chance. Instead of qualifying casual influences as chance, detailed study of these events often revealed that they were not chance at all. Negative casual influences frequently turned out to be the direct outcomes of poor planning, bad decisions, inappropriate behaviours, ill-advised comments, inflexible approaches and expectations, and prejudiced values and beliefs.

As the stories of Anthony and Alistair illustrate, musical development need not be left to chance when parents and teachers accept responsibility for matching children's present experience, skills, and psychological needs with appropriate learning strategies. So whilst none of this is to deny that chance plays a role in musical development, the task for us as researchers and educators may be to more clearly define how we can leave less to chance than results from our study suggest is often the case.

A key element in the chance dimension relates to the assumption in most instrumental programmes that a particular kind of musicality—performance from notation—will meet the demands, needs, and prior experience of *all* young learners. To this extent it is true that Anthony and Alistair may simply have got 'lucky'. What would have happened, for example, if, in Anthony's first lessons on the trombone, his teacher had encouraged him to play by ear or improvise and, subsequently, been far less enthusiastic about Anthony's achievement or aptitude had he performed far less well than he had on the B flat major scale?

We will examine the stories of two of our learners who seemed to 'get unlucky' for very different kinds of reasons in the following chapter. One of these stories relates to the question of 'whose musicality' which we discussed at the beginning of this chapter.

The adaptation of Gagné's model above by McPherson and Williamon (2006) defines eight types of musical talents that are evident in music. These eight talents are based on professional occupations and areas of the discipline such as performing, improvising (e.g. jazz), composing original music, reworking music by arranging it for a particular context (e.g. movie score), analyzing music as is typical with music theory teachers, critically appraising music of the type evident in newspaper criticism of a professional performance, conducting, and music teaching. As we have already observed, formal education settings identify musical talent primarily as a competency in musical performance, as in the case of Anthony and Alistair. We noted in Chapter 2 how much notation-based performance dominated our participants' early instrumental learning experiences to an almost total exclusion of improvisation or playing by ear.

Within this limited framework graded music examinations even help us identify the top 10% of achievers—in any particular instrument at least—with some degree of reliability and repeatability. Significantly, however, the more notation-based the performance skill, the easier assessment becomes and the more music becomes acceptable to mainstream education, especially at high-school levels. Anthony has also developed some skill in composition as several others in our sample did, but applying criteria for determining the top 10% in this area of musicality becomes more problematic. What of those learners in our study who went on to compose and improvise quite extensively, some without even basic music literacy skills? Small (1998) and others have argued against this kind of reductionist thinking about discreet notions of composing, improvising, and performing as an historical and institutional anomaly. Such compartmentalisation of musicalities may even have serious implications for the impact, quality, and long-term sustainability of musical performance itself (as being something very different from composing and improvising), and we will discuss this in the closing chapters of this book.

Anthony is now also teaching pupils himself, even though he is absolutely adamant that he does not wish to become a teacher. How would we measure or categorize Anthony's talent as a music teacher? If musicality is a higher function that is difficult to reduce to the sum of natural or acquired abilities and their development, what then of teaching music, which calls upon a whole range of different social and communicative competencies in addition to musical ones. How would we quantify the top 10% of music teachers? Do Anthony and Alistair's teachers fit the bill or did they simply fit Anthony and Alistair's bill? Whilst they may see their teachers as perfect examples of the ideal authoritative teacher prototype that we spoke of in Chapter 4, is this how their teachers appeared to other students who made less of an impression in early lessons? It turns out that it is not. In fact other students saw Anthony's teacher in a very different light. Some were poorly matched to him and found him not authoritative, but strongly authoritarian. Was this because they were clearly less well prepared than Anthony? Did they perhaps suffer by virtue of comparison with the student who turned up to his first lesson well equipped to conquer a B flat major scale in one attempt? Were Anthony and one or two other students privileged in these transactions because of an 'innate' ability that their teacher recognized in them? Or did their previous experience and flying start give the teacher cause to create a representation of innate ability that became a self-fulfilling prophecy?

In his attempt to clarify some of the most basic ingredients of innate ability, Gagné (2009) states that:

> When we say that little Mary is a 'born' pianist, we are certainly not implying that she began playing the piano in the hospital nursery, nor that she was able to play a concerto within weeks of beginning her piano lessons. Describing her talent as innate only makes sense metaphorically. It will convey the idea that Mary progressed rapidly and seemingly effortlessly through her talent development program, at a much more rapid pace than that of her learning peers. The same applies to any natural ability. Intellectually precocious children develop their cognitive abilities by going through the same developmental stages as any other child. The difference resided in the ease and speed with which they will advance through these successive stages. The term precocious says it all: They reach a given level of knowledge and reasoning before the vast majority of learning peers. And, the higher their intellectual giftedness will be, the earlier these successive stages will be reached. (p. 72–73)

Anthony comes close to making a similar statement about his ability to play the trombone when he claims, 'natural ability has helped me a lot'. But before we jump to the conclusion that he is claiming to be a 'born' trombone player, it is worth hearing how Anthony qualifies his claim for 'a natural flair'.

> I think to be a good trombone player you have to have good listening skills to get the intonation right, because there is a meter of tubing where you can put it anywhere and it's got to be in the precise position to be in tune, and if it's not you got to be able to hear it's not . . . but I think also perseverance and a lot of hard work has also got me quite far.

Syzygies for precociousness

Repeatedly in Anthony and Alistair's musical lives so far it is possible to pinpoint serendipitous alignments of circumstances that have clearly enabled them to progress far more quickly and more smoothly than their peers through various stages of musical development. It is not true to say that this has been 'easy' when such progress has been the result of serious commitment, investment, and hard work that Anthony recognizes he has made for himself and that others have made for him. If this journey is 'seemingly effortless' then it is because the confluence of these factors deceive the casual observer as they so often do: levels of parental support, the absence of conflict around the activity at home and school, parental valuing of music learning and participation for the 'love of it', the high standards and consistency of teaching, exemplar and inspiring modelling, exposure to musical events, and valuable peer and social networks have created and sustained lively music and musical lives. All these align with Anthony and Alistair's previous biological, social, and psychological experience to produce powerful syzygies for exceptional development that is precocious.

The consistency of these alignments and rapid realignments to changing needs and phases, their integrity and unity, across all micro and macro levels of Anthony and Alistair's ecological systems, is unsurpassed in our study and in the light of initial testing leaves us seriously questioning how their ability can be described as natural. If, as Gagné states, it only makes sense to talk of Mary's talent as innate in a *metaphorical* sense, maybe it would be better to not talk of it as innate or natural at all. Such talk seems to have been far more often used as an excuse to limit opportunities for the development of musical talents, than for providing them. This has often been the case where music perception tests decide which students should be given instrumental tuition, or in lagging efforts within traditional music education settings to differentiate provision on the basis of individual need and capacity. Ultimately, as we shall see in the next chapter, where we look at the lives of two other young people in our study, early indications of 'giftedness'—whatever their true origin—may turn out to have negligible impact on the development of musical talents anyway and musical talents may develop to impressive levels in spite of the absence of indications of musical 'giftedness'.

Even in times of change and transition the consistency of supportive and motivating mechanisms across Anthony and Alistair's ecological systems at various micro and macro levels is striking. A unity across the beliefs, conventions, and practices of families, peers, institutions, and the local community towards music for any period of time is unusual enough it seems. But at the centre of the particular syzygies that sustained Anthony and Alistair's trajectories is a key single influence—a music teacher. It is rare that a single music teacher is able to meet the changing needs of learners from beginner to expert, from child to young adult, as the teacher in these two accounts seems so resoundingly to have done. Similarly the primary school wind band, an outstanding local community band, and the high school band and music programme provided a natural sense of continuity and progression across these musical lives.

Stages and phases of development

Time is measured in stages and phases, it is marked by key events, changing seasons, and, in the life of children, by changing schools, changing friends and teachers, and even changing families. In sports psychology, there has been some progress to collate what is known about development into more holistic explanations that attempt to describe and define change over time. It is important to note from the outset the problematic nature of trying to 'frame' development into stages or phases as classic models of general development like Piaget, Erikson, or Bloom's work illustrates (Shaffer & Kipp, 2009). In sports psychology, however, some conceptions that have emerged attempt to bring findings into generalizable models. Focusing the debate in relation to musical development may benefit from transferring and translating this knowledge across disciplines.

Virtually all of the models of development we have come across in educational psychology and sport psychology, as well as those in music, place a great deal of emphasis on the types of support the learner receives from others, particularly their parents and their teacher. Anthony and Alistair's accounts clearly show what kinds of support make a difference to the development of expertise and suggest that self-regulation comes from safe and supportive environments that promote a sense of personal competence. Self-regulation does not appear to emerge from a vacuum where children are simply left to get on with it (if they want to) or by parent/teacher over-regulation or over-investment.

In thinking about a theory for support systems and syzygies across various stages and phases that we saw so positively influencing the musical development of Anthony and Alistair, and about the various psychological behaviours that facilitate development through various stages or phases of learning music during the school years, we found ourselves drawn to models that have appeared in sport, such as those devised by Abbott and Collins (2004) and Côté et al. (2007). The transitions in these models are different from the transitions we explored in Chapters 2 and 3, where we explained how many children's interest in continuing on their instrument changed dramatically at three key points: first, as they moved from primary to secondary school; second, as they moved from junior high school to senior high school, when final examinations and university entrance preparation takes a high priority; and finally from year 12 to the workforce or university, when life decisions are made that impact on access and opportunities for further active musical engagement. We shall see a very dramatic individual example of the impact of those school transitions in the following chapter. Our adaptation of the sports psychology literature, however, forms another way of thinking about musical development in that it attempts to define some of the consistent *intra-personal* stages that we have observed in our learners across these more macro transitions.

Bloom's (1985) pioneering collection of findings, based on studies with experts in various fields, suggests that talent emerges according to three stages: initiating, development, and mastery. His initial studies set the scene for subsequent attempts to clarify the support needed to sustain development across the gruelling years it takes to achieve expert levels of performance. Various researchers in sport have developed Bloom's model and other work by Côté (1999) into a more detailed conception, which McPherson and Lehmann (in press) adapted for music and which we use here to define the development of Anthony and Alistair's musical expertise across the years of schooling and into the early years of adulthood.

Both Anthony and Alistair tick almost every construct in the sampling, specializing, investment, and maintenance stages of Figures 6.2 and 6.3 in relation to their experience as developing brass players. We hesitate only with the suggestion that their early wind instrument experience emphasized fun, leading to skill development. Unlike some other band directors in the project, their wind band director turns this construct on its head with his explicit philosophy that 'skill development leads to having fun'. The key point here though is that both Anthony and Alistair demonstrated enough motor, cognitive, physical, and musical maturity to ensure the early success we have seen—in other words, they developed sufficient skills early enough to have fun before tasks became onerous! By their own accounts, they were having fun from day one of the programme because they appear to have benefited from a higher level of 'readiness' than many of our learners. It is easy to see why others, who were at a lower level of musical achievement as they entered the respective band programmes because, for example, of an under-exposure to a diverse range of activities that might have nurtured motor, cognitive, physical and musical skills or because of the absence of some key support systems, would have found the experience very challenging and ultimately frustrating. Essentially, the director of Anthony and Alistair's programme demanded that students progressed to specializing levels rapidly: by his own admission the programme itself was one of 'specializing'.

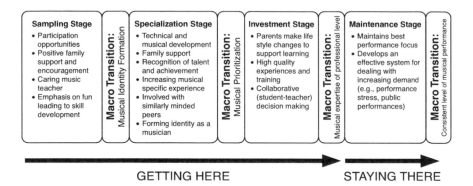

GETTING HERE   STAYING THERE

Figure 6.2: Stages for musical development. Adapted from 'Eliminating the dichotomy between theory and practice in talent identification and development: considering the role of psychology', Angela Abbott and Dave Collins, Journal of Sports Sciences, © Taylor and Francis, 2004, reprinted by permission of the publisher (Taylor & Francis Group, http://www.informaworld.com). See also McPherson and Lehmann (in press).

Thinking about 'play' and 'playing'

Anthony and Alistair were quickly able to 'play' at the high levels that their band director demanded and the relationship between 'playing' and the systematic development of skills is central to most conceptions in sports development. We believe that unpacking the semantic confusion around the word 'play' is important to understanding the

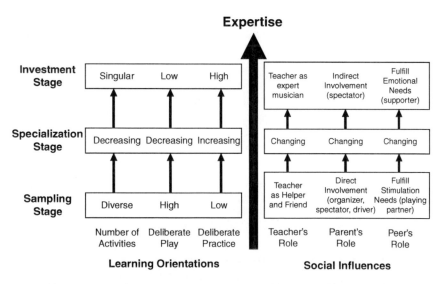

Figure 6.3: Changes in learning orientations and social influences during the sampling, specialization, and investment stages of developing musical expertise. Adapted, with permission, from J. Cote, J. Baker, and B. Abernethy, 2003, From play to practice: A developmental framework for the acquisition of expertise in team sports. In Expert performance in sports: Advances in research on sport expertise, edited by J.L. Starkes and K.A. Ericsson (Champaign, IL: Human Kinetics), 98.

processes at work here: there is a sense in which 'playing' is synonymous with 'having fun'. Even the more serious 'playing' of a musical instrument is about 'enjoyment', so that whatever the level of musical talent development, 'playing' remains at its heart. From analysis of students' practice strategies, we found that different forms of practice and playing fulfilled different roles at various stages of development.

In sport, Abbott and Collins (2004) suggest that in the sampling stage—typically between the ages of 6 and 12—practice can be described as *deliberate play* that involves loosely structured activities aimed at increasing motivation and enjoyment rather than technical skill. This is followed by the specialization stage (approximately 13 to 15 years of age) where more emphasis is generally placed on developing technical skill and where students start to specialize more in the types of sporting activities in which they are engaged as a form of enjoyable social activity. At this stage practice tends to encompass *deliberate practice* of the skills and techniques provided by specialist coaches or teachers as well as deliberate play and competition where the emphasis is on playing for enjoyment. Young athletes at this stage report feeling more positive about their involvement when engaged in deliberate practice rather than deliberate play, which in turn encourages them to take on more challenging tasks that impact on their sense of self-efficacy and ability to persist despite obstacles. We know from previous studies like that of Davidson *et al.* (1997) into the development of young expert musicians that deliberate play is an important component here too. Whilst all of the high achievers in that study engaged in deliberate play (or what Davidson *et al.* at the time referred to as 'informal' practice such as doodling and playing around), some of them engaged in it to the detriment of structured forms of practice and ultimately it appeared to hinder their progress in this very specific area of musical talent.

Practising for your own personal enjoyment as well as to improve are both important during the early stages of learning, but as skills develop further learning needs to include more and more strategic and goal-orientated practice, such as the type of practice that was reported and observed from both Anthony and Alistair when they entered the specialization stage. During this period, Anthony and Alistair began completing the intermediate grades of the AMEB performance exams and participated as active members in a community band alongside their music teacher, who helped prepare them for regional and state band championships.

A focus on deliberate practice in the investment stage occurs when young athletes are immersed in the sport and are able to set their own goals for achieving excellence. As the term 'investment' implies, there is a sense here of delayed gratification or enjoyment, the quality of the 'playing'—in the case of music, expert performance—depends upon that investment. We believe that this was the case for Anthony and Alistair in our study and for a small number of other participants who entered a specializing stage as early as primary school level. Unfortunately, as we shall see in the next chapter, the absence of investment from some parents, teachers, and schools failed to provide the support mechanisms necessary to sustain a transition into the investment phase and the ongoing development of musical talents. There is also a danger here of parental over-investment, especially of emotional capital, in their children's interests.

The final stage of the model—the maintenance stage—typically occurs after the school years and involves sustaining performance at a consistently high level.

Anthony and Alistair can be said to have maintained their playing at this level for several years already, but there are clear indications that this may become unsustainable. Anthony has been conscious for some time that other career paths, and he had a desire for a career in graphic arts, may be more professionally rewarding than music. His decision not to study music at university was an intensely practical one. Having watched his mother teach music, Anthony is adamant about not becoming a music teacher, although he has been more than happy to supplement his present income with a few pupils while at university and even now, since completing his training and becoming a professional graphic artist. Similarly, he has already experienced the competition surrounding orchestral jobs and whilst it is too early to say that Anthony will not end up performing professionally, the commitment needed to maintain such high performance levels is under serious threat from his changing life style and other competing interests.

These four macro stages of development from sports psychology can easily be reworked as a framework for explaining the existing literature in music and our own data. We will return therefore to them in the chapters that follow. As in sport, it is important to note that the road to musical excellence also involves many micro-stages of development where individuals will encounter many challenges, such as the emotionally draining family traumas described in Chapter 4. Each individual trajectory is therefore highly idiosyncratic. Negotiating the three transitions requires that support mechanisms can change in quality too: support that is appropriate for sampling is not likely to be appropriate for specialization, even if, as Anthony's teacher demonstrates, the same key individuals are sometimes able to provide both. As Abbott and Collins (2004) reinforce, the capacity to initiate and commit to these changes is vital for a learner—and his or her support network of teachers, parents, and peers—to successfully negotiate the transitions.

Two things strike us as being very significant when we look at the work of Abbot and Collins (2004) on the development of expertise in sport from the perspective of music education. Firstly, the emphasis on a long sampling stage identified by Abbott and Collins contrasts with many instrumental programmes, even those at primary school levels, where there may be limited opportunity for exploration and sampling through 'playful' processes aimed at increasing motivation and enjoyment rather than technical skills. For many students in our study, formal education provided only one kind of musical sampling opportunity. As we shall see in the next chapter, this sampling may even have been in an area of musical activity, or on an instrument, which the individual did not find motivating or enjoyable. Recorder programmes in schools are often used as part of this sampling stage, but often it might be the programme rather than the child that is doing the sampling, identifying children for future instrumental music lessons on the basis of the talent that is exposed or emerges through this experience and because of the limited available resources to extend sampling opportunities.

There is little evidence from our study that these processes emphasize the less structured and more playful activities that might increase motivation and enjoyment rather than technical skill. Nor is there any consistency about the provision of other musical activities that might bring young people to a place where a successful transition into specialization is possible. Readiness to enter the specialization stage becomes absolutely crucial to the possibility of successfully progressing through it, as we shall see in the next chapter. In contrast to the instrumental programme that Anthony and Alistair were engaged in at their primary school, several other directors viewed their band programmes as essentially part of this sampling stage.

The key to the effectiveness of either kind of music education practice is the extent to which it is able to differentiate for student learning on the basis of individual needs and abilities by providing the kind of syzygies that bring social, biological. and psychological experiences into positive alignment. This brings us to our second point from the work of Abbott and Collins (2004). These authors argue for a reconceptualization that recognizes the dynamic inter-relationship between talent recognition and talent development processes. Such a relationship is clearly evident in the musical lives of Anthony and Alistair. Their sampling experiences included a range of learning experiences both in school and outside of it, which enabled them, thanks to wide-ranging support networks, to make a swift transition to the specialization stage. Anthony and Alistair found their niche fairly quickly and were able to make the very most of the excellent support systems around them. One of the more interesting ways sports psychologists examine development is not by trying to identify the best performers at any particular moment, but rather by identifying the factors or blend of factors that, over time, may inhibit development. Such a conception sits easily with those who believe that musicians are more a product of their environment than their genetic endowment because the explanation is focused on how individuals interact with their environment and deal with the opportunities they are given (Abbott & Collins, 2004).

Anthony and Alistair have clearly become talented musicians, although it seems that neither wishes to become a professional musician. We suggest that detailed accounts of their musical lives reveal that they were indeed gifted by a wide and adaptable range of support mechanisms across micro- and macro-ecological systems that nurtured emerging skills, 'readying' them for transitions through the various stages of musical development, for which our adapted model provides a useful interpretative framework.

If this chapter has revealed how a wide range of promotive factors facilitated the development of expert musical talent, the chapter that follows will examine how the failure of support mechanisms and the misalignment and mismatching of social, biological, psychological, and environmental factors represent serious threat to it and create crises of self-regulation. As we have already illustrated, an extensive range of risk factors emerge in the lives of many of our participants and when we look in detail at some of those lives it is possible to get a clearer understanding of how critical combinations of them impact musical journeys very dramatically indeed.

Chapter 7

Lily and Bryan: exits and entrances in musical lives

The previous chapter enabled us to explore some theoretical ideas about musical development from the lives of two high-achieving young people. Our explorations were framed according to Gagné's model of musical talent and giftedness on the one hand (Gagné, 2009), and by adapting Abbott and Collins' model (2004) of talent development in sports on the other. There is a problem, however, in attaching too much significance to these theories in attempting to account for individual journeys. Many of the existing theoretical models draw on pools of highly skilled individuals and look at them as cohorts rather than teasing out the individual factors that shape each person. So, rather like reverse engineering, having recognized 'talented' individuals, we find ourselves attempting to expose common conditions that might explain why a specific talent has emerged and flourished. Previous studies like this have helped to demystify exceptional musicianship and creativity, whether in the case of classical composers like Mozart (Simonton, 1991; Lehmann, 1997) or young high achievers at specialist music schools (Sloboda *et al.*, 1996).

Our understanding of the pathways that have led to such high levels of expertise in the lives of young achievers, as in the lives of Anthony and Alistair, is enhanced by perspectives from Abbott and Collins' model (2004), with its sampling, specialization, investment, and maintenance phases. Similarly, Gagné's (2009) dynamic model of talent development—even noting reservations about the conceptualization of innate and natural abilities—is able to account for the journeys of some of our participants in the western classical tradition of high musical achievement. Looking beyond the unswerving and linear trajectories of Anthony and Alistair's musical lives, our study often charts far more complex journeys. Czikszentmihalyi (1996) refers to complex life journeys when he shows how talent is not a stable trait because our capacity for action changes over the course of our lives. This resonates with work by Haensly *et al.* (1986), which demonstrates how the context in which we live is shaped by various coalescences of abilities that either drive us to become more committed to an activity or conflict in ways that make us lose interest. Theories of musical development must also be able to account for these kinds of journeys, and this underlines the importance of 'progress mapping' ongoing development, rather than attempting to explain it only through retrospective analyses of high achievement.

Extensive longitudinal research that is presently following neural, cognitive, and motor development has already reported in its early phases that, rather than there being any pre-existing or 'natural' markers for musical development, exposure to instrumental music learning impacts upon the development and plasticity of the brain (Schlaug *et al.*, 2005, 2009; Norton *et al.*, 2005; Forgeard *et al.*, 2008). If there is a sense in which music, given the chance, may take care of nature, it becomes compelling to investigate and attempt to map the complex pathways that deny music the opportunity to have its way with young people and constrains their capacity for music learning.

We have seen in Anthony and Alistair some of the processes through which people are motivated to interact with music in significant ways when their personal life alignments are favourable. When appropriate musical opportunity and support to tackle new challenges are well matched to individual 'readiness' in terms of social, biological, and psychological experience, music itself seems able to nurture nature. But given that only about one dozen of the more than 150 pathways we followed have led to outcomes similar to Anthony and Alistair's—and recall that this seems fairly representative of outcomes from music education in the West generally—we need to think carefully about the ways in which our participants' lives are marked by exits and entrances into and out of a wide variety of opportunities for musical development. The challenge becomes understanding how the detail of social, biological, and psychological experience—personal relationships, institutional and domestic beliefs and practices, personal appropriations of music's communicative potential, music's place in personal and social identity, and the strategies that are adopted to cope with investment demands—pushes people away from musical engagement as well as pulling them towards it.

Costs and benefits of school ensembles as an instrumental learning programme for all

Unlike the young people from Chetham's School of Music in Manchester, UK, who participated in Sloboda *et al.*'s seminal study (1996) and Davidson and Burland's follow-up (2006; Burland & Davidson, 2004), our learners did not enter a common musical pathway because of any particular talent they were seen to possess. Whilst some parents admitted they found the opportunity for children to take part in valued and sometimes locally prestigious music programmes attractive, most still found their children attending these schools for more mundane reasons than the pursuit of musical opportunity. Nevertheless, this is not to deny that the values and beliefs of a certain demographic may configure expectations for schools in all kinds of areas, especially perhaps in the arts and music. Several musical directors in our study commented on the contrast in expectations at private schools, as compared to public schools, but several of the programmes we observed had, nevertheless, built up very significant status within their school and community:

> We see the band as part of the school, but it's an extra-curricular activity that has become so big that it's the high-profile thing inside the school, which is great.

Given such expectations at local school levels, what are seen as ideal entrances to instrumental learning may actually reflect institutional operational needs, rather than those of individual students. Whilst there may be a general consensus about key windows of opportunity for the development of musical cognition and other skills, and that ensemble programmes have the potential to motivate students by appealing to relational and competency dimensions of psychological needs, there are risks in blanket provision for instrumental learning. Ensemble programmes may fulfil a role that is more about the attraction and profile of music performance within the school and wider community than individual musical development (Davidson & Pitts, 2001). There are potential obstacles to, as well as opportunities for, musical development in the arrangements that all of our schools made, in so far as such arrangements often seemed unable to differentiate effectively according to previous experience, present ability, and personal interest. In Chapter 2 we touched upon the debate that surrounds the question about what age is most appropriate for children to start instrumental lessons. Recall that Jørgensen's (2001) study investigating the relationship between the age at which conservatoire musicians began instrumental or vocal lessons and their level of performance whilst at the conservatoire is inconclusive.

Since many children never get the opportunity to sample instrumental learning in any form, it is hard to be critical of programmes that attempt to guarantee a short period of sampling for all. School instrumental music programmes, not least in Australia, tend to ration such opportunities according to student outcomes from music perception tests or offer instrumental opportunities as optional and expensive extras to those (parents) with the financial resources to pay for them. In fact, most of the programmes in our study did demand fee payment at some level. The fact the take-up level for music in all the schools was high suggests that those fees were not out of financial limits, and that there was a widely accepted view that parents should support the opportunity given to their children through ensemble learning, even if they had to pay a small fee for it.

Even though nearly all the band directors studied articulated the importance of an inclusive access principle for the initial sampling level, it was clear from interviews with the musical directors that some fully expected a large number of students to make exits from the programmes within a year or two, principally because of the high demands the band leaders were to make upon the developing instrumentalists. For other directors, what mattered most was keeping all students engaged for as long as possible.

> I don't think my job is to have a band that is excellent. I think my job is to get kids involved in music.

For one director, keeping students was an economic necessity:

> So I'd much rather that they were having a good time, enjoying coming along, enjoying playing the music, and enjoying practising at home. So it feeds itself that way. If I've got to lighten up a little bit, to ensure that each kid stays until the end of the year—because at this year, so many kids leave to go to private schools anyway—I'm continually in fear of kids dropping out of the programme. So I want to keep every kid here, not only for the sake of the band and the numbers, but also for financial reasons. We need the fees, we need to buy new instruments, I need to be paid, and if a few too many kids drop out, we can't afford to run the band.

The use of an ensemble programme for initial formal instrumental music sampling has obvious pedagogic attractions. Because of the high levels of task interdependence in music ensembles, even students with limited skills may find themselves making a contribution to a highly valued and complex conjunctive task that generates a sense of competency, and that regularly exposes them to the modelling of more advanced techniques. Similarly, such groups often generate high levels of social interdependence, where peers (slightly older near-age peers, in particular), may exercise considerable positive reinforcement for values and beliefs about participation in the ensemble and music in general.

Along with school and even wider community recognition of the group's achievement, this is likely to encourage a strong sense of collective identity, which many of the participants in the study report. Sometimes our learners indicated that this relatedness may even be the most important factor in ongoing commitment. Programmes like this have potential costs too. The nature of conjunctive tasks means that students' commitment to work on these tasks by themselves may be undermined by the limited satisfaction that is obtained from playing a part that might make little musical sense and give modest musical satisfaction by itself. In the interviews, even Anthony's mother raised such concerns, and there were a considerable number of parents who expressed worries when children were learning instruments that were not seen as melody-carrying ones. So, whilst successfully playing a part in the ensemble was a source of pleasure and motivation, practising that part alone at home, which was often essential for successful participation in the ensemble, was frequently reported as a tedious and a musically unsatisfying task that neither students nor parents were able to take any pleasure from. Where those kinds of part-learning assignments were the major focus of home practice, students appear to have been at risk and in many cases this led to early exits.

In addition, students in ensemble programmes like those in our study may also find themselves exercising little autonomy over repertoire during rehearsals or performance itself, or even, as we have already noted, over the instrument given to them to play. Pupil discontent about their initial instrument turns out to be one of the most significant predictors of early exits from the programme. Regardless of the needs of the band to maintain a balance between instruments, or teachers' perceptions of what might best suit students, not one of the students who was initially unhappy about the allocation of a specific instrument continued beyond the first year, and as far as we are aware, none ever engaged with formal instrumental instruction again. Some directors went to great lengths in an effort to reconcile children's interests with the band's needs and highlighted the time factor involved:

> It's very time-consuming. I'll probably spend most of a day doing it, but I really want the kids to leave here feeling that they've been successful at playing something, and they're happy to play that instrument, even if I've tried to guide them in a certain direction because I want a balanced group.

But this was not always the case. One boy got through two instruments in the first year, both of which were based on the band's needs, and this did not reflect his desires in any way. The mother, clearly irritated, explained:

> He was not given a choice of instrument. He did not like the baritone and he was then given the keyboard (some of the wind bands had keyboard players). In both instances he did not like being the only player of each instrument.

Other students may have been happy to take on an instrument where they had sole responsibility for a part in the ensemble and risen to the challenge. This student and one or two others like him did not, and the failure to recognize basic personality traits like self-confidence and independence put their capacity for music learning at unnecessary risk.

Sadly, several pupils felt unable to register their unhappiness to either parents or teachers. They appear to have thought that quitting was easier than requesting to learn a different instrument, even when there was a personal preference for change. The negotiation and potential conflict that they thought would follow such a request was too daunting a challenge. In such cases it was rare for parents or teachers to sit down and ask whether students would like to change instruments. The assumption seems to have been that they were simply not interested in learning any instrument.

While for many participants in our project the impact of the band director was very significant, in both positive and negative ways, there was often little opportunity for students to build up the same kind of impactful relationship as they might with their 'first' instrumental teacher. Previous research shows that a deep initial relationship with the first teacher is often very significant for future engagement and development (McPherson & Davidson, 2006).

Where there were no individual lessons in addition to ensemble lessons, this appeared to deny students an extremely significant support mechanism and, in some cases, to deny them exposure to differentiated approaches to teaching. Finally, a failure to differentiate tasks in ensembles according to student ability can lead to the demotivation of more highly skilled students, or frustration for less able ones, because of the difficulty in finding repertoire that is able to suit students with such a wide range of abilities.

Initially, however, ensemble programmes at primary schools appear to have been positive experiences for the majority of participants. The 'triggered' situational interest we spoke of earlier ensured an entrance to musical opportunity that had been eagerly awaited because the school had already exposed them to performances that had produced extremely positive responses.

'It will be fun!': Lily's dream

Soon after starting her school wind band programme in Year 4, Lily expressed a sentiment widely held by our participants that:

> When I heard the band in Year 3 I felt I wanted to be part of that special group. I thought it sounded good.

Clearly, this experience was key to the motivation that had been totally absent from Lily's brief exposure to recorder in the Year 3, an experience that she had 'nothing good to say about', and was determined to discontinue. In contrast, even before commencing lessons on the clarinet, Lily was adamant that, '(I)t will be fun!' Lily's first choice of band instrument was actually percussion, but her parents objected because they lived in a small unit and were worried about both space and noise, and so Lily commenced lessons on her second choice, the clarinet. After just a few lessons she remarked, 'Now I think clarinet is better. I like the black colour and screwing on reeds!' She had originally been attracted by the sound of the instrument—'I wanted something that could make noise!' The sound of the chalumeau register seems to have been a particular attraction for Lily, who declared that she had 'wanted to play the low notes, A, G, F, and B, I get to use the bottom keys'. She was adamant that neither friends nor teacher advice was influential in her choice of instrument. She enjoyed playing melodies and, equating percussion with untuned percussion exclusively, quickly formed a view that justified her playing clarinet rather than percussion: 'I wouldn't have been able to play tunes on percussion'.

Even though exposure to the recorder had been a sampling experience that Lily had no desire at all to develop into specialism, it would have had very significant transferable impact to the clarinet, just as Anthony's piano and recorder experience had been for him. As a young adult, Lily admitted that she thought maybe she had an advantage in having learnt the recorder that gave her a strong 'kick-start', so that she was quickly achieving at a relatively high level—this reflects Anthony's experience too. After just a few lessons Lily declared, 'I know lots of notes', and she was already predicting she would play into adulthood and would not change her instrument. 'I want to become superb, I hope to be best in the band.' Such ambition was clearly encouraged by her tutor who, Lily reported, said 'I am playing well!' When asked what she would need to do to fulfil this ambition, Lily replied with comments showing a strongly developed sense of her own musical ability as being incremental, and therefore something she could control and develop, rather than a fixed entity:

> Practise my sight-reading, know how to play tunes from memory and not getting squeaks. Practising hard on my instrument will be the main influence on whether or not I become a good musician. I like the idea of working hard and achieving something.

These comments reveal some very important points with regard to Lily's own learning orientation: first, the link between investment and achievement as something pleasurable is already accepted by Lily at the relatively young age of 7 years; second, a view of music learning that is already able to articulate key component skills in musical fluency—sight-reading, musical memory and tone production. There is also a clear realization of the social potential that music making outside the band could afford, when Lily said, 'I can play with my friend who plays flute or other clarinetists and the band'.

Lily was adamant that she would practice once every day for 30 minutes, but did confess to some anxiety about chipping reeds and learning to read and write notes. Her practice plan did turn out to be over-ambitious, but Lily still managed to practice almost every day for between 15 and 25 minutes, so that by the end of the first year she had already acquired between 100 and 150 hours of private practice time, in addition to weekly lessons and rehearsals. This is significantly more than any other learner in the project. She preferred playing in a band concert over sports, and liked tackling new and difficult pieces and as she said herself she 'loved it!'

Lily's ensemble was one of several that provided students with both a regular wind band programme and individual lessons from the outset. These were often highly structured. For example, one of the directors explained how he expected instrumental teachers, in what appears to have been a rarely rigid authoritarian way, to:

> . . . work on the same system I do, which is 20 minutes of technical work, solo work, 5 minutes of aural and 5 minutes of band. If you can do your technical work and you've got good aural skills you should be able to play in band.

Thinking about the advantages and disadvantages of learning exclusively through an ensemble programme or individual lessons outlined above, the weight of evidence from our study suggests that a balance of individual and ensemble learning from the outset of instrumental learning is more likely to generate greater levels of motivation and more effective support for learning than either of these options alone. Like Anthony and Alistair, Lily admired her instrumental teacher greatly, and his importance as a role model, specifically as a clarinetist, is obvious:

> I started at an age a few years younger than my tutor did. If he is that good after those few years, I can be better than him when I'm his age.

She added that he was somebody who was 'fun, and made lessons interesting, not strict'.

A particular kind of work ethic sometimes causes educators and parents to question the value of 'having fun' or 'playing' as we discussed in the last chapter, but 'having fun' is one of the very strongest early predictors for ongoing musical engagement among our participants. With this in mind, music educators might do well to reflect upon the semantics of phrases like '*playing* a musical instrument' or 'clarinet *player*'. In addition, and as we noted in the previous chapter from studies of talented young musicians, balancing a playful and flexible approach to private practise with more systematic strategies may be crucial to ongoing musical development (Sloboda & Davidson, 1996). So far, Lily's journey sounds remarkably similar to Anthony and Alistair's and there is every indication that Lily might be a candidate for future musical expertise.

Asked about her dream instrument Lily replied:

> A new clarinet, because my school instrument needs to be repaired and my clarinet feels different to other people's—it feels like plastic. My clarinet looks a bit rusty and the reed and mouthpiece stink!

Making progress in private

The investment phase of the model that was developed in the last chapter clearly includes outlay for things like suitable musical instruments. It is a key factor in the success of many of the programmes in the study that they spend a lot of energy, through committees and parent involvement, in attempting to ensure that instruments are available to children for this initial sampling, but in Lily's case there are clearly some issues that are potentially demotivating for her. For many parents, perhaps for Lily's, buying an instrument may simply be economically impossible. Others may not see any value in it, especially at an early stage of learning where they often feel that the child needs first to display long-term investment in terms of practice and progress—a commonly expressed view among parents in the study. Others may feel that what the child is using is good enough, especially if parents themselves have little, if any, musical experience. Lily's parents, for example, never talk about music, they never sing or attend concerts. Whilst Lily mentions a broken violin in the house, she has no idea if anybody could even play it! Their sporadic listening includes some classical, a bit of Beatles, Paul Anka, Crowded House and 'Chinese singers singing in Mandarin'. Lily herself only listens to pop and TV music, and claims to have never sung in a choir and neither, she insists, does she sing by herself, with friends, or with family.

Not surprisingly then, Lily's parents feel that their lack of experience disqualifies them from offering even basic support:

> We don't know the instrument so we cannot help her. Practice is generally done in her room, so sometimes she will let her sister listen, but that is not often. She usually goes and does it, though only when she is ready. When she does practise she doesn't really let anyone hear her so we don't really know when she does it. She goes into her room and shuts the door, and will not let anyone in there. She usually practises, usually nominates a time that practice will commence.

So while Lily's parents often reminded her to practise, her own responses to an early survey reveal that whilst they attempted to force her to practise, they rarely if ever listened to her 'play'. Essentially, Lily is regulating her own practice, and this is consistent with what her mother says about her personality:

> She isn't scared to experiment, she likes to do things by herself, and she is very adventurous. She experiments with things until she can work them out. She is very cheeky, doesn't like to lose, and is very stubborn.

There is consistent evidence that Lily was very conscientious in her practice regime at this early stage, even if she did not practise at the same time each day, as Anthony did. She used the practice diary set by her tutor to:

> practise what I needed to practise—memorize a scale—but I would also goof off a lot, blow a few notes, and just test my range!

Dad, who 'is most keen and wants me to go in competitions' seemed more concerned with his daughter's level of achievement *per se* than with the value of music itself. Her mother admits that the emotional climate around practice was sometimes tinted by threats of punishment or withdrawal of lessons.

> Her father only really tells her off if she has not done her practice. He says that she will get punished, but nothing ever happens, he just shouts at her and threatens to stop her instrumental lessons, and says that he will not pay for the next one.

Her parents had quickly come to the opinion that Lily possessed some talent for music and by the end of the first year they had noticed that:

> She is playing more complicated music. I am very impressed with the pieces that she is playing, especially with her age. She is playing some really difficult things. She is passionate about the band!

This judgment indicates the contradictions present in what so many parents say about their own musical competency and about the level of support they feel able, or unable, to provide. The journey from musical sampling to musical expertise clearly becomes a far more arduous and precarious one if music educators fail to engage and mobilize key figures like parents in ways beyond attending school concerts. There is no shortage of literature or initiatives in education generally, although especially in literacy, that explicitly recognize the importance of these school/home partnerships and carefully unpacks what *kind* of support is effective (Pomerantz *et al.*, 2005; see also McPherson, 2009).

The tension and emotional climate surrounding music practice appears essentially similar to that surrounding homework but, given that music is not seen as essential in the way that other homework often is, parents may quickly abdicate responsibility for it when it becomes a site of conflict. Challenging values and beliefs towards musical talent and expertise, and helping parents to adopt positive orientations towards their children's music learning should clearly be key priorities for music educators. There is little evidence in our study that such priorities extended beyond mobilizing parental support for music camps, committees, and other practical and organizational needs. Whilst involvement at this level clearly demonstrates that parents value the activity, this was by no means the practice in all school music programmes. The motivation for such engagement appears often to have been the meeting of practical needs, rather than asking how parents might be encouraged to value their children's musical development and support it effectively.

Early into the second year Lily's mother understates the already very significant progress that Lily is making:

> She was promoted to Concert Band 1 very quickly. Usually only students in year 6 get into that band, but she was still in year 5 when that happened, so I guess that was encouraging.

By the beginning of her final year in primary school, just over two years into the programme, both mother and daughter had their eye on a prestigious high school with a strong musical tradition:

> She is really excited about it because of the band, they are meant to have a really good one. That is the only reason that she wants to go there.

In fact, Lily reports slightly more parental interest as she increased in competency, but it seems significant that her mother still stays outside the bedroom.

> Mum might walk past and listen for a while if I leave the door open. She might just comment that I'm doing well, and she might ask what piece I'm playing.

and Dad,

> . . . stops by and listens if I'm playing a piece from '66 Great Tunes'. He probably knows it because he likes classical music, it contains classical pieces he likes and knows.

In the third year of the programme, Lily was able to celebrate her by now considerable achievements, as she appears to have progressed from sampling to early levels of expertise:

> The greatest thing for me so far was at the National Band Championships. I played a solo without stuffing up.

But she had no intention of sitting on her laurels and articulated a clear strategy for ongoing improvement and increasing expertise:

> To improve, I need to tongue really fast and move my fingers quickly. Play the highest notes 'nicely'.

In fact Lily's ambition was now greater than it had been in her first year of learning, and claimed 'I will play until I die!' and 'If I was to quit, it would be because I was forced to'.

Lily clearly applied systematic practice strategies in pursuit of excellence. In fact she articulated these more clearly than just about any other learner in our study at this stage:

> My tutor tells me and I know what I must try to improve. I don't play the parts I already know, I go through that section and find the trouble spots and I go over it really slow and speed it up . . . and then I play the older pieces I like to play.

When asked what she would like to do after leaving school, Lily's first choice was a 'virtuoso clarinettist'.

> I'm off to a great start, I'm vastly improving. I can already play quite well, I like to play. I'm glued to the clarinet and music. I'll probably pursue a career in playing.

In an early test where participants are asked to select which graphic notation corresponds to the tune 'Twinkle, Twinkle Little Star', Lily displayed sophisticated levels of musical metacognition that very few other participants articulated when she explains how she went about solving the problem.

> You sort of have to play 'Twinkle Twinkle' in your mind and you have to check it. I played it on a clarinet in my head.

Apart from the satisfaction of achievement, as, for example, with the successful solo for the band in the National Competition, Lily was developing a repository of meaningful musical experiences that do intra-communicative work for her at a personal aesthetic and regulatory level. She revealed a strong sense of identity with some key pieces such as the 'Carnival of Venice . . . the atmosphere . . . it's really so . . .' and stated how she was 'honoured and feel it is my duty to do well'.

A competitor to the clarinet

Just as Lily was commencing her last year in primary school, however, she received her first computer as a Christmas present.

> It was novel, and yeah, that was it. There were so many new things to experiment with.

Comments made by both Lily and her mother suggest that Lily had a particular liking for trying out and gaining competency with new things. The computer quickly took up enough of her time for her parents to express some concern, but Lily insisted that she was still committed to playing the clarinet. There was absolutely no doubt at all in her mind that she would continue playing into high school and indeed 'for life'. But as time went by Lily's parents saw the computer as luring their 'talented' daughter away from instrumental learning, especially after Lily entered high school. In fact, soon after arriving at the high school Lily had set her heart on, the increase in motivation and commitment that her parents had expected was replaced with dramatic demotivation. They soon became so exasperated with her refusal to practise that they even talked about throwing the girl's computer—what they saw to be the clarinet's chief competitor—out of the window. They were at a loss to explain the downturn in interest and the personal computer became the site of serious domestic conflict.

The competition for young people's elective activities has burgeoned immensely over recent decades and, in all probability, more in the time-span that this project has covered than at any other time in history. This is evidenced first in the extraordinarily diverse recreational activities that the participants increasingly undertook outside the home over the first few years of the study. Second, and in Lily's case it seems even more significantly and far more secretively, young people's social and recreational lives moved increasingly behind closed bedroom doors as this project and information technology developed side by side. Never before have there been such a wide range of experiences to be sampled by young people as in contemporary urban living. Some, inevitably, are rejected and others pursued with a desire for greater competency and specialization or simply for recreation, socialization, or even just diversion.

Indeed, the philosopher Heidegger (1977) argues that routinization of novelty through ceaseless technological innovation is symptomatic of the mood of the modern age—a mood that he controversially describes as boredom. We wonder what Heidegger would have made of the technological developments in the past quarter of a century since his death. We will return to notions of novelty in the next chapter, but for now we can agree that computers and the internet have become a universal presence competing for space in all our lives. Within 5 years of the introduction of instant internet messaging in the USA, for example, it had become the most popular of all computer activities amongst young people. Interestingly, the same extensive research in the USA suggests that the time spent on a computer outside of school work just at the beginning of this millennium is still insignificant when compared to the amount of time spent watching TV or listening to music! A further finding from the same study revealed that almost without exception, and regardless of socio-economic status, young people had access to their own private music systems (Rideout *et al.*, 2010)

School transitions: transfers out of music learning?

With all this in mind, we return to Lily's musical story in high school only to discover that it is stunningly and almost tragically brief—within a year Lily had given up the clarinet and childhood dreams and aspirations completely! Lily's parents offered very straightforward explanations for this dramatic change in direction, and blame is squarely placed on the new technology that had hijacked Lily's musical journey. It would be surprising if things were as straightforward as that, but it was not until much later that Lily, as a young adult, shared with us her version of events—information that she either kept from or failed to communicate effectively to her parents, or to us, at the time. The downturn and eventual exit from music learning was, according to Lily, the outcome of a series of unfortunate events and poor arrangements made by parents and schools to facilitate a safe, risk-free transition between schools and teachers—a sad example of how unserendipitous happenstance can demotivate and thwart musical development. It reflects multiple failures to invest in Lily's emerging musical talent. Typically, the crisis occurred soon after the transition from primary to secondary school, just as it has for many other young people in our study.

Once again it might be easy to interpret disengagement like Lily' as indicating a change in student priorities, increased opportunities for extra/co-curricular activities, a change in peer groups and the influences exerted by them. Perhaps, like many other children who carried on until the end of primary school, this was simply a convenient place for Lily to stop; motivation had undoubtedly been less intense over recent months and the change of school and teacher was, perhaps, a good opportunity to make an exit without causing too much disturbance. In other circumstances, parents might even have agreed, as several did, that upon arrival at high school, the child should simply make up their own mind without parental input to decision making.

None of this is true for Lily. As we have heard, the clarinet she played belonged to her primary school band and, understandably, the school demanded she return it when she left. If her parents had ever previously been disposed to buy her a clarinet, and there is no suggestion that they had been, the downturn in motivation that they had observed over the past year was unlikely to have encouraged them to do so, and even less so as the emotional climate around practice turned increasingly sour and often led to conflict. Upon arrival at high school, Lily discovered that the auditions for the school's four wind ensembles were imminent and worse still, she had had no instrument upon which to practice for the previous two months or so. With no instrument to play, Lily was unable to audition for the band that she had dreamt of joining. Soon after the main auditions had been held, and which Lily inevitably missed, the school managed to find an instrument for her at her request, but by this time places for clarinets in the school's two leading bands—the bands Lily had set her heart on—-were already oversubscribed. She eventually auditioned and was given a place in the third band, but Lily was immediately struck by the low standard of playing, disruptive behaviour, and lack of motivation amongst players. Fairly quickly, she became thoroughly frustrated and practise declined even more dramatically. In what seemed almost an act of desperation, Lily's parents actually bought a clarinet for her from overseas at the end of the first term. It was too late.

Even now, it might be tempting to assume that Lily and her parents had simply over-estimated her ability, and that as she had matured through junior school Lily had come to make a more accurate assessment of her ability. Unsurprisingly, nearly all students in our study typically assessed themselves as being better than average during the first 3 years of engagement. Perhaps Lily's decision to quit was simply an excuse born of the reality check of going to high school and discovering that there were other good clarinet players, better clarinet players—the crashing of unrealistic expectations and dreams.

Our evidence suggests that this hardly seems likely to have been the case. Her band director at primary school had indeed identified Lily, as she always aimed to be, as one of the 'three best players in the band' and the band was clearly performing at one of the highest levels of any primary bands in the study. The director's view of Lily's ability is substantiated in the tests that participants undertook during the first 3 years of the study. In the first year, Lily's WFPS test was the highest in the entire research sample (48, average 17, range 2–48) and that score continued to increase over the 3 years of testing. In spite of the significant decline in practice time in her third year of study, Lily had still accumulated a larger 3-year total than almost anybody else in the study.

By the end of the 3 years her WFPS score was still amongst the highest 5% in the study. It seems very likely, given the nature of the WFPS, that Lily's previous encounter with the recorder had given her some early advantage in testing on the clarinet, as she herself recognized. It was an advantage that also gave Lily an edge in terms of self-confidence and motivation, just as we observed with Anthony. Nevertheless, her band director, like Lily's parents, had observed a downturn in her final year at primary school and explained it thus:

> Lily hasn't come along as well this year— the first two years she was very good—but this year. You tend to find with some girls (I don't want to make blanket statements), or with some students, when they get to sixth class, they're having a bit of an identity crisis and so it's a "Am I going to continue with this music thing?" So she's still a very good player.

The director may not wish to make 'blanket statements', but there is evidence to suggest that the transition between primary and secondary schooling is more difficult psychologically for girls than boys (Finn & Rock, 1997), and similarly there is evidence that girls actually endure more distress, increased levels of loneliness, and a greater decline in general academic performance than boys during inter-school transitions (Benner & Graham, 2009). The association of declining performance with transitions between school phases (Alvidrez & Weinstein, 1993, p. 9; Galton & Hargreaves, 2002) is an indication of a systemic problem which continues to plague young people's development to expertise in any field. Where the school system, as opposed to a private tutor and family, are the prime providers and supporters of musical opportunity, it is not hard to see why school transitions prove to be the insurmountable obstacle they clearly are for many musical journeys.

Repeating material and curriculum content is seen as one of the key demotivating factors in inter-school transitions (Galton & Hargreaves, 2002) and, whatever the standard of the flagship bands in her new school, Lily was clearly shocked by the change in standards of attitude and ability in the lower level band that she found herself in after a disastrous audition process. In our most recent interview with Lily, she compared the two experiences, beginning with her view of the primary school experience:

> Maybe everyone had the assumption that this is the way that things were done, so everyone had to work to that standard . . . everyone around me was really motivated, and there was just this expectation that everyone would play really well, that everyone would practice and put in their best efforts for the band. In high school, I don't know why they even (the students) persisted, because with me, I had to do it intensely or not at all.

In fact, it seems that several of the primary bands were consistently performing at a significantly higher level than many junior high school bands, endorsing the concerns highlighted in research about school transitions generally and cited above. Lily even admitted that perhaps she had a 'bit of an ego' going up to high school, but as she explains, 'you have to have self-motivation, but you have to be able to act on it all the time'. There can be little doubt that Lily felt that she had been prevented from acting on her self-motivation, 'I think I felt pretty much disillusioned straightaway!'

The new clarinet languished and remained almost totally untouched. Lily's older sister had some singing lessons, briefly, and she bought a keyboard that Lily enjoyed experimenting on:

> It had automatic chords and a really wide variety of instruments that sounded kind of realistic. But I didn't think to pick up the clarinet.

Even in early adulthood, Lily expresses the same fundamental philosophy that she had expressed in her childhood: 'enjoying playing is kind of pushing yourself isn't it? More for me it would be.'

Cultural heritage and compliance

The multiple perspectives of musical development seem complicated enough in this case study, but one further dimension illustrates the problems we face in attempting to understand how personality, parental values and beliefs, teaching and learning methods, and environmental opportunities configure musical journeys. Lily is of Chinese origin. Her mother speaks little English and spoke to us through Lily's older sister. Lily claims that her parents were a good deal less strict than many other Asian families she knew. She cites the fact that she went on to follow an arts degree as an example of their relatively liberal view of things.

> Well, I think all Asian parents want their kids to take a commerce degree, become an accountant, or become a lawyer, but I think, well, my other sisters did arts degrees too.

This point of view is not unique to parents of Asian heritage in our study. Parental pressure, especially during the middle and upper high school years in relation to future vocational opportunities and potential earning capacity, is frequently articulated as a reason to ease off on musical specialization. Nevertheless, just as girls in the study tended to be more likely than boys to persevere with their instruments out of conscientiousness rather than high levels of personal motivation, several participants of Asian origin expressed a sentiment that appears from the authors' own European heritage to represent a submission to parental authority in relation to instrumental practice and homework in general. However, it is here that we are reminded of Pomerantz *et al.*'s (2005) research showing that Asian children tend to be more likely to take on their parents' goals and subsequently be more influenced by their parents' views because they typically have a different view of parental opinion and values than most other children living in multicultural societies like the US and Australia. Whereas children of European heritage might view their parents' practice of making a decision without consulting them as controlling or interfering, Asian children may not because this action is congruent with their decision to take on their parents' goals autonomously.

Indeed, two girls of Chinese heritage, who both achieved very high levels of expertise on two instruments, claimed that one of the key factors was parental belief that success in high-grade music exams would be very important supporting documents when their offspring applied to read medicine at university. Interestingly, both participants and parents demonstrated relatively low levels of intrapersonal motivation for, or engagement with, music itself and both participants have significantly disengaged with music performance in social and personal contexts following admission to university. It is tempting to suggest that from the point of view of parental values and beliefs, instrumental expertise was primarily a means to an end. This may be a far more common view than is widely recognized.

Throughout Lily's story she has impressed us as being strong-willed, and that is evident once again when, at university, she made a totally unexpected re-entry to organized musical activities when she decided to join the university community wind band after more than 5 years without touching the clarinet.

> I wanted to do something with the clarinet, it's been good socially to be involved in the group and it was about recreation. I had to learn to loosen up. I found I was more in tune with making myself sound better, as in tone and maybe pitch. Except that technically, my fingers had gone out of work. So I wasn't as up to scratch as the others.

Within a year, Lily had already returned to a WFPS score commensurate with her score just before she exited the instrumental programme at high school and only slightly lower than the score achieved by Anthony, who had continued to play throughout high school and acquired such high-level expertise. Where her re-entry to clarinet playing will lead remains to be seen. That she will never fulfil, in terms of musical expertise, the promise and ambition she previously displayed seems obvious, but that is not to say that she will not lead a rich musical life.

For other participants, exits from the instrumental programme were made at very early stages indeed because of what appears to have been a total misalignment of provision and needs. For Lily, early provision was able to match her early needs. The band programme and Lily's individual tutor provided enough support to enable her to develop at an exceptional rate in the early years of the programme. In spite of other serious shortcomings at other ecological system levels, like the home, the fit of provision to Lily's own biological, social, and psychological experiences enabled her to make outstanding progress. Ultimately, however, the absence of any meaningful transaction around music in the home left Lily critically vulnerable. At an older age such obstacles may have been surmountable by other social networks, individual determination, or initiative alone, after all, Lily had shown these qualities already. In this case, however, and bearing in mind the wider challenges that Lily was probably facing in changing schools, it was not. Lily's very considerable investment seems to have paid low dividends for the time being at least.

Justifying an early exit

Others participants, like Bryan, found their entrance to the programme more or less completely unsupported from the outset and made little if any personal investment in it either. Unlike Lily, the clarinet was not an instrument of choice for Bryan. On the contrary, it was an instrument assigned to him by the band director/teacher. Bryan was adamant almost from the outset that 'I didn't really want to do it. My mum wanted me to go in it'. His comments consistently reflected a complete lack of motivation towards playing the clarinet, or any instrument for that matter. In response to being asked to name his dream instrument, Bryan, in his first interview after taking up lessons, replied, 'I don't know. I'm not really keen on instruments'. When asked to state whether there was anything that he liked or disliked about the clarinet, Bryan stated, 'It's hard to play and it's also boring'. Asked why he wanted to learn an instrument, Bryan responded: 'I don't really want to learn it'.

Bryan's other interests at this stage were soccer, Tai-kwando, and chess, and he complained that there was little time to practise, even though he was quick to add that he did not really like it much anyway. Nearly all the participants had a wide range of interests and hobbies, indeed it seems that many of those that went on to develop considerable expertise in music were actually developing significant expertise in several other domains too and led extremely busy lives. It was their ability to organize those commitments in systematic but flexible ways that facilitated their ongoing progress. Significantly, this systematic level of time-management should not be equated with regimented systems in the sense of practising at the same time every day, as we have already discussed.

Bryan's mother, however, concurs with Bryan's argument about time restrictions:

> He complained he didn't have time to practise, time was the most important factor. He had a lot on, that was the major thing. He was quite adamant he didn't want to continue.

It appears that Bryan's parents, and his mother in particular, initially thought that it would be good for Bryan to play something and join the band. This was a motive widely held by parents, often, it seems, without seriously thinking about the timing or appropriateness of the opportunity available in relation to their own children's present abilities, experiences, and needs. Just several months into the project, Bryan's mother appears to have revised her view of things and used the popular argument about natural musical talent to justify Bryan's exit from it:

> No, he's not musically orientated at all. He just tried it . . . he never struck me as someone who was really interested in music and he does a lot anyway. He wasn't much good at it, he had no aptitude for it. He's not naturally talented, he's a fairly quiet child and he doesn't like to fail. I think he knew he wasn't any good at it.

In addition, Bryan's mother also cites issues relating to gender identity as contributing to Bryan's disaffection with band.

> He didn't like going to rehearsals—there were a lot of girls there, he didn't like them then. A lot of girls in the band, there were a lot of girls, I think he felt it was a girl thing. A lot of boys dropped out, so I think it was peer pressure.

The literature on gender identity and musical participation is extensive, but in our study gender is not often highlighted as a key issue. Perhaps the fact that our ensembles were wind ensembles alleviated some of the tensions found, say, around stringed instruments, which may be seen as more exclusively female. Some of the delineated gender meanings—in the sense that Green (2001) developed the concept—may be more easily side-stepped here than in string-based ensembles. Nevertheless, only one director highlighted gender issues, commenting that 'I try to promote both boys and girls on all instruments'. Whatever the truth of the comment, the ratio of girls to boys on flute was 27:3 at the outset of the programme, and clearly suggests that gender bias was very much at work. Bryan's mother's comments are supported by evidence in the study that boys were far more likely to quit the programme, especially if, like Bryan, they were under-impressed by it. Girls, on the other hand, were far more likely to tolerate personal dissatisfaction out of conscientiousness (Faulkner *et al.*, 2010).

Making a re-entry

In a study into the development of musical expertise, this would have normally been the end of Bryan's story. More likely, in fact, it would probably never have been told. No expertise had been developed, no investment made, at best he would have been an anonymous statistic in the 'Quit' camp. Whatever theories of musical development suggest about optimal ages for entrances into formal instrumental lessons, there is clearly a sense in which those theories are extremely unhelpful unless educators, parents, and carers have been able to invest appropriately enough to bring children to a place of motivational and musical readiness that coincides with the cognitive and musical window of opportunity, and the specific kind of provision that is going to be made available to them. In Bryan's case, and for very many other young learners, the mismatch is glaring. Rarely, if ever, is there an attempt to provide opportunities on the basis of diagnostics, beyond the controversial use of music perception metrics to allocate instruments or coerce instrumental choice. Put simply there was a sense that 'this is the opportunity, take it, now or never'.

'Never' is a very long time, and because of the nature of our study the story of music in Bryan's life does not stop with his extraordinarily brief excursion into formal instrumental learning. One of the greatest challenges for music educators in the twenty-first century is negotiating interfaces between formal music education and the extraordinary role that music plays in young peoples' lives, never more so because of the burgeoning of everyday music technologies and the subsequent power that music has acquired as a technology of self.

Like all of our participants, Bryan continues to listen to huge amounts of music. It begs a very important question about what is listening expertise, how does that develop, and how is it relevant to music educators and researchers like us? In the UK just a few decades ago, for example, developing appreciative music listeners was seen as a very worthy outcome for music education (see Pitts, 2000; Cox, 2002). Supported by the introduction of recording and radio, the 'musical appreciation' view of music education was one on the key foci of twentieth-century music education, but we can assume that these educators would not have had the music on Bryan's playlist in mind. Some of our learners, as we explore in more depth in Chapters 9 and 10 turned out in young adulthood to have developed the most extensive and eclectic play lists, and used them purposefully to regulate self in ways that previous generations could never have imagined. They have developed sophisticated social networks to share those lists and devote very considerable amounts of time to managing them to effectively manage self. These young people have developed technical expertise in areas that many of us that are researching the whole question of musical development have not.

More recently the music appreciation movement in music education has been in demise. 'Listening', whilst always recognized as the core of all musical activity, has, as a discreet musical behaviour, been seen more recently as somehow inferior to playing or composing music because of a view of it as something passive. This is not the reality that DeNora (2000) reports in her seminal study of music and everyday life, and neither is it at all the impression that participants in our study give us. Bryan, for example, holds extremely strong views about the state of commercial popular music and its lack of musical originality, in opinions ironically not so far removed from Adorno's (1997) classical criticism of popular music as an attempt to pacify the masses:

> I think music is pretty stuffed up nowadays. It's pretty consumerist. I just don't think a lot of people have an idea of what music is. All they know is like from TV. I think people won't stumble across a lot of good stuff if it's not there to be stumbled across. Bands like U2, Chilli Peppers, Sanity, . . . they have a market that they just keep hitting towards.

In defiance of Bryan's mother's claims that he was 'not musically orientated . . . and . . . had no aptitude for it . . .' he even articulates a developmental view of listening expertise when he states:

> Like with Chilli Peppers, they used to be really good. Even the album Blood, Sugar, Sex, Magik, that's such a f . . . ing amazing album. But now, they're too easy to listen to.

Bryan listens a lot and explains:

> Yeah, well I'm a musician and I download a f . . . load of music from the net. I'm obsessed with getting new music.

Hardly any participants in the entire study dare to express the idea, let alone with such total lack of reservation, that 'I'm a musician'. The term has been overwhelmed by the notion of specialization and professionalism outlined in the opening chapter of this book. As an identity construct, it strikes at the very heart of the debate about musical talent—if only very special people are musicians, surely only very special people are musical. It would be controversial indeed were Bryan's claims to musicianship based on his sophisticated listening skills alone, but, like many of our participants, he went on to find his own informal pathway to further musical development. In spite of his brief childhood experience of the clarinet and wind band, Bryan has found that musical development, even through stages of specialization and investment, is not dependent on the pathways that music educators often map out for young people.

Quite by chance it seems, Bryan's aunt bought him 'a really horrible acoustic guitar for a birthday or something'. He had no friends that played the guitar as far as he can recall, but at about 13 years of age, Bryan had a few guitar lessons:

> Count them on two hands, no maybe one. Just the basic things like figuring out songs and looking at guitar tabs and that sort of thing.

By the age of 15 Bryan would occasionally hook up with a few guys he knew, although they were not particularly friends, to play cover versions at a local 'legions club'—an Australian working and servicemen's association. In the interim, Bryan's progression was a private, bedroom affair, supported by music he was downloading on his computer.

Whilst Lily's computer was rather unfairly blamed for drawing her away from music, Bryan's proved to be his most important facilitator and motivator. Bryan soon emerged as something of a trend setter and musical leader of taste, bringing music that he was listening to to his own circle of friends, so that a few of them even took up the musical cause and the guitar. After the transition to university, Bryan struck up a friendship with John, a bass player, and they started playing regularly until they decided to set up a band.

> Mid-break coming up, we just got two more people together . . . they hadn't been in a 'band band' before, just a few things playing covers . . . then we started playing and we liked it, so we went off for a while and worked on it and came back and recorded a demo and then we started getting shows. We were lucky, there was a band offering us the support show and, you know, we then started getting plays on fBI radio a lot.

The radio station Bryan speaks of is Sydney's most popular community radio station. It is dedicated to unsigned artists and under-represented genres and has over 350,000 listeners every day.

The group spends a lot of time together and John is now Bryan's best friend. They compose their own Indie songs, and do regular gigs, but Bryan is adamant that it is not 'like just business or anything like that'. In an insightful comparison with his earlier wind band experience, Bryan explains how in his present group:

> You don't feel pressurized to stay in it, because, you don't have any kind of . . . you don't have your mum or you don't have a boss, or a teacher, or anyone who's guiding it. It's your own thing.

The consistency between interviews that our participants gave most recently, at around the age of around 20, and their earliest comments, made more than a decade ago, is frequently striking. This is significant because retrospective narratives are often criticized as running the risk of being highly reconstructed and selective. With many of our participants we find that this is not the case, and that their memory of how they thought they saw things in the early years of the project is, in fact, very similar to views expressed in the real time of experiencing them. So Bryan is as equally damning now as he was as a young child about the primary school ensemble experience: 'I hated it!'

Even his mother confirmed this in a recent interview:

> It was just that they (the school) were asking people to do it, not that I thought Bryan was remotely musical. His father wasn't and I'm not remotely. And, um, but it was the clarinet. He absolutely hated it.

Bryan explains:

> I still hate um. I just still hate reading music and anything like that.

In high school the only attempt to facilitate Bryan's re-entry to more institutionally directed pathways was when the music teacher, who had noticed that he had gained some facility on the guitar, encouraged Bryan to take part in a special project:

> (It was) like music for plays or something, you were supposed to go away for a week and I hated it so much. It was that whole theoretical side of it!

Not the direct route: summarizing Lily and Bryan's musical pathways

The musical journeys of Lily and Bryan could hardly have been more different from each other, and neither could they have been more diametrically opposed to the musical lives of Anthony and Alistair in the previous chapter. Any attempt at plotting Lily and Bryan's journeys on the kinds of models of developing expertise that we developed from those life stories leaves fairly gaping holes, stops, starts, regressions, and sidesteps. Certainly the phases of sampling, specialism, investment, and maintenance, and the transitions between them, are a good deal messier than the smooth progression we noticed in the previous chapter, yet they have quite clearly both developed significant levels of expertise in different areas of music and in very different ways.

The empowering syzygies that characterized Anthony and Alistair's musical journeys and created such a unifying sense of musical direction from childhood to young adulthood are noticeably missing from Lily and Bryan's stories. When, in adolescence, Bryan became less reliant on regulation by 'others', he was able to bring a range of social, biological, and environmental factors into positive alignments that supported the growth of expertise. However, as far as the original instrumental programme in primary school was concerned, little if anything seems to have lined up in favour of Bryan's musical development. The absence of supportive domestic constellations is common to both early alignments. Lily's passion, ambition, and commitment were enough to compensate for these shortcomings because she had been highly motivated by listening to performances of the band, so that even though the recorder experience was totally uninspiring, it had left her in a state of preparedness for the clarinet in particular, with its common finger patterns, which allowed her to capitalize on her initial aspiration to be 'the best'.

In many ways, it appeared that Lily might have been destined for a stellar trajectory. All the indications are that Lily's first clarinet teacher was extremely effective in motivating her and in helping her to develop systematic and metacognitive practice strategies that supported her ambition. However, their relationship did not develop in the ways that we saw in Anthony's story, and neither were there significant community links either, as there was with Anthony's emerging involvement with the community wind band. When a key phase in her development was marked by a complete misalignment, Lily was left on a collapsing trajectory. None of her psychological needs for senses of competency, for feelings of autonomy, or for experiences of relatedness were any longer being met by the clarinet learning experience, and whatever resilience Lily had already shown, there were simply no resources available to her.

This chapter, and the previous one, should leave us in no doubt about the impact of domestic environments on musical development. Whilst our quantitative data provided us with correlations between engagement or achievement, and one-dimensional features of environment, like reminding children to practice, time spent practicing, the use of rewards and so on, we have, as highly privileged observers of domestic life, sometimes been able to compile nuanced accounts of individual family cultures and process, values, and beliefs. In some cases, researchers spent significant periods of time discussing the music in the lives not just of our direct participants, but of parents and siblings too. Individuals only have one life of course, and what we call our musical lives can never exist in vacuum-sealed compartments within that life. Nor, as a rule, are individual lives entirely separate from other people's lives. Family life, in its myriad computations and dynamic forms, is what individual lives often construct. So, in asking in detail about music in individual's lives, we often gained deep contextual insights into family histories, dynamics, and conventions. The following chapter provides one such case study: it traces the lives of the Hulme family.

Chapter 8

A family dynamic

The current chapter is unlike any other in this book, in that it considers music in the life of a whole family at two time points in 1999 and 2009. The family in question is not obviously dominated by musical activity and no one in the family thought of themselves as a performer or even played a musical instrument at the time of our last interview with them. To this extent, they are quite probably representative of a great many of our participants' families. Nevertheless, all members of this particular family display strong and interacting musical selves where beliefs, values, and activities have been developed that promote music as a part of everyday life.

The story of the Hulme family enables us to illustrate that whilst musical engagement can be intermittent and vary from active participation to listening, it can still be highly significant in realizing an individual's identity, in family dynamics, and in everyday life, whatever the degree of engagement. We acknowledge that for many people musical engagement includes categories of participation ranging from dancing, teaching, and socializing to the strict definition of playing an instrument. The chapter shows us how, just as syzygies may align to facilitate performance opportunity—as they did for Anthony and Alistair throughout their musical lives so far, and in Bryan's dramatic musical re-entry—they can equally transpire against it. Nevertheless, syzygies may align to facilitate different kinds of musical opportunity and engagement that lead, for example, to the development of expertise as listeners or dancers. This chapter also demonstrates that progress in music often has little to do with any sort of innate capacity in music, but rather is to do with one's overall beliefs and motivation.

The decision to focus on the Hulme family emerged in 1997–1999 from observations of the monthly practice videos sent to us during the first 3 years of the study. We were particularly drawn to the video material because, unlike any others submitted, the young clarinet student–Lucy–was not practising alone, but rather was sitting alongside her slightly older brother James. The videos provided fascinating case studies of sibling interaction and music learning, showing how James was teaching his younger sister. James was a tough task-master and the 12-year-old's instructions seemed to be modelled on phrases and concepts he had learned from his own adult clarinet teacher and other adults he had heard instructing children. If we were to plot his behaviour on the model of teaching styles discussed in Chapter 4, James would sit squarely in the 'authoritarian teacher' sector. Comments like: 'Well done, Luce, good girl' or 'Yes, well, not quite right, but let's try again and see if we can improve things' sounded as if James was trying to take on the role of an adult. Whilst the behaviour provoked wry smiles from the researcher, it was obvious that James was earnestly attempting to help support Lucy's learning. Jane Davidson and Stephanie Pitts wrote about the family in an article entitled 'People have talents. . .' (Davidson & Pitts, 2001) which captured not only James's capacity to teach his sister, but other issues that related to this family: their beliefs about musical ability and their priorities and passions. This current chapter revisits those data.

Intrigued by the video interaction between the children, Jane Davidson decided to meet the whole family, and spent several hours with them discussing music and many other topics over afternoon tea, evening practice, and dinner in 1999. Some of the emergent and striking outcomes from that meeting can be usefully explored in our current discussion. At the time of the original home visit in 1999, Jane had only seen Lucy and James on the video and was not aware of an older sibling called Sean. At the time of this meeting, Sean was 16 years of age, James was 12 years of age and Lucy was 10 years of age.

Introduction to Sean

In 1999, Sean had already taken piano lessons for many years and had played the trumpet in his school band since primary school. Sean's parents believed his interest in the trumpet came from the inspirational school band leader who had undertaken many exciting projects with the students. At the time of Jane's visit, he was planning the latest project—a band tour to Europe. Whilst Sean appeared enthusiastic about music, he seemed more stimulated by the camaraderie of the band, rather than the instrument itself. He felt that 'playing music was ok', but was somewhat uncertain about his musical future. Sean was quiet and witty, and during Jane's visit to the home he was present through some of the family discussion and the meals. Like many teenagers, he was quick to excuse himself from the group talk to go to his own room. After the family discussion, Jane asked Sean if she could interview him in his room; his space, his world. Sean's bedroom had the typical spillage of books, gadgets, and games around the place, but there was no music stand or instrument to be seen.

Sean was very happy to discuss his musical tastes and he even played Jane a few tracks. His overwhelming preference was for rock music listening. He played examples and discussed the qualities of the strong bass and screaming guitar solos and vocals that he enjoyed. Music was clearly important to him, and something he used regularly. Rock music in particular was a topic he and his male friends often spoke about at school. Sean considered school work important and his main focus was mathematics. He was clearly a very successful scholar and felt that he would probably go on to study mathematics at university, hopefully following his Dad's career as an accountant. When asked what he preferred most, he did say that music was good for socializing.

Introduction to Lucy

Lucy was full of fizz, wearing her heart on her sleeve and in love with painting, dancing, and life in general. In contrast to Sean's quietness, Lucy was chatty and giggly. She confessed that: 'Sometimes I can be a pain in the neck, other times, I can be an angel.' She was particularly aware that lately she had needed to be quiet around Sean, who was having to study hard. Whilst Lucy did say that she enjoyed her music-making, this was most definitely a secondary activity to dancing and art work. She spoke at length about all the different kinds of dance she did, about her art projects, and her out-of-school social life—she was able to list a very extensive range of dance classes, clubs, and cultural activities. Lucy was a whirlwind of plans and projects.

By the time of this interview Lucy had already given up playing the clarinet, although she was having lessons on piano. Both Lucy and her parents were keen to emphasize that James's teaching had nothing to do with Lucy's decision to stop playing the clarinet. When asked in detail about her musical interactions with James, it seemed that Lucy's first motivation to learn the clarinet had been to emulate James to get into the school band, but once there she clearly felt that she had little affinity with the instrument, and as she had hated getting up early for the school band rehearsals, she had given up. Her mum said that Lucy was very busy and that the clarinet was yet another extra-curricular option and so she had not wanted to 'push it too much'.

Complexly, whilst James had taken one-on-one lessons on clarinet, Lucy had not, so James had been her only one-on-one teacher. It was an interesting position for Lucy to be in. On the one hand, she had been playing and was being taught in the band ensemble, but on the other hand, she was not dedicated enough, or perhaps not sufficiently good enough in the eyes of her parents, to be given private lessons outside the context of the band. James had thus become a surrogate teacher. Lucy accepted her brother's lessons, making comments like 'Oh, James, he's good, but he was a bit strict' and 'James made me laugh when he was the teacher'.

In the sessions observed on video, Lucy displayed a lot of patience in listening to didactic instruction from James and she sustained her motivation and attention through long practice sessions. As she and her parents said at the start of the interviews, Lucy was evidently satisfied with James teaching her, because by the end of her interview with Jane, she stated that she did not really need her piano teacher, 'because I can be helped by my brothers'.

Family musicking

Through family discussion, it was evident that all three children had joined the school band, each one inspired by the older sibling and also by their teachers, especially Sean's dynamic secondary school band teacher. Additionally, James looked up to Sean's capacity to play the trumpet, which he regarded as a tougher instrument than the clarinet. All had learned the piano, and of the three of them, Lucy was the most dedicated pianist. She enjoyed it far more than the clarinet because of its fun, creative, and relaxing outcomes: 'You can make up your own tunes and play for yourself for fun.' She liked her lessons, but did not practice all that much. Piano was a low-level activity. In fact for all of them, piano was something that they used for relaxation.

In 1999, the musical futures for both Sean and Lucy seemed somewhat ambiguous. There was a slim chance that Sean would keep on playing the trumpet after his trip to Europe, but the most likely scenario was that the end of school would mark his performance exit point. This was the case for several of our participants who had continued through high school and saw prestigious overseas trips like this as a chance to 'go out at the top'. Students often made decisions to stop playing after such tours well in advance of the tour itself. It seemed likely that Sean would give up playing in order to focus on accountancy. In addition to his trumpet-playing skills, Sean was evidently a dedicated music listener, and his rock music identity seemed quite fixed. It was something that brought him together with his friends and which also gave him a musical niche within the family, as Sean was the only rock listener. Lucy, without doubt, was already a dancer by self-definition and music was a vital part of that experience. She described in some detail how she enjoyed the music she listened to in her various dance classes. In contrast, the piano was a companion through periods of self-reflection: 'sometimes I just go and play on the piano to be by myself'. The clarinet was something to do at school and something to connect her to her brother, but her motivations and connections to the clarinet did not outweigh her need or desire to stay in bed for an extra hour in the morning. Lucy's three kinds of musical engagement are discreet in terms of musical style and the form of musical engagement, but also in terms of personal and social function, and the psychological needs that they meet.

And then there was James

James was different to the other two siblings in that during Jane's visits he was the only self-defined musician. When Jane met him, James was highly enthusiastic about his band playing and had ambitions to take music as far as he could, even though, as a 12-year-old, James found it a little difficult to imagine what he would do as a professional clarinettist. He also enjoyed other kinds of creative work and thought that writing might be another possibility for a future profession. James's parents predicted that he would go far with his career because he was a good 'all rounder' with an 'outgoing personality'. His mum, Suzie, said she could imagine him doing 'amazing things as an adult'. James was incredibly vivacious: 'I just go up to anyone and start a conversation' was his description of how he got to know the people in the local park where it was his job to exercise the dog.

During Jane's visit, James asked many questions about her research and enquired what musicians could do in their careers. He was also keen to play his clarinet for Jane, unlike his siblings, who both declined the invitation to play. Seated on the edge of his bed, James played several tunes, with his music resting on his clarinet case. He also showed Jane all his sheet music: the music played in band and in his lessons. James recounted how he had recently made a considerable amount of money for a charity by busking in the local shopping mall. This experience had a double impact on him; it had motivated him to practise more in order to be able to increase his earning potential and it had galvanized his love of performance. James chatted at length about what he enjoyed about music and how it was his passion. 'I'd hate not to be able to play, not to have that privilege' (Davidson & Pitts, 2001, p. 165).

It was evident that James loved the affirmation of who he was through praise he had achieved in recognition of his music performance achievements. James was also extremely proud of his teaching of Lucy. 'I want to help her to get better.' In fact, James noted that both he and Sean had also helped Lucy with her piano, because they were older and so more experienced. James's view was paternal, but he was critical of his skills as a teacher, seeming to take some responsibility for Lucy having given up, despite Lucy and his parents' comments to the contrary:

> It was kind of hard with Lucy, because she was good at the time, but sometimes I'd go too far, I'd go out of her span. I was still young then, so I'd kind of got to where I was,

but I wasn't trying to teach her trills and stuff . . . I could have done better if I was older, like me now and her when she was, because I'd have known what to do. (Davidson & Pitts, 2001, p. 165)

Whilst this account of sibling regulation is the only highly detailed one that we have from our study, a great deal of evidence indicated that siblings often impacted each other in very significant ways, in both positive and negative senses, especially during the early years of learning. Older siblings in particular provided role models to be emulated or avoided, unwelcome interference or positive encouragement, duet partners or, in the case of James, surrogate teachers. These highly individualized dynamics reveal another layer to the complexities of musical development rarely touched upon in the literature.

Identities

One story that emerged from the face-to-face meeting with the Hulme family that could not have been predicted from the video presented some interesting themes for discussion (see Davidson & Pitts, 2001). The three children were actually adopted, coming to Australia from Chile and Columbia. Their parents, Bob and Suzie, were Caucasian Australians of Anglo-Scottish heritage. Although there was some confusion in early discussions with the children, it emerged that both James and Lucy believed that their lives were being influenced in two very strong yet distinct ways:

i) Their biological inheritance (the Latin American self) included their physical appearance—all three had olive skin and black hair, and both boys were quite small when compared to their Caucasian classmates—and the capacity to express themselves and their feelings through dance and music.

ii) Their environmental development (membership of Bob and Suzie's family unit) resulted in them acquiring the skills of their adopted parents through environmental circumstances. Lucy, for instance, had 'got' art skills from Suzie, who was an interior designer; James had 'got' some classical music listening interests and capacities to understand mathematics from Bob, a music-loving accountant.

Sean was older and a little more circumspect in his views generally, but he could see that his abilities in mathematics had been heavily influenced by Bob's assistance with his homework. The Latin American association with music and dance culture was something he did not accept: 'I can't remember anything about where I came from. I was a baby. It has nothing to do with me.'

Suzie believed that it was crucial for the children to know about their cultural heritage, so they all attended a network for Latin American children adopted into Australia. The network also provided a way for Suzie to learn about Latin American culture and support her children as they grew up and negotiated their own identity.

Educational style

Hoksbergen (1997) describes adoptive parents as 'educators who find themselves in a very special situation' (p. 1), indicating that it is indeed a parent's role to educate—something often not fore-fronted in discussions about generic parenting. With adopted children, that education may include informing about all sorts of social, cultural, and biological matters that might not emerge in the course of a genetic family's interactions. Benson *et al.* (1994) present evidence from a large-scale American survey suggesting that a high proportion of adoptive parents display common tendencies:

> Adoptive families in this study typically evidence a high level of strength in terms of warmth, communication, discipline, and cohesion. Less functional parenting styles, such as authoritarian decision-making, are rare. (Benson et al., 1994, p. 6)

If we consider our findings about parental impact on early instrumental learning in Chapters 2 and 3, this statement could well be a description of ideal parental supporters of musical development: warm and supportive, offering a disciplined framework for practice, and making sure they are informed about what needs to happen when. Benson *et al.* (1994) report that the most common parenting style in successful adoptive families involves 'acceptance of the child's difference' (p. 58). Bob, James's dad, seemed particularly skilled at enabling James to reflect upon his own behaviour whilst still showing him love and stability. For example, James was very socially able, although his confident nature sent a shudder down his father's spine at the thought of the potential difficulties he could encounter owing to his fearlessness. Bob offered this take on his son's personality as they discussed his teaching skills over dinner:

> James: Sometimes I try to control Lucy and she doesn't like that.
> Bob: You try to control a lot of people though.
> James: I don't like to do it, it just comes.
> Bob: See, what you haven't done is recognize that people have their own space, and you should respect that space. You're a big influence, but you don't own anyone. But you'll get that. (Davidson & Pitts, 2001, p. 168)

This parenting act was both pointing out a potential weakness, but also acknowledging that it could only be ameliorated if James was able to acknowledge his tendency to dominate others. In fact, both boys, but especially James, were respectful and in admiration of their dad, who was described as: 'very smart', 'wise', 'a keen music listener', and 'a sports guy'. He was someone they both wanted to emulate and Sean certainly wanted to follow in his father's career steps.

Musical practices and parenting

As Davidson and Pitts reported in their original interview study, the supportive parenting style revealed by Bob and Suzie corresponds closely with advice given to parents on supporting instrumental learning in the home: 'the young musician may require an environment which is facilitating and encouraging but allows personal space and freedom to develop creativity' (Hallam, 1998, p. 81). Successful young musicians and their parents reported the strong influence of the home environment and parental support, often manifested as an interest in the child's musical development rather than a high level of musical skill or experience on the parents' part (Sloboda & Howe, 1991). As with the general approach of adoptive parents reported by Benson *et al.* (1994, p. 6), the parents of successful young musicians sought a balance between imposing discipline and encouraging self-motivation (Sloboda & Howe,

1991, p. 18). Thinking back to Chapter 4, the model of teaching styles discussed there might be equally useful as a model of parenting styles in that the qualities of *demandingness* and *responsiveness* need to be carefully balanced in support of musical development or indeed in support of development in general.

Not all adoptive families display the positive characteristics that we observed with the Hulme family, and similarly not all successful musicians have enjoyed the balanced approach described by Sloboda and Howe (1991). It is clear, however, that the Hulmes were attempting to provide their children with a rich array of stimuli and that music was one of the elements that featured strongly in the home. They aimed at this delicate balance of encouragement and self-motivation.

Intriguingly, Suzie believed that being the parent of adopted children she could be a little more objective about them than children who resembled her physically. She even commented that she did not 'put characteristics' onto her kids in the way that she'd heard friends doing: 'Oh, you know, "he's just the model and personality of his dad type of comment".' Her children were clearly not the 'model' of anyone else in their family, so she refused to try to ascribe her children such characteristics. Suzie felt it helped her to try to treat all of the children equally, working hard not to push them too hard, but equally not letting them give up: 'With Lucy it was a weighing up of whether or not it was worth all the hassle of getting her to go to the band.' In the end, it had been decided against pushing that activity.

Of course the children were clearly seeking out their identifies with family, friends, and role models, so it is not that surprising that at least the two younger children wanted to believe that their Latin American roots helped them to become musicians. Varying positions within the family and the different roles ascribed to the different influences are worthy of discussion because they introduce the notion of different sorts of alignments and how these might shape self-determination beliefs. To start the discussion, it is important to note that researchers like Plomin & Daniels (1987) and Dunn (1993; Dunn & McGuire, 1992; Dunn *et al.*, 1994) have shown the significant range of inter-related factors on both the perceptions and the positioning of the realized competencies of siblings.

Birth order and sibships

Dunn (1993) has shown how older siblings often take on the roles of teachers and that sibling boys tend to be more protective of their younger siblings if they are girls. It can be argued that the Hulme family fall well within this paradigm. Both boys had helped Lucy with piano, and James was particularly protective over her clarinet skills, regarding this as an area of expertise where he could help her out.

In terms of birth order, Isaacson and Radish's (2002) observations around first and second borns reveal that first borns tend to occupy a position of attention, respect, and admiration. The second child has, from the start, to cope with the attention already placed on the first born. Furthermore, it is difficult for younger children to out-perform the older child, by virtue of their age disadvantage, and it seems that inadequacy can be a common feeling for the second born. There were certainly several participants in our study who cited these feelings in relation to perceptions of instrumental competency in the early years of the project. Some children deliberately avoided instruments that older siblings were playing for this reason, whilst others deliberately chose them for exactly the same reason. Sibling rivalry has been researched at length, and it seems that parents are often complicit in this sort of rivalry, favouring one child over the other, or emphasizing one child's strength as another child's weakness and so on. It has even been argued that birth order directly impacts the big five personality traits of openness, conscientiousness, extraversion, agreeableness, and neuroticism (Sulloway, 1997). Sulloway reports that first borns are often more conscientious, more socially dominant, and less creative than later born siblings. These are traits that we have already discussed in relation to the development of various kinds of musical expertise.

Davidson and Borthwick (2002; Borthwick & Davidson, 2002) undertook some work on sibling relationships in a musical household and met with a family weekly for 18 months, engaging in musical play and helping with other homework. They noted that ideas about genetic inheritance were used by the parents to place different children into different niches: the elder son, who was most like the mother, was regarded as the more musically talented, and the younger son, who was more like the grandfather, was regarded as the most artistically able, the grandfather having been a painter. Desperate to please the mother, the younger child fitted into his ascribed niche and tried with all his might to become the painter his grandfather had been. Towards the end of the 18-month research period, the younger boy had made some 'astonishing progress'—as reported by the father—and was starting to develop a different sort of musical niche than the older brother, who was most definitely seen as the classical music specialist.

The representations parents make of their children easily become self-fufilling prophecies. When we consider the Hulme family, it is evident that there is some playing out of niche identification going on: James being the most musical one, Lucy a dancer, and Sean the most serious mathematician.

But, what of these children 10 years later? What had they achieved as adults? Was Sean the most high achieving? Had he become the accountant he had talked of? Was James in his brother's shadow? Was he still enjoying the 'privilege' of being 'able to play'? Was Lucy still being 'looked after', protected, and 'taught' by her brothers? How had her artistic interests developed? Had they played out their roles as Jane had observed, and she and Stephanie Pitts had written about? What role was music playing in their lives, individually or collectively?

Musical lives in 2009

Jane Davidson returned to the family to speak with each family member in turn 10 years after the initial set of interviews. These interviews, which had so marked Jane's thoughts and research, could not be recalled by a single family member. Nevertheless, everyone was enthusiastic to offer assistance and all were eager to describe their current lives at this stage. Lucy was now 20 years old and still living at home with both her parents and James, now 22 years old. Sean was 26 years old and still living in Sydney, but in a house-share with his friends. Jane attended the interviews at various locations around Sydney with Paul Evans (see Chapter 4). Paul is the same age as Sean and he was able to bring contemporary cultural ideas and knowledge to the discussion of current musical tastes.

Lucy's musical life

Lucy was now a strikingly tall and attractive 20-year-old who had the same effusive bubbly nature her 10-year-old self had presented. She had left school and was studying for a Diploma of Children's Services in Early Childhood with aspirations to go on and take a bachelor's degree in early childhood. She was also a successful dance teacher—dashing off after the interview to teach a jazz dance class—and added extra money to her pay packet by working in a clothes shop. When asked about her life, it was clear that Lucy had stuck with her dance and artistic skills, but music had also remained a significant part of her life. Lucy selected music for her dance classes, loved going to night clubs to dance and socialize, and she still occasionally sat down and 'tinkled' on the piano. Her survey, completed as part of the study, showed someone who listened to music a great deal, using her MP3 player and hanging out with her friends, or else out socializing at a club or bar.

Lucy's clarinet had been forgotten about, but lessons on the piano had continued up until year 10. Her most recent teacher had been a perfect guide, allowing Lucy 'to play funky stuff'. She would play with the teacher and sometimes with her brothers. There was a uniting force to the piano; it brought the three of them together.

When asked to look back on James's role as teacher, Lucy was very generous:

> Ah, [laughs], no it was alright, me and my brother get on really well, there's no rivalry there. [Laughs] He's a good guy. Um, yeah, I don't know. Just him teaching me, I thought it was funny. I didn't really mind. I thought "you're my older brother, so go for it". Yeah, yeah, he helped. When he was playing piano it probably made me want to play it too.

The transcript seems to imply that the role of older sibling asserting his agenda on the younger sibling is present, but it is certainly not ill-willed nor demotivating. Indeed, there was a true and genuine fondness between all three siblings, rather than any overt rivalry. Lucy spoke enthusiastically about her close relationship with James, which was indeed largely based on their sharing of music listening. Lucy still deferred to James as the musical expert:

> My brother likes a whole lot of different music with different beats and good rhythms or something, he can sort of listen and be relaxed and study as well. He has big speakers, and I've found that I've got some chill-out music that he likes to listen to on the speakers. Whenever I get something new I show him and see if he likes it as well.

When asked generally about her life, Lucy does not hesitate to put her family as her main priority, with her dancing and music on a par with each other in terms of her everyday exposure to each form: 'Music is basically just a part of my life, I listen all the time.'

Sean's musical life

True to his own prediction, Sean was now working as an accountant, having developed his mathematical skills throughout university. His mum described him as very much 'going along with the flow' and being 'extremely happy living with his friends in a house-share'. It seemed that Sean had remained the quieter, highly diligent older boy with a sense of loyalty to his friends and family. He was certainly nowhere nearly as involved in the arts as Lucy.

The researchers met with Sean in a trendy café in Surry Hills, Sydney. He was on his way out with a group of friends for the evening. The sense of love and loyalty to the family was present, as was his witty, reflective personality. He was also clearly very influenced by music: he loved playing his music in his car. He was the proud owner of a Mitsubishi Lancer that he enjoyed because of its engine size, speed, and the overall 'cool' he associated with it. Just as it was for some other young men in our study, playing music in the car was an important vehicle for the (loud) presentation of Sean's personal identity.

Sean reflected on his band experiences as fun, but something of the past: his teenage, not his adult persona. As an adult, his working life was very separate from his social life and his social life was strongly bound up in the music he and his housemates enjoyed, and specifically the music he could play in his car, usually very loud. Sean was indeed the shyer, older brother, who was consistently high achieving and sensible, with limited patience for musical performance, but with an enduring interest in music listening as something to connect him to people.

James's musical life

James was incredibly busy, so Jane and Paul met him in a bar in North Sydney, on his way to a social event with some friends. He revealed a hugely dynamic personality, and was energized and upbeat from the very start of the meeting.

At the end of his sister Lucy's interview, she had confessed that James would always be the person she would turn to for help, for unlike Sean, who could do just about anything but could not explain clearly to her how he did it, James could both do it and explain it. In the conversation with adult James, those reflective and explanatory qualities radiated from him. Two key constructs emerged from an interpretative phenomenological analysis of that interview that relate to James's current beliefs about music and self; *Latin American inheritance* and *past and present engagement*.

Latin American inheritance

Jane began the conversation noting that there was Latin music playing in the bar, so she reminded him of their conversation about adoption and the role of the family of origin in his life. James responded:

> That's so strange that you bring it up! I listen to a lot of South American music. I don't know why, it's just I like the beat. Not that I seek it out or buy it in stores or anything, but I do sort of listen to that beat, that style of music. I mean, I do listen to other kinds of music and rock and stuff . . . but I find that the stuff I like listening to is the South American. I couldn't tell you any names of any artists because I don't collect them, but definitely if I hear that sort of beat the mood it creates I feel is something different about it.
>
> Jane: Right.
>
> James: My friends would say, as soon as that kind of song comes on: 'Oh this is your song, James.' They'll say stuff like that.

Paul: Do you know what kind of style? How would you describe it?

James: More guitary. I'm trying to think. There is definitely a style with a name. But I've never, like I don't collect it on my stuff. But definitely if I hear it I'll be like 'Hey, I like that'. Umm . . . I don't know, can you rattle off any names of any styles you know and I might be able to . . . I could show you the style, I can give you samples, I don't have any burnt . . . Sort of like Cuban/Latino stuff. Cuban/Latino is . . .

Paul: Jazz, or?

James: A mixture of jazz and funky hip hop rhythm, more traditional so . . . and then strange cause um, I think there's a style called [] which is really big in South America which is all, like, a mixture of hip hop and Latino and beats and that's what I love, which I can't explain. I don't even understand the music or what they're saying, but it sounds like . . . yeah.

[Jane and James continue to talk about James's Columbian roots.]

James: And that had a very big impact on my cultural, I guess, awareness that you were saying at Multicultural Day I remember in primary school we would always do the traditional, we'd try to emulate the traditional dances. And um, I mean I don't really tell many people about my sort of background. When they say 'Where are you from?' I say 'Oh South America' and they say ['When did you come here?'] and I say 'I was adopted', but from other [] from that group they make it a big thing about Latino and stuff and they'll make a big impact on making everyone, you know, I found that frustrating.

Jane: So how do you feel about that? I mean, obviously you're interested if you want to learn Spanish, there's something there that you want to find out about.

James: I'm really considering going there . . . and going around Columbia, because as I get older I'm much more interested. I, not even intentionally, I go on Google and stuff, reading up about it, meeting people that, I mean I'm sort of attracted to people from there, more then the Aussie girls and stuff. Like, there's no particular reason, but I'll look twice or something.

Actually I had a dream—this is weird—I had a dream the other night that I was travelling back to South America, like I was with this girl that I felt this connection with, who turned out to be my sister. And um, in the dream I was going back to meet my mum or something, then I woke up and stuff.

Like any adopted child, James has a curiosity about his roots, but unlike his brother and sister, who do not dwell on it or wish to pursue it, James has given himself an association with Latin musical culture which frames his own passion for music. Even his friends link him to 'that sort of music from his roots'. This offers a vague connection to a sense of identity that tantalizingly encourages him to find out more about his origins.

Past and present engagement

When interviewed in childhood, James had been very motivated by the profits of busking. Reflecting on this experience as an adult he noted:

I went busking with a neighbour and we made like $60 in an hour, because people thought we were cute I think, playing along and people just threw money at us. And um, one guy was—like the first time we went busking—my friend went off to get a drink and this guy invited us to [play this song], and he actually just stopped and listened. Cause no one does, they just kind of throw their coins and keep walking. And I think he was in the symphony orchestra, I remember him saying something like, you know, 'keep up music' or something 'it's a good expression of yourself'. I remember him saying that to me and I can see him in the corner of where I was in a [tracksuit], and something about what he said, I was like 'yeah, this would be cool' . . . I felt the energy of the music. Not just to sound corny, but I really did enjoy being in a band . . . I couldn't play by myself in my room or anything but as soon as I, like, if there was a concert or something. Yeah. And then I went in year 11 to Montreal Jazz Festival with our band. We went all around Canada and America in jazz festivals on a jazz tour, and one of the stops was at the Montreal Jazz Festival and that was amazing. And that was in year 11 and got me—I was going to stop at the end of that and just focus on studies for year 12—but it kept in me for another year. And it got me a lot more, doing a lot of musical things with friends and stuff.

The dramatic turn around in the story of James's musical pathway was not at all what might have been anticipated. The young and highly motivated clarinettist had developed into an enthusiastic saxophonist, who had toured North America—rather like his brother had toured with his school wind band. James's life was jam-packed with musical activities: clubbing, listening, and socializing. Given the high positive motivation displayed at 12 years of age, it was an interesting turn of events to learn that he had given up performing at the end of his school career.

Reflecting on his experiences, James gave some insight into this:

Looking back, the real reason I picked up the clarinet was because I liked using my hands and . . . I wanted to be a drummer and I still think I should have cause when I hear songs I kind of . . . I can feel the rhythm section more than the other instruments. Yeah and also, at the assembly and the clarinet, they got me to say 'I'm going to play the clarinet in the band', and then I was just like playing an instrument. And then as that went on a few years later I found out that music, sort of um, if I was kept busy playing music doing the stuff at school, I found that music covered the sports and covered the school kind of, so it was kind of like this crazy organizational thing that I had. That was something weird thinking back on it now actually.

So, perhaps in the end, James was not really dissimilar to those students studied by Sloboda and Howe (1991), that unless a key and meaningful instrument is found, the desire to persist wanes. The link between James's love of Latin rhythms and the desire to play drums does clarify his sentiments towards being a drummer. Furthermore, it seems that he was somehow very concerned to be seen taking part in key school activities to stay 'in' with his peer group:

I wanted to be busy and my better friends were all involved and I wanted to be involved along with them, yeah, cause it kept me connected to my friends because they were in the band. Um I remember that was one of the reasons why. It wasn't the fact that I enjoyed it from when I was younger, it was more that my friends were doing it and I wanted to be involved. And like I said it was sort of in my mind to get involved, so I get to see my friends there and get to do the trips they do—band camp was a big thing at [school]. Like being involved with that I got to go there and stuff. And then when I was in the second year of playing band at [school], I got promoted I think it was from third section to second or first section cause I did this one little line that I thought was really simple but no one at the back could play it, I just said I'll play it to demonstrate and then for some reason he promoted me up to firsts. And then that was another sort of big on my musical sort of . . .

Jane: Map?

James: Yeah map. It was so stupid probably looking back on it. And yeah that gave me more confidence for some reason and so I remember that being pretty big. But I can't remember any internal desires to play when I was early on, like when I was young. There was nothing really driving me.

Jane: So what switched in to—because I was actually referring to this bit where you said 'Oh I got here and then I was going to give up and focus on my exams for school for year 12, but then there was some moment and I actually kept going with my music'. There must have been something in the music that you found particularly appealing, was there?

James: Yeah, definitely the energy. Like um, Benjamin's Big Band, the youth band I was involved in all through high school, the director [name] put in a lot of energy and just being involved in any band he was part of was, like, any musician would have found incredible because the energy he gave off just made everyone just put in that much more. He left after the band tour in year 11 and everyone knew with him leaving the band would, like, wouldn't be the same. And it wasn't—he did leave and I was always prepared to just go 'Yep, I'm going to leave' like some of my friends, but it was the Montreal Jazz—the experience I had—that definitely wanted me to keep on playing. Sorry, my high school, it just got really good []. Yeah, I just remember just smiling sometimes when—cause I was in the jazz band and I would just sit there and, like, other people would be improvising something and then that feeling you get when everyone gets in the groove—it's just like, I would smile. I feel like a 'dork' actually, yeah, um. I remember leaving with the biggest highs after band practice. Like I said before, I could never get the same high when I was just by myself in my room. Unless I heard a really good song . . . cause I can, like, sit in my room and listen to some really good jazz pieces and stuff and get that, almost the same feeling. Or if I go to concerts..

Jane: Right, so it's not necessarily to do with doing it yourself, it's to do more with being in it?

James: I enjoy it, cause sometimes you'd get to a really tricky part of the piece and you'd pull it off and you'd get that sort of satisfaction, like 'this week I made it, last week I stuffed up these two bars or these two progressions' and then you'd be like 'Oh crap' and then you'd sort of strive for it one week and be like 'Yes!' and that feeling of making that sound was pretty good. Cause sometimes, just listening to it you'd be blown away, I was blown away and was like 'yeah I love this'. It was definitely because the teacher left that I stopped.

Here we see someone immersed in the sound, the challenge, and the camaraderie of playing. But in the next breath, his opinion changes:

Jane: So, looking back now, would you consider starting to play again now?

James: I would love to but—I don't know—I felt that everyone around me was progressing a lot faster than I was, especially in year 12. And their improvisation skills were just, like, incredible. But mine—I didn't particularly like improvising—I didn't find myself particularly good apart from blue scales. And they're still involved in bands. I go and support them all the time. But I was happy sort of giving it up for some reason, just because I thought that I had reached my sort of peak and I was happy that I had got it and the [band was all falling apart] and . . . like I'm happy going out partying and listening to music and watching my bands. Telling people I'm not involved in bands isn't such a big thing anymore, it used to be a really big thing, like 'yeah I'm a part of [Benjamin's], I'm part of the school band, jazz band, concert band, all of that stuff'—you could rattle it off and they'd be impressed, like 'What do you play?' and you'd tell them what you played and it was like, 'Oh!' and you'd play for them sometimes.

This story seems somewhat contradictory. It reveals someone who truly loves music, but who no longer needs the performance aspect. The performance element was undoubtedly highly motivating for James early on, as was his own teaching experience with his sister, and from his own descriptions practising at home together or in the band on a tour were activities he enjoyed doing with friends. Could it be that his self-confessed need to keep up with others, to be seen to be doing the 'right things' has ultimately had a role in stifling his desire to continue playing? The psychological need of relatedness is salient here: the peer group alliance, the camaraderie of the music-making. James was certainly no longer making the progress he initially envisaged, but the crucially motivating teacher had moved on and the band had changed, so that crucial 'other' external stimuli had vanished too.

James, of course, had some of his own theories on this point:

James: Throughout high school, I think my musical expression, the part of my life that music played was important. I don't know why, I enjoyed telling people I was involved in the bands. Now it doesn't feel as big a deal, like I don't tell, people might ask, 'Is there a clarinettist in the room?'

Jane: Do you think being James when you were a young teenager was more to do with your identity in the music?

James: Yeah definitely. And the sports. A lot of people know me for the sports.

Jane: Yeah I was going to ask you about that, but what's your identity now? Who are you now?

James: I'm like the guy in my group who has sort of settled down, got his life kind of planned out—I've got work lined up next year, he's going to go to Europe, he's very active, plays a lot of sports—I guess if someone had to describe me they'd say, like, 'Oh yeah James is like the balanced one'.

Paul: Your friends aren't like that?

James: Oh, my best friend's a bit more, like, not lost but still a bit, plans the immediate future instead of more. Kind of just getting through their degree.

Jane: Can I ask you a cheeky question in a way, but it kind of relates to something you said on the stairs as we were walking down here, you said 'Accountancy is the most boring—whatever you said—the most boring . . . '

James: It was probably boring. I cannot see myself taking it up as a lifelong career.

Jane: Right, cause that's something your mum said quite categorically yesterday, that she could not envisage you being an accountant. So why did you do it James?

James: Oh because I want to get to be a chartered accountant. When I started, when I was at the end of high school I really wanted to do chiropractic science . . . I loved using my hands, like I was doing design and technology courses, like woodwork and all of that. I was doing carving outside of school, just random things with my hands. I loved just sitting down using my hands like carving . . . And then, in year 12, I found business studies was my best subject. I never tried, I just got it and I was good at it. Funny that you said that thing about busking before because . . . seriously a day before we had to hand in our university application I changed to business. I got it, I enjoyed business first year, second year, third year and I did marketing, finance, accounting . . . but by the time I'd done my summer vacation the only subject I'd focus on was accounting, like, my accounting major.

So I thought if I get it, 'cool', if I don't I'm not going to be 'cut'. So when I went along to the interview I was so relaxed. Everyone around me was like sweating . . . And then one interview led to the next and then I got in . . . So I thought, 'If I can do this without making an effort, I may as well go ahead with it'. Accountancy is pretty easy—it's boring, but it's easy.

Paul: So you're good at what? In general in your life, what are you good at? You're good at music..

James: Everyone knows me for sport. I'm very hyperactive—tennis, soccer, golf, skiing, I love.

So, on one level, we see that James's attention has shifted to sports and his accountancy work. At the end of the interview, however, he confesses that he could just do carpentry all day, illustrating how his pathways and attention focus are continually shifting, re-aligning his motivations and passions. This sense of self in relation to friends and activities is rather different to Sean's more singular sense of who he is in relationships, or indeed to Lucy, who is very clear about her dancing and her aspirations as an artistic early childhood teacher.

But what of that musical 'gene' he spoke of, what of the passion for rhythm and sound?

James: I'm creative in that sort of—not like fine art creative, but just the way I do things, like I'm . . . yeah . . . when it comes to solutions to problems I can look outside the box a bit more, or if I don't have the tool I'll just make up things..

I don't think I was ever really good at music, I just enjoyed it that much. In everything I do, I think I'm good generally at a lot of things, but excelling in any one of them I wouldn't say I succeed and excel at anything.

Yeah I can't think of anything I excelled at—I never excelled at music and that's one of the reasons I stopped—I found everyone around me was just getting better. Um, uni, definitely average in general. Like I probably got like a 70 average now that I've finished. Sports? Yeah I played soccer for heaps of years. Golf? I've got an average handicap. Nothing, I just love playing, tennis is the same.

Paul: So you're not exceptional but you've got it covered, you could do it.

James: Yeah I could take on anyone, give anyone a good game.

Jane: So this seems to be something to do with investments as well—there are some things you can do to a certain degree and you can get so you're really proficient and you're really enjoying it, but to go that extra mile, it takes an effort that perhaps you're not prepared to . . .

James: Yes, I enjoy my space and my personal time. Yeah, like I'll just get on my bike with no particular destination and just ride. I'm kind of enjoying that more. I used to when I had my kayak I used to get up at 4.30 in the morning and go kayaking for an hour and a half by myself and then some of my friends were getting pissed off that I wasn't asking them so they came along but I wouldn't go out of my way to ask them because I kind of liked being on the water when it was absolutely dead quiet and everything was waking up. I used to really enjoy that. I mean, don't get me wrong, I love going out clubbing—I would say that if we have a look at my immediate last month 80% of it would be with my friends and stuff—definitely, maybe higher. I mean, I haven't even been home in like the last four or five nights.

Jane: So, you're a busy person doing lots of things that you enjoy.

> James: Yeah. I'm like, I have random moods but sometimes I'll have to be around someone and other times I'll be in a group and just want to be by myself and then other times I don't care, I'll just go with the flow.
>
> Jane: And do you use music in those circumstances when you . . .
>
> James: All the time. I can't be anywhere without my [music], in my car I always have music, I always have heaps and heaps of music, my laptops full of it, my cars full of it, yeah music has to be there . . .

So, it is clear that as James is progressing through his life, he is rather good at whatever he turns his hand to, yet there is not one singular focus for all his attention. Despite music having lost its performance status, it is crucial to his daily life. It contributes to his everyday existence, indeed to his sense of who he is from his Latin roots to his car, his friends, his social world. Speaking about his listening for the day he comments:

> I came home from work so I was listening to this guy called [] who does—all my friends call it—elevator music, but I don't think it's that at all. It's um, I could play it for you now if you want. That was on my way home, then coming here on the bus I was listening to that [Reggaeton] style I was talking to you about before and that was just for no reason. That's just on my favourites list so I choose it for some reason.
>
> [Fiddles around trying to find the song.]
>
> Jane: That's alright, don't worry.
>
> James: Going through this phone isn't' really a true reflection of my music because it's more sort of the [] stuff, all the artists you probably know of. A lot of dance stuff on here actually. Oh here we go.
>
> [Plays the song.]
>
> Jane: Is that all instrumental?
>
> Janes: Most of his stuff is instrumental. I like listening to this stuff . . .
>
> [Puts on a different piece of music (a heavier metal piece)—more discussion of the music, but difficult to hear.]
>
> James: I like listening to that stuff more when I'm a bit angry—so that's my vent— I don't go off doing random things, I just listen to some music.
>
> Jane: And that regulates how you feel?
>
> James: Yeah because I'm always around music and definitely it's good, yeah. It definitely regulates my moods, sure. Like if I'm down I'll listen to some up music for whatever the mood is, I can't say it's definitely jazz or what. Even some dance songs for some reason I'll listen to and I want to get pumped up or calm not or if I'm upset then . . . I find myself when I choose songs that I like. If I go through my favourites it's the rhythm section that I listen to—the rhythm section's got more of a part of the song than sort of just the general songs when people are singing.

So, James returns to his musical 'ground', which is the rhythmical base he discussed throughout the interview. It is also evident that he has a piece of music for every eventuality. His music is a central part of his life. It was very surprising that he has taken accountancy training and read business studies at university. Even his mother was surprised by his career path and commented: 'He's too creative to be an accountant.' Neither James nor his mother thought he would stay in the career, but whether he would ever return to music, take up carpentry as a career or push himself to his limit in sports remains to be seen.

Conclusions: theoretical threads

Ibarra (Ibarra, 1999) developed the concept of 'provisional selves' as a term to explain how each of us 'tries out' identities before settling on one at least for a while. From the data presented in this chapter, this type of provisional exploration is most evident in the case of James. It is interesting that James had displayed a childhood musician self that had stayed with him, not as a major career self-determining feature, but rather as a pastime. Of course, in part James was not so clear about his self in terms of career pathways as his brother and sister were. There seemed to be so many options available to him because of his all-rounder abilities and his changing interests: sports, carpentry, and even journalism. His accountancy—which could have been a clear area of focus and self-identification for him—was not a niche. His mum could not see him staying in the job. James thought it was a job he would only do for a 'short time' before taking up something more related to travel, adventure, or carpentry. James seemed to be still working through his provisional selves, whereas both Sean and Lucy were much closer to an identified whole.

Of the theoretical ground we have covered thus far in this book, we could see that for James, music was not wholly fulfilling in terms of the self-determination theory. Whilst he was evidently competent—he could teach his sister, play in a big band, and tour the USA—he was not sufficiently competent to keep up with many of his colleagues. Whilst music was a totally related activity for him both in playing and in listening, it was clear that he had not always felt autonomous. Firstly, he was apparently reluctant to practice; secondly, it seems that he preferred making his music in a group situation, rather than being alone; thirdly, he had never quite achieved a status or indeed encountered a teacher who had given him sufficient rein to have control over his musical learning. Contrastingly, his carpentry and other self-created objects, such as his legendary ability to make beautiful PowerPoint presentation presents for friends, had been completely autonomous activities that had brought him a great sense of competency through the praise given by others. He had felt socially related by connecting with people through these activities. It should be noted that James was a music addict—he could not resist getting his MP3 player out to show Jane and Paul all his collection and displayed a considerable and discerning skill in differentiating between styles of music to satisfy different personal needs. It reminded Jane of her encounter with the 12-year-old James, who had insisted on showing her all his music and playing for her in his bedroom. Now, the interest had seemed to transfer from producing music to consuming music.

From the range of data presented, it does seem that there was a lot happening in James's internal world that made various elements of self harder for him to reconcile. Sean was happy to be an accountant and happy to know that his musical identity was offering him social opportunity and emotional regulation, with that loud bass pumping away in his car. Lucy was also in a clearer identity-space: she was social, loved arts, loved children, and loved dancing. She had two main identities: dancer and early childhood educator. She loved music as an expression of her dancer self, but also as a social force. Competency in music had never really been a concern for her as it was only ever an activity for relaxation, not high achievement.

We can see how Sameroff's theoretical notion of transactional regulation may be in operation through those complex and entangled interactions that configure the shifting responsibilities of caregivers, parents, teachers, and other social networks and institutions, to the learner him/herself. Without doubt syzygistic alignments and realignments were part of the experiences of these three children. Music had been a fairly constant part of their experiences, but never to such a degree for any one individual for them to be sufficiently committed to the dedicated practice required to achieve a high degree of competency. Even the best player, James, was very concerned that his lack of dedication would put him so far behind his peers that returning to playing would just be too difficult a challenge to face.

It was clear from the first interviews with parents at the very beginning of this study that family dynamics would have a significant impact on the musical development of our participants. Did parents supervise practice, give reminders to practice, listen to practice, or get involved with the projects at school? What were family beliefs and values about music and what kind of music experiences formed part of family life? We have already heard how crucial Anthony's mother was to his growing expertise, and we heard about the impact of family on Lily and Alistair. The Hulme family adds much to our study, the interpersonal dynamics of the family showing how music was developed, supported, and then continued into something highly meaningful to all members but in very different ways to the performer expertise that Anthony, Alistair, Lily, and Bryan all demonstrate. This case study also shows how the dynamics of parenting never stressed musical performance as a potential career pathway for the Hulme children. It is both interesting and surprising to see that both boys decided to move into accountancy, a career modelled for them by their father. What if Bob had been a musician? Suzie was a designer and this had strongly influenced Lucy's path to pre-school artwork. The Hulme family provide a unique illustration of how development can indeed be much more the consequence of environment and opportunity than simple genetics. Of course, the Hulme data also reveal that, as belief systems, theories of genetic inheritance can be useful: saying that you have music in your bones can certainly help you to explain a passion or indeed develop a passion for Latin-American rhythms, for example.

Chapter 9

Tristram: speaking about my own musical life, development, and identity

Using cultural heritage or genetic inheritance to explain a passion for a particular musical or dance style or genre brings a sense of cohesion to how Lucy identifies herself. Things become connected with each other, sense is made, and an identity is formed and performed. Another of our participants, Damian, now a young archetypal Aussie outdoor guy, sees his enjoyment and considerable potential as a bass player in the primary school ensemble as turning into a key component of his outdoor identity as a teenager. Damian's mother had commented how, at the age of 8 years, 'He came home with a bass guitar—his eyes lit up—he was the only one who could manage it. It's the only bass guitar in the band and he feels special.' More than a decade later, Damian uses this experience as an explanation for his passion for the 'bass' in music. He told us that the first thing he did, on recently purchasing a car, was to insert customized bass speakers for the playing of *his* music. Rather like Sean in the previous chapter, Damian emphasized how much the 'bass' in music had always mattered to him at a physical and visceral level, from that first experience on the bass guitar and the special status that it afforded him.

As young adults, our participants had strong views on what musical experiences, past and present, good or bad, meant to them and how these experiences had influenced them at musical, personal, and social levels. Because this is a study about their musical lives, there is a real sense in which these are the most important views and interpretations of all. As music education researchers, we may have paid too much attention to what we think are, or should be, key features of young people's musical lives or even to the qualities that we believe constitute a life that can be called musical. We may have paid too little attention to voices that provide 'a commentary of the individual's very personal view of his own experience as he understands it' (Watson, 1976; cited in Tierney, 2000, p. 539). In this chapter and the one that follows we will be giving two of our participants the freedom to provide such a commentary with no more than a contextual introduction. As we subsequently turn to the final two chapters of this book, we hope that the theory developed there can be seen as emerging from a dialogic authority.

On the one hand, this dialogic authority comes from the personal view that our participants have of their own experiences as they understand them. With various levels of mediation, we have attempted to share these views with the reader throughout this book. In the previous three chapters we have used qualitative methods, specifically Interpretative Phenomenological Analysis (IPA; see Chapter 5), to develop categories and constructs of our participants' musical lives, through which we have been able to review early data and analysis, and attempt to contextualize interpretations. Such classificiations enable us to understand the role that various phenomena play in musical development, and in explaining the impact of various experiences and our participants' perceptions of them we developed a range of constructs:

- The teacher and a flying start.
- The role of music examinations and programme expectations.
- Syzygies for precociousness.
- Thinking about 'play' and 'playing.
- Cultural heritage and compliance.
- 'It will be fun!' Lily's dream.
- Making progress in private.
- A competitor to the clarinet.
- School transitions—transfers out of music learning?
- Justifying an early exit.
- Making a re-entry.
- Parental views of music learning—for the love of it or the good of it?
- A girlie thing?

In the following pages, we take a further step on our methodological journey, with the detailed reflective musical life-stories of Tristram and Sarah, which moves beyond IPA to description. In doing so, we invite the reader to make up their own minds about these very personal views of musical lives, development, and identity.

The other dimension of this dialogic authority comes from our understanding or interpretation of our participants' views of their musical lives, along with all the other extensive data that has been formulated and collected throughout this study from various measurements, surveys, video analysis, and so on.

In turning to almost purely descriptive data, we do need to recognize, nevertheless, that the narratives told in this chapter and the next were elicited with the intention of exploring the specific role of music in people's lives. There may have been no moral, social, or personal imperatives for the telling of these stories except that we asked these young people to tell them to us. Tierney reminds us that life-history texts exist somewhere between history and memory, and that memories are recalled for reasons that are important to someone (Tierney, 2000, p. 545). We have already seen how retrospective accounts in our earlier case studies were consistent, even down to small detail, with information we had collected long ago—in real time as it were. The fact that participants knew that we were already privy to a great deal of information about their lives may account for this level of integrity. Given the detail we already know, we feel inclined to concur with Connell and not 'spurn(ing) the effort that respondents themselves make to speak the truth'. As Connell (1995) continues, 'An autobiographical story is evidence for a great deal beyond its own language' (p. 91).

The extensive stories provided in this chapter and in Chapter 10 are composite texts formed from several conversations rather than just one. Some repetition has been cut, as has the interviewer's voice. One of those interviews, used in this chapter, formed part of the survey and interviews carried out by Paul Evans discussed in Chapter 5. Further interviews were taken later by the authors themselves—in person, by Skype, telephone, and through e-mail communication. Participants were asked to talk about music in their lives around the time of the interviews, and to reflect on music throughout their lives with special reference to their experience in school. Interviews were highly informal and conversational. Questions were either open-ended or aimed at clarification or expansion. Subsequently, those edited texts were sent to the participants for further commentary, approval, editing, and amendment. We express our sincere gratitude to these participants. We believe that the stories told here provide key evidence for interim theory about how musical skills, behaviours, and identities develop in the musical lives of young people. These accounts are particularly fitting case studies to close this section of our book. As young adults, the two protagonists—one male, one female—engage in deeply personal accounts of emerging adult musical identities. They provided insights into the conditions and experiences that have brought them to unique places as highly skilled musicians, where music plays very valuable but very different roles in their everyday lives.

Tristram's background

The potential significance of a sampling phase in early instrumental musical learning in developing musical expertise has already been discussed in earlier chapters. We believe that it is under used in formal arrangements that are made for musical development, and that lessons could be learnt from Abbott's sport psychology model, which we reviewed earlier. Tristram, however, is almost unique in the range of musical instruments that he sampled in some depth at early stages of his development. He 'sort of played the violin in infants and sort of stopped at about year 2, but (I) started off on piano and stopped playing that in about year 4'. The tactile and visual seems to have been important to Tristram from an early age. In his first interview, aged 8, Tristram commented, 'How the piano has all the keys set out before you. I like the sound of the piano', and how he was attracted to the sound of the violin too, 'how it was a string instrument. I liked using the bow and plucking on it'.

Tristram's older siblings had:

> . . . said it was good being in the band. My brother (12) plays the trumpet and my sister (17) plays flute and piano sometimes. They had already been in the band at X school—I like instruments—hearing sounds of the different instruments. I like music itself.

When the time came, Tristram chose to play percussion in the school ensemble programme. Initially, he thought that in doing percussion he 'could still do piano easily, because they are both percussion'. He also claimed to like 'making loud noises' and the role of being responsible 'for keeping the band in time'.

Tristram's combined scores on Gordon's (1982) Intermediate Measures of Music Audition (IMMA) tonal and rhythmic measures ranked him as between the top

8th and 15th percentiles of our sample soon after commencing in the ensemble programme. Considering the extent of his previous experience, this hardly seems to indicate exceptional potential. Furthermore, his teacher was quick to articulate some concerns about Tristram's potential: 'He plays percussion but he's not very coordinated. I think it's by sheer force of will and intelligence that he manages to play.' But Tristram had recognized this deficit too: 'I don't think I'm going to be excellent because I am not double handed. I am right handed and the left hand sometimes gets out of time.' Tristram's assessment of the problem may have been correct, but he already had a proposed remedy: 'keep on practising—if you keep on practising gradually it gets you better'. General school reports suggest that Tristram showed a high level of conscientiousness both in terms of work and relationship ethics at an early age:

> Tristram has achieved excellent results through his dedication and commitment to all that he undertakes. His enthusiasm for research and his wide general knowledge will ensure his continued academic success. He has demonstrated maturity and kindness in his relationships with his peers and is an asset to 3F. Tristram will be a joy to any teacher lucky enough to have him.

Whilst Tristram's early exposure to instrumental learning did not reveal any extraordinary capacities, he did report that lessons were enjoyable. His mother's early comment that 'Tristram loved playing pieces that he liked for his piano teacher' indicates some degree of personal autonomy. In his first interview Tristram expressed the view that he hated exams. We could never have imagined then how prophetic that statement would turn out to be in term of his later music development.

Tristram's mum was a primary school teacher and throughout all the interviews and especially in the most recent one, Tristram testifies to her support. Her belief in the importance of music is confirmed in a decision, made since Tristram has left school, to direct the primary school choir, even though she has little formal training herself.

Several key issues arise from this introductory discussion. Firstly, Tristram was always interested, as a player of instruments, in the tactile and visual senses as well as the aural. Secondly, Tristram was privileged amongst our participants as having had fairly extensive sampling opportunities in instrumental learning in his childhood. Thirdly, like Anthony, there is a clear sense that his parents believe in learning to play a musical instrument 'for the love of it' rather than because of the 'good of it'. Fourthly, Tristram had early experience of autonomy around his music learning and the sharing of chosen pieces with his piano teacher and at home. Fifthly, Tristram was not seen as particularly musical, and certainly not particularly well co-ordinated, by his music teachers in the primary ensemble programme, even though he had had considerable prior musical experience. He was, however, seen as being very intelligent, enthusiastic, kind, and mature for his age. Finally, Tristram showed an early and strong resistance to formalized assessment and testing.

This is Tristram's recent account of his musical life so far.

Tristram's musical life

It was a really big thing at my school to be *in* the band, because it's what X school does. It was just *the* thing to do, everyone. Also it was fun, got to show off. We had a very big band programme, and, I think it was like, if you played drums you were cool. I actually didn't like playing drum kit. I preferred percussion, particularly the timpani. Well, it's more that I like being the band or orchestra side of things than playing drum kit. Which is why I got into vibraphone. They had a xylophone and a glockenspiel and they had a xylo-marimba—a horrible instrument (chuckles)! The way it was done at X school was you would have one person specifically on tuned percussion and another on untuned and timpani. And I played timpani. There was some vague kind of audition process. You just sort of blew on a few different instruments—obviously a great indication of what your skills are going to be (laughs). They also said 'just indicate if you really want to play something' and at the time I just really wanted to play drums. Can't remember why at all. It was percussion in general, so they gradually found that I didn't like playing kit very much, and moved into timpani and then into high school into mallet percussion. I ended up enjoying that the most, which is why I focused on it so much. I just felt like I didn't fit on the kit—just the appearance of the kit drummer—cool person. Whereas mallets seems like a different way of playing and it was also something that not many other people did, so it was a chance to try something that not many other people would know how to do.

Both my brother and sister had been through the concert bands, so to an extent it seemed like it was the thing you did, almost the inevitable. And a lot of my friends were talking about doing it as well. I knew I wanted to keep playing in high school. When I got into YY school I was very glad because my brother had been there and I knew it was a very musical school. He had been through the jazz programme himself. My sister played flute a bit, but it was mainly purely within band, it wasn't more in general. But she plays in the University of Chicago orchestra or the wind ensemble. Pat, my brother, he played trumpet a lot, in the orchestra and in the jazz programme, and doing music in Higher School Certificate [HSC]. I think he played through year 12, he gave up after that, but I'm not sure how long after that. He moved out reasonably early and he took his trumpet with him, and his girlfriend played trumpet as well. I don't know how long he kept it up, he doesn't play anymore.

I probably was a good player: I got into the top concert band in the beginning of year 5, the second level one, not many people in year 5 get into the top level one. There's some skills which take a while to learn—how to tune timpani in particular. I probably struggled most on playing kit, because I just didn't enjoy doing that sort of stuff. I tried out for the jazz band at the beginning of year 6 and didn't get in so I said ok that's it. Before that it was, 'This isn't what I want to be doing'. I like playing all the other things and I just didn't enjoy the kit drums very much. Didn't see myself as a drummer. I was already getting this image of what a drummer is, as distinct from a percussionist. And I wanted to be a percussionist, somehow that would have been more of a musician at the time, probably not now [chuckles]. Sort of trying to be all controlled and serious and studious.

A lot of people dropped out by the end of primary school but I just enjoyed it, doing something that a lot of other people don't do. It gave me a whole lot of friends. Some of my friends did it, some didn't, so it was sort of mixed bag. I didn't want to be the person who gave up. I felt a bit of a need to compete with my brothers and sisters maybe, but I didn't think it was really like a conscious thought, but a sort of factor in that. It was just something I did.

The music programme at high school was fantastic, particularly the jazz programme. I guess I was in year 7, in high school, the music department was looking for people to start learning the bassoon 'cos they hadn't had anyone for several years. Yeah and the school owned quite a good instrument and they wanted people to be actually using it. So a teacher came around and gave a demonstration to the class and I thought I'd give it a try because I wanted to play percussion, but I also wanted to play a melodic instrument. And I'm not sure, I don't really know, but I don't think many people just start on the bassoon as their first instrument, or their first wind instrument anyway. I seemed to be all right at it. There was another person who started at the same time as me and he gave up fairly soon, but I kept going. It's sort of difficult to tell whether people were glad that there was a bassoonist, or whether it was actually me being a good player. When I first started out I'd often do half an hour a day and towards the end it dropped off quite a bit 'cos I was just getting sick of playing—it was becoming more a chore than something I did for enjoyment. I would still practice quite a bit, but it wasn't focused. About half way through year 7, I joined the junior concert band. YY has a very strong jazz programme and I wanted to be part of that, and I didn't like playing kit. There were two people playing mallets in year 12, so they were leaving and there was a big gap, so the director of jazz, just said, you know, 'Do you want to try vibes?' So I tried it next time and sort of found I liked it. Eventually I got my own vibraphone. It's just gathering dust in the corner here at home. So it was vibes in jazz band and bassoon in concert band in year 7, and eventually orchestra as well, and eventually State Wind Ensemble. So it was both concert bands, the orchestra, the full jazz programme—the three stage bands. I had to leave orchestra in year 10 because rehearsal was same time as State Wind Ensemble. I think I left concert band at the same time, they changed conductor and I didn't really like the new person. I was still playing bassoon as part of music class in years 11 and 12 and I did composition for extension. The State Wind Ensemble was incredible to play in 'cos it's also playing real concert band music, which you don't get very much over here. I also got involved in the choir and the vocal ensemble. That was combined with the local girls' school in years 10, 11, 12 and I was also in musicals. I was just in general chorus in year 10, then had a singing role, like a solo role, in year 11. It was a lot of fun because it was something I hadn't done before and singing and dancing and acting.

I'm now in third year uni, studying arts, linguistics. I don't do music subjects at uni. It was a possibility in the first year, but it was sort of very difficult to fit in with time-tables and I ended up not quite being able to get it in there. I thought about going to the conservatorium to do music at uni through year 12. I think I was just over playing. I wanted to look at other things. There was just so much. I mean particularly going through year 12, playing the same pieces all the time. I was just getting sick of it. Just because of HSC. I'm involved in the one of the revue societies which always tries to have a strong musical component. It's Law Revue. I was in the cast. Um, well I tried out for the singing roles, but just doing sketches, dancing, and in the combined, the choral number. I sort of thought about whether I wanted to try out on percussion. They always need percussionists. Yeah. I stopped playing bassoon after, just before the HSC, or like after the practical music exam, because I just. . . I stopped playing because by that stage it was becoming more a ritual. Not something I enjoyed doing. Also the instrument actually belonged to the school so I no longer had access to it, so that was another factor in it. I had spoken to my parents and if I was going to study music at uni then owning a bassoon would have been a possibility. But then I decided I didn't want to, it just sort of happened. I kept up vibes until the end of January because there was a tour thing to the United States. And after that I just stopped playing. Still have a vibraphone which we're probably going to donate to the school. I just haven't played anything in years. I just wanted a clean break from school and while I still have the instrument, well, I had the big tour after school with the band going around the world, and that seemed like a fitting finale in many ways—London, Barbados, New York, and Florida. Didn't want to play after that. Sort of felt like I was played out. I really hadn't been enjoying school towards the end, I just felt boxed in and locked in to what I was doing, so I just wanted to get away from it all of it. I still listen to a lot of music, probably three hours a day for four or five days a week. Still try to do some writing every now and then I'll listen to just about anything. I very rarely find something I don't like, perhaps particular groups of people I don't like, rather than styles.

Well a lot of it is in the car, and I've also got an MP3 player and often just on the computer I'll put a CD in. And it will be a random mix of those kind of styles that I mentioned before. Generally in the car I'll try and get into things I don't always listen to, so trying out different things, just random CDs from my parents' collection. Um, but on the MP3 player particularly, generally things like that, just sort of random. Also my teacher had quite a lot of CDs, particularly of vibes players but also interesting and um, not so well known, musicians, ones that my teacher had got from the States. Things I was trying to play. I was playing with a few friends at school, we'd share a few CDs, but not a great deal. Occasionally I'd play music that was related to what we were playing in orchestra, but usually it was because I already knew the piece from my listening, rather than playing something and then wanting to find a full professional recording of it.

School music teachers were very important to me, particularly at high school not, very much in primary school. I had the same teacher from years 9 to 12, for music, and by the end we were very strong friends, and there were about six of us who had been in the same class for years, so we were pretty close, spend most of our time together at high school yeah. It was just sort of a core group which was fantastic—it meant we could bounce ideas off each other quite a bit as well. We've gone out of touch since then.

I ended up having three bassoon teachers because two got positions overseas. Well, they were doing study overseas. First one, he's the one that sort of demonstrated the instrument in year 7. I don't really remember him that much. I think we had him for about a year, year and a half. He was nice, but, yeah he just sort of disappeared for a while, and we got the next teacher who said, 'Yeah I'm your new teacher, didn't you know, didn't he tell you?' But she was great. Has worked with the ballet a few times and freelance bassoonist and bassoon teacher. And she was really nice, really friendly. Very prepared to help me with things. And so she got me very interested in contra-bassoon—not something you can really do in high school very much. Even very few bassoonists are able to play it. A lot of technical exercises and particularly extending my range. She was pretty much focused on bassoon (more than my previous teacher).

I think also at that stage I was giving up playing percussion generally and focusing on vibes, and was focusing on the two instruments, rather than all the percussion as well. I did two bassoon exams, she just mentioned the AMEB thing, and I did fifth and sixth grade AMEB on bassoon, but I don't know, I just really didn't like the whole AMEB system of cutting you off from the outside world (laughs), it is a bit like that. It was probably more the teacher's decision. But particularly when it came to pieces, she would give me a choice of different things, she would say you know, these are all really good pieces you should do one of them. I would take them for a few weeks and whichever one I chose would be the one to focus on. She got a permanent teaching position in Melbourne, so um, then, the third teacher just for year 12 was just a few years ahead of me at YY school, it must have been quite a few years because she had finished her BMus at uni by that stage. She wasn't as good I think, not really, she hadn't had the professional experience, but she was very used to dealing particularly with school students. She was really enthusiastic. Sort of like, you know, 'You're playing the bassoon for the HSC, here's something that would be really good, here's some pieces that would be really really fun to play', as opposed to just technical exercises. I'm thinking the previous year she'd been the bassoon and lower winds tutor in the State Wind Ensemble. And then after HSC I stopped, just wasn't into playing anymore.

Then there was the head of jazz programme at my high school. He was an incredible band leader and just a really nice person. He exposed me to so much more than I ever expected to do. He's very much about education shouldn't just be what's on the page, it's living, it's the world. I think in his thesis project in education he did a critique of the entire education system through the lens of how guitar is taught in schools. He's a guitarist and bass guitarist which would mortify you know, classical music teachers. He also really detested the concept of art music, never talk about art music versus popular music, all music is music. We'd often talk about stuff like, in between taking the band, we'd talk about what his problems were with things and how he'd prefer things to be done. I think a lot of my experience in music was shaped by him, particularly like looking at the way people talk about, you know, you have classical music and you have everything else, how can you really have that distinction at all?

Then there is one person who started out as concert band conductor then became the choir conductor, um, she became the concert band conductor after about half-way through year 7, then reshaped it into something that was worth listening to. It was just sort of fun, and she wanted to make music fun for people. When she did the choir she wouldn't just do serious choral stuff, she'd also do things like African music and other things, like clap with your hands. Yeah, she wouldn't just choose pieces on how famous they were but she would look at the band and what the make up of it was and would try and find pieces to fit that.

A lot of teachers throughout the school were very good. One was completely insane, but the good type of insane teacher—like eccentricity rather than mad (laughs)—they were good in that way.

My parents would be a big thing too. Dad really likes listening to jazz, also likes listening to blues—which I'm not such a huge fan of. He particularly likes swing. It's stuff that he was playing in the car. And mum very much just listens to opera quite a bit. She's a school teacher now. She wasn't when I was at primary school, but she has retrained since. She now plays it to her year 1 and 2 classes. It's something that people often don't listen to, people just don't expect it to be so nice. The big essential classics stuff. The famous stuff, but it's famous for a reason. My parents didn't listen so much in the home, but we started to have more quite recently, but particularly in the car or like long car trips, we'd switch CDs quite regularly.

One of the major influences would be my school music teacher in years 9 to 12, because there was that certainty and you'd see her five times a week at least, so.

I probably thought I had a talent for bassoon or something like that. People were glad that I was around, and they appreciated you. Music was somewhere I could be myself. I could try things out a lot more—be more adventurous. At school I had a very conservative façade and was trying to keep up appearances quite a bit whereas in music I could just do whatever I wanted—do things that I enjoy doing. And getting into the visual arts as well and since then I've also started writing poetry. Particularly towards the end of high school I started to detest the whole system. In high school, and also doing art, I got to do my own thing. I never really considered employment as the ultimate point of doing anything, no idea what I would like to do after I finish my degree. But uni's like that (laughs), so I have no idea what I'm doing in spite of doing everything I am (laughs). It was something that was *mine*. Something I can just go and do by myself, don't need to worry about other people, by the end of high school everything has to matter to other people. But I could still make my decisions about it, a sense of ownership about it, a control over my own life. Um, doing art as well. Again, it's being able to create means you don't have to be, you know, strictly measured and assessed. Difficult to say what comes first whether you're good at it or whether you like it. I think by the time I got to the HSC I wasn't sure whether I was good at playing the instruments. I did quite well with my composition and like the performances they were good, but they weren't great. And sort of like before HSC I had sort of already been thinking, 'Why am I doing this? Am I really good enough to be able to do this, particularly with bassoon'. Through the State Wind Ensemble I met a few people, particularly one who was in year 9 playing stuff ten years beyond what I was dreaming of doing. She was a child prodigy, effectively. She was an incredible player, I was nowhere near as good, and that sort of put a bit of a blocker on what I was doing there. It was sort of a direct realization that there's so much more to go, particularly since she was three or four years younger than me and much, much better than I was. It just seemed like, oh my god, this is . . . ok . . . you can do it, but I can't. So I started out trying to do all three performances on bassoon for HSC, but I ended up doing one and two vibraphone pieces, because they are more free. One of them was baroque, Bach, it's from the third suite, the Bouree from one of his flute sonatas or is it partitas? Violin and flute music does actually fit very nicely onto the range and also under the hands. On the vibes there was none of us in my year that started after me but as far as the technique was going it was, I look at it now and say 'Well, how can you really say?' But at the time I felt it was technically brilliant, so I ended up doing two pieces. One that, um, a very recent piece with no metre at all which, I forget, well it was a contemporary piece, blues piece, transcribed. It was difficult to start with but because of no strict metre, you could be a lot more free with it, not really master it but just, portray it. That's probably the best word, portray it, follow the way the music went, rather than trying to impose anything on it, just like, by the run of phrases, just work out, use that to decide tempo and dynamics.

I couldn't do stuff like that on the bassoon. Well, I sort of had a go every now and then, trying to improvise and found it just seemed so foreign to me on that instrument. It's almost like I had to start again and it seemed like too much effort for something you don't usually do on bassoon in any case, at least that's the impression I got. I don't know if there are many jazz bassoonists. I've heard of one which is quite incredible. With the piano, that was still learning, so it was more limited to what music I was given by the teacher.

But often with pieces I learnt there came the feeling like I'm just getting it, I'm not able to *own* the piece, I'm just making it. And as time went on it became more and more difficult to find the sort of desire to make it. I sort of felt like I could be playing better. It always seemed people were able to move a lot faster. Well, with the getting better and better thing, I always felt like if I put in more effort I would be getting so much better, and it's difficult to practice. Like, playing the HSC was sort of like, that was it. It's you know, the big, the end of high school, which is the big chance and uh, I didn't react well to the HSC at all. I really got pissed off with it. You have to choose your pieces so far in advance and get them as perfect as possible. It sort of felt like I was just being completely limited in what I was able to do and I wasn't . . . I mean the teachers were really good, they got me to do other things too but it always came back to doing the same thing over and over again and trying to get that little bit better and it became infuriating towards the end. It is the freedom of music that attracts me the most. There's so many different types of things you can do and there is something for everyone. I mean, I'm a really eclectic listener. I was kind of trying to avoid looking at the HSC at all. I was also getting very annoyed with school in general. I sort of just felt like I wasn't able to be myself towards the end of high school, so that became a very big thing and playing my instrument wasn't something I was able to do myself, it was just something I was doing. It was in the mindset of 'this is my school persona'. I really liked music and I really liked spending time with the people in it. But I just sort of had a big collapse in my ability, in my confidence in being able to play at the same standard as the people around me, this was probably part of it. It's sort of just, it was harder and harder to find time to play stuff that I wanted to play as distinct from the stuff I had practiced for the stuff, for HSC. I may have had the niggling doubts for a lot longer, but sort of when it came to a head, it was probably the biggest. You know, this is the big mark. There was nothing negative before, even moving the percussion instruments, especially the vibraphone, it's an incredibly difficult instrument to transport but it's just what comes with playing it. It was the HSC, day in, day out, the same thing.

I was also getting more into the visual arts side of things, which is how I found interior architecture as a degree. I just really enjoyed making art, thought about design, particularly set design. I enjoyed the theory side of it but not the work side, I just changed to an arts degree, chose four subjects in the first semester, did best in linguistics and enjoyed it most so decided to keep going.

In year 10 and 11 I sort of felt like everything was going right. At the time it was the right thing. I was playing the State Wind Ensemble and going overseas with that. I was in the musical, in choir, I was playing well. No, it seemed like, this is the big thing, 'I'm going to be a musician or a composer or a music something'. Not so much the theory at that stage, that came later. Particularly it was composition and performance. I really enjoyed composition. I still, every now and then, have a go at doing it. I attempted to write songs but I'm not a lyricist, I'm good at harmony rather than melody anyway. Still trying to you know, like spoof lyrics for revue later this year. I did two compositions for HSC. One was a duet for xylophone and vibraphone which I played with my then teacher. Sort of looking at rhythms, crossing, like alternating beats, various melodies trying to weave through each other. The other was for voice, clarinet, violin, and cello. It was the first song I had ever written, trying to write my own lyrics, which was kind of more daunting than I expected. I loved composition, I could do whatever I liked. I started out doing two vocal pieces and then half way through I just completely canned one of them because it was going absolutely nowhere. So, just fiddling around on the piano and then on the vibes and the school xylophone I just came up with the other one, sort of almost out of the blue and it felt so good to be able to create something from absolutely nothing. Through year 12, probably as a way of getting away from having to play the same thing every time, my vibes teacher introduced me to lots of free jazz ideas and often we'd spend quite a bit of the lesson time just playing off each other, which was just fun because you could anything you wanted. There were absolutely no limits.

That's the thing about uni too, like I changed from architecture to linguistics and arts: if you don't like something you're doing you can change it, which is very different to the way the school system is set up (laughs).

I also did some arranging for a friend for a piece he wrote in year 9. I wanted to see if I want to try arranging this for something else, and eventually around half-way through last year I came up with the string quintet version of it that he was really happy with and hopefully at some stage we'll actually hear it played.

If it wasn't for the high school I wouldn't have picked up vibes because none of the places have them except my school, and wouldn't have picked up bassoon either. I'm not sure . . . not liking school in general by the end of it, more and more just school, but THAT school. It sort of felt like I was being straight-jacketed into 'this is what the young man is'. I wasn't able to be myself, which is why I first went into music and art, because they were very much about who I was, but by the end of it, even music performance, that wasn't really being mine anymore. It had felt safer to do it than try to do other stuff which I wasn't so interested in. Things that, you know, sports, I'm not a particularly sporty person. I did lawn bowls, but I did that with the people who played music anyway (proudly), I was a school representative in lawn bowls! (laughs) I think I was, you know, I was able to think of art as not being a school thing, it's like art I was being judged as myself rather than being judged as this image of a musician or a music student or whatever. Cos art, my art works would actually be myself entirely.

Um, at uni I cut ties with a lot of people from school. Going into interior architecture, that's a very insular degree. I just didn't see people. And also just didn't want to see a lot of people. There's not many electives, everybody does all the courses together. And it was sort of two or three people I see reasonably regularly from the high school period.

Probably would pick up a lot more music now. Just cos I'm, if I hear something I'll try and find it again. So going thorough CD shops just looking at what's there, which I certainly didn't do at high school. I very rarely got into new music in high school. I didn't listen to the radio at all. Like The Killers, I only got into last year, as part of a revue. We were doing a dance number to one of their songs, and I really liked it so I bought three CDs. I listened to a lot of classical music which a lot of people don't listen to so. I'm more able to talk about music, certainly when I'm around university music students. When I'm in the car, it's not very environmentally friendly but I can turn up the music as loud as I want and sing along, usually I'm the only one in the car, so I can completely choose my own music and I've got an MP3 player and I change the music on that quite regularly. When I put my shuffle on it could go anywhere. My friends seem to enjoy it. I am told I have incredibly eclectic tastes. I find it's a good way to introduce more music to them as well as them introducing music to me. Particularly the classical side of things because a lot of people just don't have much experience with that and even more so with opera, I didn't listen to it at school at all, I couldn't stand it. I think more since school I've started appreciating music as drama more, like pieces moving into each other and the theatricality of music which I didn't really understand at school. So sort of even with CDs I pay more attention to why is this track after this one—are they actually trying to tell a story? And opera was part of that: previously I had listened to music that was very nice and beautiful but after that it was like, actually this is a story, there is something going on here. I've got a 10-stacker CD thing in the back of the car so I put in ten different CDs and I'll put in things I listen to all the time but I'll also put in completely new things and find it's a good way of getting to know completely new music and sort of expanding horizons a lot more. I will listen to just about anything. Recommendations from friends. With classical stuff it is just things we have at home. Classical, pop, jazz all mixed up. I think at the moment I've got *The Magic Flute*, Dvorak's ninth, Scissor Sisters and The Killers! If I don't like something it's generally just a song I don't like, not a genre or an artist. I think I've sort of opened up a lot more in the last few years 'cos I sort of tried to maintain that persona through high school that I sort of listened to classical and jazz and that's it. I was trying to pretend other types of music didn't exist. It was just something I did, makes no sense now whatsoever. More recently, if I like something I'll listen to it. Doing the revue I'm being introduced to a lot of new music and it's opened up new worlds. I'm also going out a lot more recently to clubs and places like that and dancing along is exciting. With friends, mainly around Newtown or Oxford Street, so it's sort of like dance music quite a bit and karaoke as well, which is an interesting experience (laughs). What would I choose? Dusty Springfield is good for a laugh sometimes. Plus if it's something everyone knows then everyone sings along, particularly choruses—'You Raise Me Up'. I like to test that piece, because it's almost so 'Danny Boy' . . . but not quite. Everybody knows it, so it's very easy to sing along. It's just sort of joining in, doing your bit. Just a shared love. For me it is about being someone different, shedding all pretensions about myself. If I sing badly, I sing badly—who cares, everyone's singing badly together (laughs)—particularly with copious amounts of alcohol, it tends not to have the best effect on the voice. I am going to a party tonight which is eighties themed, so . . . wonderful eighties music. Auditions tomorrow for the boys only dance, which is a very, very fast hip-hop number and also possibly some choral practice and after that there's another party. There'll be music there but I'm not sure what type or if there's going to be dancing. I've got into dancing a lot more recently too. I was in the review last year as well, in the combined dances which is all very choreographed and sort of going out dancing however I want and it's a good way to meet people and find out what people are like as well.

Generally, I don't sit down to listen to music very much. I'm doing things and it gets to a particular track and I'll stop and just listen to it because I love that particular song so much that it will distract me from what I am doing. It's not so good for the study side of things. I had been to a few Sinfonia concerts at school and a few things with school like Sydney Symphony. But last year I went to the Tchaikovsky Violin Concerto with the Sydney Symphony through the Classical Music Appreciation Society. It was wonderful, the first time going for myself, not going to study the music, so just going to listen to it and lose myself in it. I think I'm more of an appreciator, but it doesn't feel like something I have to do anymore. Sort of like, I do it, I listen to it, I love it, but I don't', you know, it's not, kind of, wouldn't fight tooth and nail if you tried to take my music away from me. Like it's not all, it's not everything I am now. But it was in high school I think, yeah, say in year 10. I still love it, but I have got other things I can do. Still do some art works every now and then. Also involved in revue, like it's musical but it's also sketches and acting and design, it's pretty famous in New South Wales, it's a gigantic cast this year, about 60 people. Everyone had to audition for vocals to sort out SATB parts, but I also auditioned for solo singing roles. I haven't ever had any singing lessons apart from within choir practice, but I enjoy it. It's an option. I'm also auditioning for the guys' audition-only dance. I'm also trying to get in some sketches as well. And also one of the editors of the student newspaper this year, which gives me lots of opportunities just to write and edit. I tend to write absolutely on the spur of the moment type things and I've had a few published which is quite scary. I think we had been looking at a few poems in one of my courses and when I was on my way home I just sort of had this idea in my head, like, oh my God, I just have to write this down. Outside of English classes I had never written poetry before. Often my poems are about getting an emotion out. I sort of find sometimes that it's just a way of getting frustrations out and almost sort of cleansing myself of them, so they tend to be a bit angry in some ways. So I'd possibly think about going into publications, going for postgrad work and possibly going into academia. It's something my grandfather did and something my sister's doing now, so I know it's always an option but I'm really not sure, it's awhile off now. And I'm also getting involved in student politics, which is very complicated and sometimes very bitter. This is who I am now. I'm not sure. I think I've done too much queer theory to attempt to define identity by action (laughs). It's who you identify as, rather than what you do, as being your identity. Behaviours don't in themselves create a person. They're sort of an aspect of those that come from the identity rather than . . .

Now, I am just singing when I can. I'm having fun with the video camera at the moment so I'm just trying things out, but I've never done any video shooting before so I'm not really sure what it's going to end up like. And also doing photography a lot more recently, generally for social things and also just for social things and also just trying out different ways of taking photos and getting a good picture.

Musically, lots of things stand out though: playing on the beach in Barbados, listening to Tower of Power playing in San Francisco, completely different experiences, learning to appreciate music from within and without at the same time. So making and loving music with other people, linked experiences, but not quite the same. Joy, absolute love of life!

It might seem surprising, given the extraordinary richness of Tristram's musical life, that he makes no special claims for 'musician' status. This is in stark contrast to Bryan's self-identification as a musician in the recent interview which we discussed in Chapter 7. There is a strong sense that Tristram may well have identified himself as a musician just a few years ago but alignments have changed. Since then, a crisis of musical confidence and frustration at the monotony of Higher School Certificate music has changed the way Tristram identifies himself. In any event, Tristram is clear that identity is about *what* and *who* one identifies *as* and *with*, rather than something that others ascribe to us. Such a view questions the very basis of a great deal of music education and music psychology research that has traditionally defined musicianship for other people, having observed and even tested their actions, in much the way that we originally did in this study.

Bryan's self-assigned musician status, and the role that this view of self has quickly come to play as a central construct of his personal identity, remind us that musicianship takes on different forms in different people's lives. This is especially true when we relinquish our privileged grip on the term and accept that because 'musicianship', 'musician', and 'musical' are constructs, other people can construct them too. In some instances, the terms may take on many and varied forms even in the context of an individual life. We have heard how Bryan and his mother shifted definitions of *being musical* for entirely pragmatic reasons that justified Bryan's engagement or disengagement with various kinds of musical actions. Constructs of musicianship or non-musicianship may be discreetly compartmentalized by time or space in strictly historical senses, as they were in Bryan's case. For others, like Anthony and Alistair, one or two key ideas about musicality, musical identity—and the practice of those ideas—have formed a relatively constant and linear thread through childhood, adolescence, and early adulthood. For other people, there may be a far more complex and dynamic interweaving of musicalities and musical identities through the various fabrics of ongoing social and personal lives, as there seemed to be with Tristram.

From this perspective, what we identify ourselves *as* or *with* is always interim, in spite of the appearance of permanence. The interviews that formed the basis of these case studies add to the illusion. A process of reification means that situated and transient identities are locked into a place, page, and time. In reality, our selves are never like this and Robert Weber (2001) reminds us of the astonishing possibilities for the changing and shifting self in the post-modern age in his provocative account of *The Created Self*. In his sense of changing identities, Bryan's sudden acquisition of a musical identity is rather like one of Weber's dramatic self-transformations: plastic surgery, changing a name, and public identity, or even gender realignment and sex affirmation. Ibarra (1999), similarly, has developed the concept of 'provisional selves', a term that captures how each of us 'tries out' different identities, along with strategies to deal with them, in order to work out a personal 'self' and emerge as a participant or specialist in a specific domain.

The idea of 'emerging' as something has, however, the kind of finality about it that is not true of real lived experience. We may attempt to petrify seminal events and give particular significance to them as marking our 'arrival' as *something*—say a 'concert pianist' in making a debut solo concert, an 'author' in publishing a first academic paper or book, a 'composer' in having a composition performed in public, and so on. But, having arrived, there is always another destination and other possibilities, especially in the increasingly mobile, flexible, diverse, and often frontier-free worlds that our participants have grown up in.

Tristram's history seems to capture what this changing self might look or sound like musically, from his early sampling of musical instruments, his rejection of drumkit 'coolness', his strong sense of being a mallet percussionist, his impressive journey as a bassoon player and composer, only to make a dramatic realignment as a young adult as an aspiring writer, dancer, and singer, having rejected instrumental music almost entirely—for the time being!

Even more so than Tristram's musical biography, the story that we are about to tell illustrates the dynamic nature of musical identity in our lives. It reminds us that any developmental view of musical abilities must account for the roles that are ascribed to music in constructing, maintaining, changing, and presenting ourselves. Music is a technology of self in at least two senses. In one sense, music has huge potential for regulating mood and behaviour. With the growth of personal music technologies, this is true for our participants as with no previous generation. In another sense, music is a technology of self at the level of working out who we think we are, reworking who we want to be, and in showing other people how we want to be identified. We have heard examples of both these kinds of functions throughout this book but especially in the last three chapters. As adolescents and young adults become increasingly concerned with setting themselves apart from parents and others, music often plays very important roles in that process of constructing and representing self (see; MacDonald *et al.*, 2002; Miell *et al.*, 2005). Those individuals who engage in solo music performance have particular opportunities to identify and present an identity or persona to a larger public audience (see Davidson, 2005). None of our participants have engaged in such activities as much as Sarah, who appeared earlier in this book as the horn player whose mother had concerns about her stamina for an instrument for which there was a lack of motivation. The story of music in her life is the subject of our final case study.

Chapter 10

Sarah: speaking about my own musical life, development, and identity

Our final case study focuses on a female who developed exceptional musical theatre skills at an early age. Her mother identified her at a very early age as somebody who liked to share her identity as 'an entertainer' with an audience. In contrast to Tristram, Sarah's involvement with the school instrumental programme was relatively short lived. She played the French horn for 5 years and we would have been denied this account had our study not embraced a larger view of young people's musical lives. Soon after Sarah had started playing in her school wind band her mother explained how she had 'jumped at the opportunity to join', just as Iris had.

> She'd seen the band at school, and seen the orchestra playing. She's very musical and has been asking for piano lessons for 2 or 3 years. She jumped at the chance to join the band. There was no decision to make—she was in it! The only decision was what instrument she would learn.

The decision was the French horn but, as with many other participants, this was not Sarah's instrument of choice. Instead, it was a decision made on an assessment of her aural ability and the prioritizing of the bands needs. The argument is common in music education; difficult instruments can only be played by people with high levels of aural acuity and because those instruments are needed in the school band, students that score highly in music perception tests are encouraged, even coerced, into playing them—not least by using the flattering line of reasoning that only the 'gifted' few can play these kinds of instruments anyway. As Sarah's mother explained just a few months into the project, 'Not many people play it—it may open more horizons for her. Why be one of thousands when she can be one of a few—if she's got the ability?'

But Sarah's mother also noted that 'Sarah is not over the moon about it' because she had wanted to learn the saxophone:

> I don't know, because she's not happy and I don't want her to lose interest. I'm a bit concerned—she's not the type to stick with it if she doesn't like it. She's not patient, she's a perfectionist and wants to plays things on it straight away.

Her mother commented in her very first interview how Sarah had wanted to become an 'entertainer of some kind from the age of two':

> As soon as she could talk, she always wanted music on, and she showed great interest in maracas, castanets, bells, sticks, and her musical mobile. She learnt all the lullabies and

pop songs from my era, and she loved Michael Jackson far more than the Playschool [popular children's television show].

Her mother had identified Sarah's excitement for novelty at an early age too; her 'endless pursuit of new experiences' and openness to them. A passion for singing and dancing was evident very early on, so that even before Sarah had began in the primary ensemble project, she was involved in extensive extra-curricular activities through the Sydney Theatrical Centre: 'She does drama, tap, jazz, and singing—it's her life at the moment. She loves an audience anywhere, anytime.'

The arts are clearly important in this family. Sarah's mother spoke about the importance of the role of music in the Jewish faith and culture, with high levels of participant singing and dancing at festivals and in the synagogue. At a micro-level, Sarah's mother has always been interested in dance and from an early age Sarah, almost uniquely in our study, was taken to musicals, shows, and the ballet. In data collected during the first 2 years of the study, she was described by her mother and various teachers as: very creative, enjoys art, strong-willed, can be quite lazy, lively, not meek and mild, bright, bubbly, happy, loyal, outgoing, talkative, free spirit, bubbly, quite sensitive, gets frustrated if she can't do things properly straight away, quite sensitive to others in sad situations, picks things up very quickly and has already worked out by ear many tunes on the horn, has a good aural memory, has some very mature thoughts, is protective of other people's feelings.

The confusion that Sarah's parents felt around her learning the French horn was obvious throughout the primary school programme. Torn between a sense that Sarah had been identified as a promising student and her lack of commitment to her instrument, they expressed concerns on several occasions that she was on the verge of giving up. That was certainly not true of Sarah's commitment to music in other areas, and her commitment to music theatre performance was matched by a significant parental investment. In fact, by the age of 9 years it had become a considerable financial outgoing: 'We have the school fees and the cost of her going to performance school as well is phenomenal.' Sarah's parents had, nevertheless, recognized what they believed to be her 'real talent' and clearly did their best to support it:

> She likes to put on shows and concerts and organizes everybody—she is a leader, but she is also a follower in the sense that she likes to know people like her. It amazes me that she can play the piano by ear and her voice amazes me.

Later, when Sarah moved to high school and became unhappy at what she saw as an increasingly narrow academic emphasis at her new school, her parents even supported her audition for, and subsequent transfer to, one of Sydney's leading performing and visual arts high schools. Sarah had given up the French horn by then, but her musical life, as we are about to hear, can hardly be defined by the terms of that particular musical engagement alone.

Sarah's musical life: a personal account

I think that everyone is really different, they all interpret music, sound, any sound, in their own way. Musical ability is not just about playing music, it's also about listening to it, creating it, maybe not even by physically playing it, but just gathering ideas in your head. For me, that's another form of musical ability. Even if you never really put it into action, the concept of it is just as strong. I guess that's a bit contradictory, because music is sound . . . but the idea of it.

I think musical ability has a lot to do with upbringing and in terms of family life. Just where you live, the context of it, and natural talent and a talent that is worked on progressively.

My parents were fairly neutral about my music. They've always been very supportive, but at the same time I never really cared about what they thought. So the fact that they were neutral in a way helped me just do my own thing. They never really influenced me that much. It's always been my own drive. I think they used to be interested in music, they used to be more musical. I don't think they are as much now, not any more.

I've got three younger siblings, so the one closest to me, she's 16 years old, she's not at all interested in music or anything like that. She's like the black sheep of the family. When she was really young, at primary school, she played the flute, but not even for a year, probably for 6 months. She hasn't picked up an instrument since then. And she doesn't really listen to music. I mean, she listens to some music like the radio, but she just turns it on for like light entertainment, it's more subconscious, it's not a conscious thing that she is choosing to listen to. She has an iPod, but I don't know if she really uses it that much. It's more of a gimmick because everybody else has one.

When it comes to my interests, I imagine she doesn't understand them. Not that she would want to. So I think it could be that a lot of it is because she is holding back, because I'm so interested in it. But then the other two younger siblings, who are 6 and 10, are really into it, like maybe even more so than I was at their age. They're both learning two instruments each at the moment, they're both learning piano and my little sister also learns the violin, and the other one is also learning the euphonium.

You don't have to learn an instrument at the school we all went to. It's optional and my parents would never force them to. But they both really wanted to. I think it's really in them, like half of it is, like even if they were living by themselves but knew what music was and didn't have anyone else talking about music in any way, they would still be drawn to it, no matter what. But a lot of it I think is to do with that fact that because I am so much older than them, they have looked up to me, and my whole life has been about music and so it is probably just natural to them.

I started singing like you know, as a toddler, so I was doing that. So singing has been the main instrument of my life. That's something that I've never ever given up. So I started that when I was younger. I had singing lessons and all that from a really young age. And I was trained up until maybe 16 years old, then I decided to break away from that because I felt like I was being pushed into one corner, vocally. And I didn't want to do that, so I decided to look at the voice as an instrument in a really different way. I think that that was influenced by the music I started to listen to, music I've studied. I'd always been taught that there was a right way and a wrong way to sing and the same in any instrument. So I was always taught, you know, to sing in pitch, in tune, you have to sing with a certain sound, an aesthetic sound I guess, very technical. I guess technique was the most important thing. Then I started to listen to music, and it was just that there is, there are different kinds of aesthetics in the voice, not just one (laughs). There are so many important people that have influenced me. A big one would have been Elliot Smith, Bob Dylan is a huge one, the Velvet Underground. A lot of them you might not know because they're quite new. But lots of old school bands from the 60s. Even more so I think the new age things, like electronic music, had a lot to do with it, things like that. Things I had been taught and things I was hearing they were clashing. I had been taught to sing in more of a musical theatre kind of way. I had no problem with that for a long time, that's really what I thought I was going to do. You know. And that made my parents really happy. Because, I don't know why, it seems to be a common thing with parents. But then, yeah I started, I guess I started mixing with different people, listening to different things, I became a lot more independent. I was finding the whole thing to be rather smothering and very mechanical and very, what's the word I'm looking for? Can't think of it right now . . . Formulated, that's it. It is formulated, yes.

It was something about the music itself, the music I was listening to. So lyrics I guess, but the sound itself was just so different, all these different melodies clashing together, it was so sporadic, unconventional, just a really different way of writing music, putting notes together. Just things that . . . I mean that it influenced the way I play now. So when I am writing a song and I play it to someone who might be interested in that kind of thing, I don't know where the song's going to go. I don't know whether they like it or not. It still sounds nice but it's just really different. It's just a different way of composing I guess. I never spoke about this to my parents or my singing teacher. I don't have a singing teacher anymore, but with friends, definitely, yes friends, all the time, mentors, things like that I guess, loads and loads of mentors. I mean some of them are friends, they are all friends actually, but they are maybe older than me, and my old art teacher from the performing and visual arts high school, he really directed me in that way, definitely. So I talked to him about it. And I've got lots of friends in bands now, some in famous bands, so I talk to them about it because they are actually in the profession, the industry. They are actually trying to do what I try to do and so on. We talk about what we are actually going through, the publicity side of it and whether people actually like it or not I guess.

So I went to primary school and I never stopped singing basically. And then I started playing French horn and I didn't know what a French horn was. They just gave it to me and said that's your instrument. So I never actually, it wasn't something that I chose. And I think that's why I didn't really feel like someone connected to it, I mean not enough to be completely interested in it and devoted to it. So even though I never really wanted to give it up, when I did, it wasn't that big a deal. The French horn, it's really hard, I found it really difficult and I think that has a lot to do with the insecurities coming in as well. You know if I couldn't play it and then all my other friends were playing instruments that were maybe a bit easier to start on and were doing very well, I would just feel like, 'Oh I must be terrible at music'. Well I was really young, but . . . yes, it's a really tough instrument. I would talk about it with my parents and my teacher and they would say like, 'It's a hard instrument, you must be good if you're doing it'. But I felt like I wasn't good. I didn't think I was good enough. But I've always been a bit of a perfectionist so I don't know, I don't remember how I played at that age and I don't know whether as an outsider that would be considered good or not. I loved playing it. But I think I was just very, I don't know, I've always been kind of laid back. And when I was told I was going to move and couldn't play the horn any more, I just went with the flow I guess. There was a huge, sort of gap, like a hole in a few years of my life. I was very impressionable I guess, because I was a young teenage girl. So not playing an instrument like French horn—which I was always teased for, people said it's like a nerdy instrument, things like that—I guess it wasn't that big a deal for me to stop.

So I stopped when I was 13, the end of year 7, when I left primary school. I went to Shore High School which is the same sort of school but on the side of the shore. The only difference is that they aren't as musically well equipped as my primary school was. So I went there and actually did enquire about picking up the French horn again at my new school, and they said you can't because we don't have one, you will have to go and buy one, and I couldn't afford it so . . . and I'd always been really, really busy. I was busy with my music and singing, my dancing and singing, things like that. So I, you know, it's not like I wasn't occupied or something. I just moved on, and it just dried up. And I never took it up again. Then later I moved to a new high school, a performing and visual arts high school, because I realized that there was a gap . . . musically, I needed something, not necessarily because I wasn't playing, but because the first high school I went to, it had nothing to do with any of that music or art stuff and everyone was telling me I had to do maths and science . . . for HSC and things like that, and I didn't want to. So I moved to a high school that did a lot of arts, performing arts, and I started playing bass guitar. I got into the school doing singing. I actually auditioned with a previous life thing, you know, a musical theatre song. Then, as I started going to the school and became friends with a group of people, that all changed. I started in different things, it wasn't that I just abandoned it. I was just broadening out. I was just really narrow minded I guess, I was really naive as to what was out there (laughs). I took up the bass guitar in year 11, end of year. I started playing with a friend. We both sang and she already played guitar, like an acoustic lead guitar. Already, we wanted to take it further and I thought we needed a bass guitar and didn't know anyone, so I tried to start playing and I taught myself how to play it. But there's a bit of a catch because . . . I've always taught myself by ear and I never really, I still haven't bothered to learn the notes. I kind of know them, but I don't know the notes, like if you ask me what the second or fourth string was, I wouldn't be able to tell you straight away. I would have to really think about it. So it's all by ear. But I think that's just as good as knowing the notation. I don't know if it's really my preferred way of learning, it's just the only way I've done it so far. Well not when I played French horn, obviously. I learnt how to notate and things like that and singing when I was younger but now, I just haven't bothered yet. Like I am still learning by ear and I just feel like once I have, once I'm okay with that, I'll move on to the other. I can read chord symbols, but I mainly just work it all out by ear, just everything. If I had to play from chord symbols on the bass, I would probably find that quite hard, but I could play it on the piano. But playing the bass it's the first time I've played a stringed instrument and I guess I find it a bit more difficult, I don't know.

Even though we started just the two of us, it's always been a collective, there have always been people coming in and out, but the two of us sort of, I don't know we were the leaders in a way. But at the moment right now, there's five of us in that band but at the same time I'm also in other bands. I'm in several other bands as well so. It's all very . . . all my friends are musicians, every single one. So there's a lot of swapping . . . around . . . which is good. That doesn't mean that they are studying music, not necessarily. What I mean is, and maybe some of them aren't even playing in a band, but they're still musicians. They might just be listening to music, but they are still musicians in my eyes. I think so, yes, they don't have to be studying it, like I am studying arts. Art was just as strong as music, always, my whole life. And it was, I was considering doing music but I decided, I don't know, I looked at it. I'm not rushing through anything, you know. If I'm going to do this art degree, then maybe do music after that. I'm kind of driven by the idea of just learning for the rest of my life, feeding on knowledge, going to uni, travelling and learning different things really. So it's not that I put art . . . it's not that I chose art above music. It's just that I'm at this point in time, in the mind frame that I am in. I mean now it's, I'm just focusing on art, educationally.

For Higher School Certificate I did two music units, a drama unit and four units of English, so all arts I guess (laughs). If I had my life over again I would never have given up French horn and I would probably have learnt a dozen other instruments (laughs). I never learned piano and I really regret that. And my dad was a pianist so, I constantly asked him to teach me as a kid, and he always said, 'No, I want you to learn, but I don't want to teach you because you won't listen to me, so I'll get you another teacher', but he never did. He played his whole life and he was really good and he got a scholarship to go to the Conservatorium after school, but his parents didn't let him go, that really, really affected him and he plays less and less now. I think it made him, really . . . it just shattered his confidence basically. Yes and I think, but that's why he's so, he pushes me so much to do it. And my parents constantly tell me that I should concentrate on my music, more than the art. They always used to use the expression that I am hiding behind my paintbrush. I still don't really know what that means. But that's what they say. I don't know if they think I am more talented in music than art. Maybe. I think so. I think they don't understand my art. I think they can relate to the music more. Well they think they can. I never felt that I had to do what my father couldn't. They've never been like that, they've never been living through my life. But they were just sort of saying, you know, you have this real opportunity, and we didn't really get that so . . .

Now I just think that they are just like all parents, they think that their kid is the most talented person and they don't want to see them waste it, and they know that I am not the most persistent person. Like I let people, not walk all over me, but I let other people go before me and I've always done that, just because I'm just so relaxed. Yes. My parents see it as a weakness I think.

Right now, I just a played a gig two nights ago at the Seymour Centre, University of Sydney, which is just up the road. That was with my five-piece band, actually there were only four of us playing. We had broken up recently, so we weren't playing together, but since we broke up I started writing music by myself and I've been really concentrating on just solo stuff and it might sound silly but, when I write my own music I write a bass line first but they're not like a bass lines, it's like a melody. Because I'm a singer, when I write bass lines it could sound like a vocal melody. And then I write the vocals or the lyrics over that. So I've got a bass part, vocals, and I might put synthesizer to it, or keyboard or, and I would have the idea. I'll know what other parts I want in my head, but I won't be able to do it. Then I will consult my friends who play the guitar and instruments and they'll, I'll tell them what I want, drums and things like that. So for this gig I got the band together, the arrangements that I write, they're written for lots of sounds, they need everything, five-piece band with typical guitar, bass, and like drums and things, vocals. Because then there's just so much going on, they need all these different synthesized sounds and even orchestral sounds as well I guess, like trumpet, like brass, things like that. It's never done in one night. It can take, you know, I can have the lyrics. I can have the lyrics down, but I can't hear anything and then I'll just, something will inspire me. I don't know what it is, anything, it's usually when I am really bored. So it's, some people are inspired by the things they see. But if I'm really, really bored and I'm just in a state of mind where I just feel so, like nothing, like everything is just completely numb. Like at work or something, all of a sudden like sounds will just pop into my head. I think I don't know how that happens because everyone else that I know, that I've spoken to about this, they're very different. They are inspired by things that they like and that they love and that they see at the time. For me it's the other way round. I'm inspired by the opposite of what I like.

I work currently at a cinema in the city. I usually do five to seven hour shifts at a time, maybe three shifts a week. I can't believe I have time to do all this. I don't sleep very much. I work at night, and go to uni during the day. Some days I'll maybe only have two hours at uni max. But most days are full, because my course asks a lot of me, it's really full time. Most days will be like ten til five. I've got to fit in time to practice with the band and time to listen to music. And I live out of home. I have a very, very buzzing social life. Because I live with two friends and people are always over and they think I'm never home. I just immerse myself in culture, I am always reading, watching films, doing things like that. Yeah, really busy.

Nothing is really set in stone with the bands. The band I spoke about earlier is the only one that really is. I don't like the idea of a set band and I don't like the idea of a leader. Although I know that somebody has to direct something. Like there has to be some discipline otherwise nothing gets done, but I just feel like I am so lucky to be, to know all these people who put music as their first priority in life and I take advantage of that as much as I can. So if I am writing something, I can just call anyone and they'll help me, or they'll be a part of it. Everyone is a part of each other's musical life I guess. So I write my own things and then everyone sort of joins in. There's no set band, so it's really a collective I guess, a big collaboration.

I don't think I hide behind my paintbrush. I put art and music together, but if I have to separate them then I guess it's that music is a lot more personal. Like lyrics-wise and sound, it's really personal, it's about my life, my relationship, emotions, my ever-changing emotions, things like that. Whereas art is not as connected to me as music is. Even though I love it just as much. On a conceptual level anyway. 'Cos I am always, I'm always drawing. I think I find art more difficult though. That's not a good thing or bad thing. It is just different. The two merge all the time. I consider them to be together, both in performance and personally. I still think that I need to be educated musically. I definitely think that, I want to do that. I think it's very important. It doesn't have to take over. I just haven't done it yet. I guess. For me personally, I find it hard to,

I think it would just strengthen my ability to compose music, and to even understand music more. There is a point when I am writing music where I have to stop, because I can't. I don't think I can go any further, because I just don't know enough. I'm just not able to. I just have to stop. I need to learn. I need to learn how to notate again, I think. Things that I've forgotten, a lot of it. It's a real shame. Because it's really important for me to know. It's extremely frustrating. So for me that would help. But I use other ways to write it. That's where the art comes into it. I guess not using musical language in the conventional way, I just draw things instead, draw the notes, draw the sounds, all different things, different ways it's played, the depth, the length of the accents, if I don't remember something. I mean I remember most of it, so that's OK. But it's just little things I guess, little changes in the music. If I don't remember what the symbol is, I'll just create my own symbol.

One of the bands that have been most influential, recently, over the past four years would be 'of Montreal' which is a band from America. They are a sort of new age, developing ideas sort of band. So new bands like that. The reason why they inspire me is because I think their lyrics are really smart, they just write so intelligently. Their melodies are just nothing like anyone could ever think of, I don't how they do it. It's just so incredible, always changing. They really question music, like the barrier. What can be considered music? They really question that and any band that does that in my eyes is really fantastic. It is just that their sound to me is really pleasing I guess. Then there are lots of obvious old bands like 'The Beatles', 'Velvet Underground' a big one. Elvis Costello, the way he fits a million words into one sentence, he's amazing. There are just so many. I could go on forever, in terms of famous bands. But my friends, all my friends who play, they're all huge influences. And in school musically, it would have been a select few of my friends, who play too, for whom music is their life even more than it is mine, I guess.

My art teacher at high school was really influential, but no music teachers really. There were others like my old singing teacher, she really helped me develop my voice, because she started teaching me how to visualize music and that helped me a lot technically, technique-wise and interpreting songs. And also, because I've done drama all my life and those teachers who have taught me how to do that, not necessarily that the teacher would help me with the music, but their ideas, I would take on their ideas in terms of performance, I guess.

When I was younger, I did so many memorable performances. I was always performing. I went on tour to America, to Los Angeles, and performed in Disneyland. I guess that whole child star thing knocked it out of me. Yeap, when I got older I just thought 'yeap, like the Mickey Mouse Kid', very sickly sweet. It was the Australian Institute for Performing Arts, just a group ranging from ages twelve to thirty and I was always in the lead role in those things, that's probably why they stand out more for me. They were mostly quirky pantomime things. I mean I've done lots of famous musicals in the past but many of these were specially made-up ones. I was always doing shows. When I wasn't travelling overseas to do them I was doing them here with groups, I was part of this group with six girls here, doing shows at socialite kinds of functions, singing and dancing. I love it. I really, really love it. It's probably why I am still doing gigs now with my band. I love performing, I love being on stage. I wouldn't go back to what I was doing before. I've just moved on. At the time I loved it, I did, but now it's like, 'Oh, I don't really like that'. But yeah, I do really miss performing. I guess just the fun of being a different person, playing someone new, escaping from myself, that's what it was like then. But now it is more like being myself, when I am on stage now, it is more like being myself, when I do perform, like really opening up myself. I like it both ways. I like other people listening to things that I create. I think that everyone should listen to each other's music.

It's still unclear what I'll be doing in a couple of years. I don't really know. I haven't got a specific thing I want to do. Other than just continuing making music and art, but travelling is a big thing. Travelling, things like that. I'm learning languages outside of uni at the moment. Yeah, I had forgotten that. I'm learning German on Saturdays. So, I am very ambitious. That is probably a problem, rather than a good thing. I just want to do it all at once. I probably need to take things easy. I was travelling for three months earlier in the year. It was leisure. Like it was a holiday. But I had no money, for me it was very much a musical and visual journey. That's what it was for me. Learning, I mean, I learnt a lot. I wrote a lot of songs. Made a lot of artwork. Just opening my mind, really opening my mind. I was meant to play with two other people while I was in Toyko. But I didn't end up doing that. In Japan you had to do sound checks and things during the day and it would have been so time-consuming. I was only there for a week, and there were so many other things I wanted to do and see. So I thought I could do the gigs some other time. I am always singing, I will just sit in parks singing and composing songs. I'd like to see more of the world, learn more instruments. I always wanted to learn the trumpet. But I could only attempt it half-heartedly. I would want to do it, but to be really good at it, I just won't be able to put in the time. It would be just completely time-consuming.

I have an iPod. I listen all the time. Always at home. When I am not listening directly, I'll be singing some songs so I'll be thinking 'Oh, I wanna listen to this band right now'. I go through phases I guess, emotions. It depends on the emotions I guess, during the day. Or I might listen to one band for a few weeks just because they are really jolly and stuff like that. And then I just go completely off them. And might not be able to look at their music for a long time. I'll listen to something else and come back to them later. But I am always searching for new music; on the internet, various sites, reviews in newspapers and magazines, friends, live gigs, everywhere. Last gig I went to was 'SigurRos', last Saturday night. Actually, it was very phenomenal, it took a lot out of me. It was very draining. I thought I was going to cry at the end. And I don't really cry that often. So it must have really affected me. It was just beautiful. They had snow-guns (laughs). It was very emotional. I think I really admire Jonsi, the lead singer, being a singer myself. You can sort of hear how he has really developed his sound, it's just so developed, got his own style. It's trained, it might be classical trained, but it's a trained voice, but it's so different. Lots of people could learn to sing in a certain way, but you couldn't learn to sing like he does. And there's a lot of musicians like that out there, a lot of singers. You can't really make that voice, like he does. He would sustain these notes for a long time, just, never ending. Sounded like we were in a echoes, beautiful cave. One of the best concerts I have seen.

I am going to another big one in a couple weeks, like big famous bands, that you have to pay a lot money to go to. It depends when they come but there could be a big bunch in the course of a couple of months. A lot of my friends who are in bands are always doing gigs. I am constantly going to their gigs, once a week, maybe twice a week, or all the time.

I really like classical too, I used to go to classical concerts a lot more and I don't go enough. I don't find out when they are on so much as I do the other things, I suppose. I see a lot of people from overseas, like a lot of world music, a lot of that is classical as well. But definitely not as much as the other stuff. They are often more expensive, and the scene is different. It's the scene I guess. Mozart and Wagner are regulars on my playlist. I like them just as much as popular music. It's a been little while actually, because my computer crashed, and I lost a load of music so I haven't got so much on me right now. I listen to a lot of soundtracks. A lot of films that I like use a lot of classical soundtracks. I mean I was listening to a soundtrack yesterday . . . ah can't remember what it was right now. Lots of composers.

Influence works both ways with my friends and my music. I perform with a lot of people, very much sort of centred around the Inner West of Sydney, I suppose. A lot of people from the same school I went to. Could be . . . people I play music with, that's about ten to twenty people. But having said that there's lots of other people who play music and I would go to listen to. I just haven't had a chance to play with them yet.

There are probably about ten people that I compose with quite regularly. Quite a wide group, I mean all of us, whenever we are together, we just start playing together, start jamming, start dancing to music that we are all making. I'm renting with two friends, two girls, both musical, one sings, both sing actually. One's not in the band though, but the other girl is, plays the cello, guitar and sings. The girl I mentioned earlier too, we started the band together. We play all the time. We're best friends and we just connect on that level on a musical level. Her ex-boyfriend, I met him through her, we actually connect the most right now musically. We just went to Byron Bay a few weeks ago to record music, and to play and to compose together. He is classically trained with guitar and piano. So he's got that side behind it. He plays really conventionally, I mean he doesn't just play conventionally all the time, but he can. That's sometimes good because I can get carried away with sounding a bit too crazy. And then I bring in the other ideas. So we play a lot together. And he also sees music on a very spiritual level, which I am trying to do, but I have never really been a spiritual person, well not religious I guess. Not that he is particularly religious, but he goes to India a lot and is very interested in meditation. Things like that influence his music a lot and that therefore influences mine. Letting go of everything in everyday life and all that allows him just to completely focus on music. He deferred uni and he is hardly working at all, just does music all the time, meditates three hours a day and then he writes music. My close friend, she is just the opposite, very focused on music, but more of an image thing I guess. Still a great musician, but just different. I guess the idea of creating an image of a musician, of the music she likes, creating the image of that. Trying to capture that. She's studying art too, she is studying time-based art. She wants to do sound for film. Everything is always connected to music.

I'm happy with my university course. The teachers are really good and its fun and because it is on a separate campus to the main uni we're all very intimate. It's a nice, really close knit and tight community. It's a good course. But I am so busy. And I'm not really in the right mindset right now. I wanna go to Mexico. It is a good course though. I guess because I am finding I am so busy, I feel really dry, I'm not making enough art. And I should be, because I am at art school and I don't use it enough. And when I am not at art school, I use it a lot more. I don't quite know how that works, trying to work it out. I took a year off. Wrote a lot of music and played with my band, did gigs all the time. And then went travelling. We haven't got our next gig lined up right now. We've got some demo discs, they are shockingly terrible, very unprofessional. Maybe it gives them some charm I guess. Acoustic stuff.

If I had to summarize myself in terms of my musical identity I guess I'm very colourful, open to anything, always expanding I guess. I don't see myself as a really exceptional musician in terms of technique I guess. I'm not, I'm not a great musician. I don't think I am. But I've always been, the fact that I am always making music, and listening to it and thinking about it, kind of takes over that in a way, I guess. I guess I'd define a musician like that technically, in a conventional sense and I'm not really good like that, although I want to be and need to be, for personal issues, not to justify myself at all, but to be better. Because I am so limited musically, I can't, I have less decision making. If you know more, you can then decide whether you want to take it on or not, but I can't do that. The technique might take over from the passion I suppose, so maybe that was a subconscious decision because it would take over everything. Maybe that's why I haven't done it.

One of my best friends is probably one of the best musicians I've ever heard. She is a saxophonist. And she is just mind-blowing and one hundred times more passionate about it than I am. She's at it. She's out there doing it. She plays in the band Bridezilla. She is just doing it. I mean I am friends with all of the girls in that band, but especially her, she is seventeen, but she's been in the band since she was fourteen. There is a big age gap among my firends, it isn't just people in my year, I mean I have a friend who is thirty and we are going to start playing together. I mean we are all connected by music rather than social status. I wouldn't give it up for anything else I guess.

Sarah's postscript

This story is indeed an artistic, creative one and, as Sarah argues, mainly a musical one. But the story does not finish here. As part of the development of the detailed case studies featured in this chapter and the previous one, Tristram and Sarah were asked to review the respective chapters, make minor changes to transcripts where necessary, and add any further interpretations or explanations. Underlying the idea of the transitory nature of the musical identity as part of the ever changing self, Sarah has added the following epilogue to her history some 18 months after a major interview. The story told above seemed to suggest that a particular kind of musical identity was emerging as Sarah reached adulthood. If the reader had been lulled into a sense of security about Sarah's musicality and musical identity, this postscript reminds us of the dynamic nature of personal identity, the musical self and musical development well into adulthood.

Sarah's latest musicflash

It mentions my sister as being the black sheep because she wasn't as engaged in music as the rest of us . . . well I probably did say that at the time, but I think I meant it more in the sense that she didn't have the same creative interests growing up as the rest of us did. But now I would say that it is actually me who feels segregated from my family, in terms of my interests, philosophically, creatively, etc.

So these days there is not as much emphasis on music in my life. While I still listen to it, sing around the house, look out for emerging artists and new music all the time . . . I am not as immersed in it as I was previously. I still go to live performances, gigs, and and all that. But I wouldn't call myself an active musician. My partner is an active musician and I fully support him and love his music. I am, however, interested in sound, specifically sound in art. I am still studying a Bachelor of Visual Arts at Sydney College of the Arts and one of my current classes this semester is post-object art, which predominately focuses on sound. We look at musicians/artists/progressive thinkers going back to Luigi Russolo, John Cage, Fluxus artists like La Monte Young, Yoko Ono, Robert Morris, and contemporary artists from around the world today who incorporate sound within their practice. This notion of sound particularly interests me. Of course, I still love music, but at the moment, my focus is drawn to contemporary art. My love for travel has also been developing. I took a year off uni in 2009 to explore Nepal, Cambodia, Vietnam, and Laos, and just last month I came back from a 16-day trip to Japan. So I am still an avid traveller, and have developed a soft spot for Asia. I am applying to go on exchange in 2012, to continue my studies of art either in New York, Baltimore, Vancouver, or Glasgow.

Kind regards

Sarah

Multiple musicalities and transient states

Early in this volume we questioned a singular view of musicality and musicianship. Our data repeatedly confirm the idea that musicality cannot in any real sense be thought of in the singular. Hood (Hood, 1960) used the term 'bi-musicalities' in an ethnomusicological context over 50 years ago to reflect typical Western classical forms of musicianship (dominated by playing music from notation) and fluency in other non-Western forms (or the reverse, since his first example was taken from musicians in the Imperial Household in Japan who were also expert performers of Western classical music). In Hood's (1960) context, the discussion revolves around music performance. Our study suggests that more than a binary view of musicality, there are multiple musicalities and unlimited possible fusions of them in the lives that our participants are living. Multiple instruments, multiple music styles, multiple modes of music making from tinkering at home, public performance, dancing and listening, to the performance that, as Sarah argues, we are all capable of having in our heads. Not only does Sarah provide a model example of these musicalities, she also highlights another fundamental problem with notions of musical development and musicianship—the idea of transient musicianships.

Given that most music researchers themselves may represent good examples of the transient nature of musicianships, some having been or continuing to be active performers or composers or conductors as well as writers and researchers, it seems surprising that so much research persists in the reifying of musicianship. All of the authors of this book have engaged with music as music performers in the classical Western sense. We all studied both at universities and at world-leading performance conservatoriums and we have all performed as professional soloists and ensemble performers. We have all continued to teach aspiring performers in a range of conservatorium and university environments, worked closely with music educators, and taught music at all levels from kindergarden to tertiary. We have been active community music facilitators, carried out music research in a wide range of fields, and written and published academic work about music. We have arranged music that has been recorded and performed widely. One of us has a particular interest in jazz, another in Zimbabwean marimba, and another in staged music theatre works from the medieval to the contemporary. We all have eclectic, but different listening preferences. A snapshot of our own musical lives at 5-yearly intervals over the past 40 years might leave the reader in some confusion about what it is that has constituted 'musicianship' at those various time points in our lives and how our own personal musicalities have developed. We have had our own syzygies (and intermittent absences of them) that have shaped our development in idiosyncratic ways along musical lifelines. Our recent trajectories around this particular project and the writing of this book are examples of the kind of transactional musical development that we have been trying to understand in the lives of our participants and that we will attempt to summarize in its closing two chapters.

Chapter 11

Music in our lives: a developmental explanation

One of the distinctive features of our longitudinal study is that we have been able to trace many points along musical lifelines from childhood to early adulthood. This has allowed us to identify specific developmental periods where our participants' musical learning appears most influential or most open to change. In these two final chapters we draw upon the many varied developmental periods that emerged during the musical lives of our music learners, and relate these to the extensive theoretical explanations offered throughout the text as a means of framing more generalizable hypothesizes about musical development.

Our aim in the last part of this book is, therefore, to proffer emergent frameworks aimed at a deeper understanding of transactional processes in and around musical engagement and their subsequent impact on musical development. Understanding those processes is, we have come to believe, essential to deeper knowledge both about how musical skills develop and of the role that music plays in our lives.

We have already used the term syzygies to describe a unity or alignment of key and often wide-ranging transactions—across social, biological, psychological, and environmental spheres—that create promotive conditions for significant musical growth. Anthony and Sarah's stories in particular demonstrate how the syzygistic alignment of these spheres of influence propelled their musical journeys on unique and relatively stellar trajectories because of the quality, consistency, appropriateness, and challenge of the transactions that configured them. Two or three other individuals in our study have had similarly purposeful pathways towards significant levels of musical expertise. Most journeys, even to high musical skill and achievement, have followed more complicated routes, and what marks the diversions and detours, cul-de-sacs, winding tracks, and high-speed freeways of those journeys is the quality of the transactions around individual musical lives. Some of the transactions may be beyond anyone's control, not least our young learners. In far more cases than educators and parents may be willing to admit, however, such transactions had a high level of other regulation in spite of repeated claims that what mattered most was the development of self-regulation. Throughout our study, we have become increasingly mindful of the range of transaction scenarios that are possible in any particular circumstance. Reflecting on these possibilities has enabled us to develop some theoretical ideas to which we will now turn.

From a detailed examination and categorization in our study of interactions around musical engagement, we have formulated a taxonomy that highlights key transactional sites and issues. In order to understand these transactions we return to Sameroff's

(2000, 2009) model of transactional regulation and development, and consider how, within and across different layers of ecological systems, transactions are able to create the positive alignments that we call syzygies. As stated above, syzygies are created when transactions align biological, social, and psychological experience, present abilities, needs and dispositions, ambition, and aspiration with present provision and resources. These syzygies are prerequisites for medium- and long-term sustainability of musical development that goes beyond the 'triggered situational interest' (Hidi & Renninger, 2006) discussed in earlier chapters that partly explained our participants' early, although often very short-lived, enthusiasm for instrumental learning.

Reviewing the literature outlined across this book, it seems apparent that a test of syzygistic influence in our participants' lives is the extent to which musical engagement and transactions met their psychological needs. We have developed a model to assess the impact of musical engagement and transactions that focuses on how activities in and around music satisfy and stimulate a sense of competency, autonomy, and relatedness. In doing so, we hope to provide a tool that may help explain how such syzygistic alignments or, conversely, misalignments, are formulated around music in young lives. The potential benefit of such a model seems to be for those individuals who are responsible for the regulation of musical engagement with the avowed aim of supporting musical development—music educators. Ultimately, however, the stories we have reported, alongside empirical evidence discussed in early chapters, demand that we focus on the nature and provision of musical transactions themselves, rather than extra-musical transactions, e.g. the social circumstance of a music performance. This is why our explanation attempts to address what it is within music itself that offers regulative and transactional power.

Transactional regulation

Sameroff's (2000, 2009, 2010) model of transactional regulation explains how the effects of child and environment interdependently create a 'transactionally regulated development' where constructs of self and other gradually shift from largely external other directed transactions (other people and environments) to self-regulation. As such, it provides a means of understanding how 'children affect their environment and environments affect children', and how 'environmental settings affect and are affected by each other' (Sameroff, 2009, p. 19). An elegance of the theory is that it offers flexible constructs that recognize how in fact self-regulation may also include elements of other regulation and *vice versa* (Sameroff, 2010).

In this way of thinking, development is not simply a straightforward process of other regulation to self-regulation. Likewise, our study provides ample evidence that development to levels of considerable musical expertise was rarely, if ever, a linear path with steady, regular progression of other to self-regulation. Even where progression appeared smooth, transactions around this development were more critical to it than any other factors. It is not simply that Anthony and Alistair were highly motivated and self-regulated because of certain traits they may have possessed, although these traits did appear to coincide neatly with the particular kind of experiences and transactions that were provided for them. Rather, we observed that the teachers, parents, and participants in our study were all involved in many different settings that were constantly changing and being shaped by their participation (Sameroff, 2009).

Figure 11.1 shows Sameroff's (2000) modelling of self to other transaction. Here we see that the ice-cream cone figure is not smooth, nor can it be: transaction implies friction, friction creates traction, and traction is essential for any and every journey. Indeed, one of Sameroff's key points is that social, biological, and psychological experiences 'foster and transform each other' (Sameroff & Fiese, 2000, p. 20). As we have seen in our case studies, this fostering and transformation of social, biological, and psychological experiences explain adaptive and maladaptive musical functioning. In infancy and early childhood many of these experiences are, to varying degrees, regulated by other people. This relatively long period of other regulation is at the heart of human development and enables us to be able to achieve complex functioning in activities like music. The ice-cream cone is clearly an incomplete representation of human maturational development because, at the other end of life, old age and degenerative processes increase dependence on 'others' once more. However, for early life it offers a useful framework to explain our data and others like it.

In continuing to clarify this other to self-regulation model, we should remember too that in adolescence others often exert a very significant influence on the way individuals behave. So whilst other regulation may move away from an obvious emphasis on physical and social regulation in infancy provided by primary carers, it becomes a less conspicuous but still very significant agent around psychological, social, and cultural needs as children grow up and become young adults. This kind of other social regulation is most evident in adolescents in areas of musical identity and culture, along with other forms of individual or collective identity tagging (see the work of Green, 2001, 2011). This explains, for example, the continuing transactional regulation that Lucy's brother, James, continues to exert over her musical development even in early adulthood, as we saw in Chapter 8. The impact of other regulation is evident also in some of Sarah's largely informal musical collaboratives.

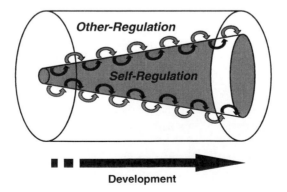

Figure 11.1: Transactional relations between self-regulation and other regulation. Reproduced from Child Development, A Unified Theory of Development: A Dialectic Integration of Nature and Nurture, Arnold Sameroff, pp. 6–22, © John Wiley and Sons (2010).

Similarly, formal education, in whatever guise, is an example of other regulation. Whilst educators might claim that their aim is to assist individuals to become independent and self-regulated learners, there is ample evidence in our study of an acute paradox between that aim and the strategies often used in this pursuit. We have numerous examples that indicate how ambiguous and even contradictory music teachers and parents can be in their regulation of music learning and musical engagement. Recall, for example, Tristram when preparing for his Higher School Certificate (HSC), and how difficult and frustrating he found the system's constraints on the playing he was able to undertake, in spite of the best intentions of his teachers to negate the impact of those limitations.

Whilst we expect adults to exercise a very considerable level of self-regulation and independence, the evidence is overwhelming that they too often find themselves regulated socially and psychologically by others for all kinds of reasons normally surrounding issues of power, status, and identity—their own or their children's. This was true of both parents' and teachers' musical values and practices observed in our study. For example, at least two of the school music programmes had longstanding traditions of excellence and were led by highly respected music directors who exerted considerable authority over the parents and their principal. This meant that their music ensemble was the most prominent extra-curricular activity at the school. These could be compared to three other schools where the music directors struggled to gain recognition of the usefulness of music to the children's education and the importance of the ensemble within the school more generally.

On another level, we also observed how children of the same age and grade level react when given positions of authority within an ensemble, such as playing the lead part in their section. In at least two schools, children auditioned for positions at the beginning of the year, whilst at others the children were rotated, so that all could experience what it felt like to play each part in the section. In these ways, the various transactions in which the participants were engaged offered signs for some that they were more capable than others. As is probably equally true in team sports, any transaction that result in decisions concerning prominence or authority within the environment in which learning takes place can have an impact on each individual child's evolving sense of competence.

Promotive and demotive factors in regulation

It is our belief that theories of self-regulation may have over-simplified developmental processes by over-emphasizing the significance of individual autonomy (Sameroff's I-ness) at the cost of its contextualization in transactions with others (We-ness) (Sameroff, 2000). Whether they are teachers, parents, other key figures, or even environmental conditions over which individuals have no control, the first thing we notice about regulatory others is that their agency can be both adaptive and maladaptive. More surprisingly perhaps, precisely the same behaviours can actually constitute promotive factors or risk factors to musical development. This is because their agency depends on the alignments they configure in individual lives and not simply on their quality alone.

As reported in Chapters 2 and 3, we observed this in the early years in the ways parents/guardians supported their children's practice. Some parents held fixed perceptions of their child's musical ability, believing that music was something you either do or do not possess. Such perceptions would have been relayed to their child in subtle and often unconscious ways, and would explain how some of the unsuccessful learners came to feel that they did not have the necessary ability to cope with the demands of learning music. In fact, in one of our articles we reported that some of the parents seemed to give up on their child as a potential musician much sooner than the child had come to feel the same way. Typically, these mothers tended to steer their child into other activities where they believed they would have more success (McPherson & Davidson, 2002). This was in contrast to other mothers who held a more incremental view of musical ability, who tended to provide ongoing support of the type needed for their child to establish a good practice routine plus also cope with the emotional and physical demands of learning.

We could also recall the case of Lucy, who was apparently not remotely demotivated by James's authoritarian teaching style, indeed, she was promoted into improving. Many children with an older sibling exercising such authority would not have tolerated the behaviour. Lucy's continued desire to play the piano with James and to relate to James as an informed expert in many aspects of her musical life, even as an adult, is perhaps because of rather than in spite of his rather authoritative style. So, one woman's 'meat' is potentially indeed another man's 'poison'.

Acknowledging promotive and demotive factors is essential. Nonetheless, efforts to definitively and exhaustively explain what factors promote musical development are destined to fail because of the complexities that are actually involved in this agency in real musical lives. Thinking of the leadership/teaching/parenting styles discussed earlier in the book and the examples just given raises problems if we take prototypes like authoritarian, authoritative, permissive, and uninvolved as having impermeable boundaries. It is true that some styles have typically represented greater risk or greater promotive factors than others to most of our participants in our study. But a teaching style of any kind actually becomes one of the spheres of influence that needs to align with participants' previous biological, social, and psychological experience in syzygisitic ways that are uniquely individual in every case. In other words, the key here is about matching. Musical matching, as we discuss later in this chapter, is a fundamental component of musical development because it is central to music's expressive and communicative function. Musical matching or mismatching may represent the most impactful promotive risk factor of all. This is why we will need to probe more deeply into the transactions of teaching and parenting styles later in this chapter.

Sameroff's (2000) use of the terms 'promotive' and 'risk' factors implies individuals who are vulnerable. Usage of this term has often therefore been linked to studies of psychological resilience that attempt to account for why some children succeed in the face of very serious adversity. Very few of our participants appeared to be 'at risk', but Sameroff (2000) argues that the term 'promotive' factors can be applied to any children regardless of whether they are high- or low-risk populations. We think the term is particularly helpful for understanding the syzygies that we observed in lives that demonstrated sustainable musical development, or even in periods of significant musical development in lives that were otherwise, or previously, notable for lacking it.

The term 'demotive', although not used by Sameroff (2000), has already been used in discourse about second language learning motivation. For example, Dörnyei (2001) defines demotivation as something that 'concerns specific external forces that reduce or diminish the motivational basis of a behavioral intention or an ongoing action' (p. 143). To extend this thinking, we use the terms 'promotive' and 'demotive' factors as a means of defining the agency of various transactional factors in musical development.

There are some problems here in using Dörnyei's (2001) definition because it calls for a much clearer distinction between self and other regulation than Sameroff might endorse. According to Dörnyei's definition, if a child comes to believe that the costs of continuing to play or practice are too high then this is not, in itself, an example of demotivation. If a child develops an affinity with a different musical style or instrument, as Sarah did, this is not demotivation for the original style. Our data do not support the notion that our participants came to hold views like these apart from as a transactional process of some kind. In Sarah's case her emerging personal style and demotivation for music theatre traditions can clearly be seen as emerging from transactions around peers and a particularly influential group of older musical mentors and their introduction of, what were for Sarah, novel musical styles. The only exceptions to this principle are two or three participants, like Bryan, who entered the instrumental learning programmes with significant motivation deficits that were only increased by early transactions in it.

The terms 'demotive' and 'demotivate' are helpful to adopt because they help us distinguish between the myriad of distractions that may draw young people away from music and the negative qualities of the experience of and around music itself that are very often imposed externally by the way others behave. Music educators have no control over the extraordinary range of recreational activities and hobbies (including different forms of music making) that attract young people and even distract them from investing time and energy in formal music learning, as our results have clearly revealed. But teachers and parents do have significant power to regulate behaviours in and around the musical engagement of the learner. If external regulators like parents persuade or influence children to give up learning their instrument because they believe that their child lacks musical ability, or that academic subjects lead to better job prospects long term, then these must be regarded as demotive factors. Frustrating or boring learning experiences and poor or inappropriate teaching, equally, are demotive factors, unless pupils have the psychological, biological, and social resources to turn those experiences into positive challenges that they are able to rise to, manage, and use to motivate engagement. However well intentioned, any parental processes that undermine the value of children practising or make that experience a source of anxiety and conflict are demotive factors. To clarify then, demotive factors are the antithesis of promotive factors and we are concerned with them primarily in so far as they describe the impact and agency of transactions in and around musical engagement and not simply the transactions themselves.

The failure to recognize that the impact of any factor is dependent on individual context, and assumptions that educators and parents may make, that specific external behaviours or contexts inevitably constitute either promotive or demotive factors might account for the prevalence of the 'one-size, one-style fits all' provision of music education experienced in many Western settings. A lack of understanding and insight into the detail of how factors acquire promotive or demotive agency might therefore explain our failure to differentiate music teaching according to biological, social, and psychological experiences and resources. In such educational settings, transactions are easily dominated by an emphasis on the teacher, teaching, and prescriptive content, rather than on the learner, learning, and flexible content. In other words, our data suggests that there is often a failure to differentiate other regulation. In this respect, effective music teaching might be characterized by the same qualities as effective parenting of adopted children, like the Hulme family, the recognition of 'difference'.

We have shown throughout our text that in order for sustainable musical development to occur, alignments of experiences, provisions, behaviours, relationships, and contexts need to form in relation to biological, social, and psychological experiences. It is clearly the role of the other regulators, like music teachers, to attempt to create syzygistic alignments of promotive factors, in so far as individual learners are not able to control conditions for themselves. It follows, therefore, that the extent to which syzygies are created in early instrumental learning will be critical for future progression because failure to create this kind of promotive unity often results in a mismatch or misalignment that will threaten developmental trajectories. When these misalignments are chronic, acute, or widespread they will lead to the kind of demotivation and disengagement that we have noted throughout this book and in Chapter 4 in particular.

Promoted to make music

Working on a theory for musical development, it is imperative to recognize that our study revealed very strong initial levels of motivation from almost all children, who displayed strongly promotive dispositions towards music learning prior to the commencement of instrumental lessons and in the very early stages of them. The issue here is not what Deci and Ryan (2002) call 'amotivation' or a general apathy towards the tasks and activities because a lack of interest from the children at the very beginning of the study was only really evident in two or three participants.

For us, one way of explaining people's attraction to and motivation for musical participation as observed in our study is the now well-researched concept of 'communicative musicality', which shows how various elements of human communication are facilitated through a coordinated relationship with an other. The most important of these relationships occurs between mother and infant, who act as partners in a music-like dialogue that forms a foundation for the infant's future development (Malloch & Trevarthen, 2009). The single most important lesson from this body of research is that the attraction of music to humans more generally is fundamental to the human condition: human beings have been promoted to make music for at least

50,000 years and we are promoted to do so from birth. This attraction is explained first and foremost by music's communicative socializing function (Blacking, 1976; Conard *et al.*, 2009; Cross, 2009). In other words music as transaction! Humans are designed to be musical (Wallin *et al.*, 2000; McPherson & Hallam, 2009).

At the beginning of our study, parents and students alike were optimistic about the role that music might play in these young people's lives. Added to this motivation was a high level of initial situational motivation around the wind-band programmes themselves. Sadly, however, it is clear that in a large number of cases, demotive factors such as the fixed view of musical ability that parents or their children held as mentioned above immediately began to form misalignments that undermined musical self-image. The capacity and willingness to self-regulate musical development soon came into serious misalignment with programme expectations. On the one hand, the presence of relatively highly skilled musical ensembles in some of our primary schools promoted a sense of optimism that capitalized on children and parents' beliefs that music did matter and that it was accessible to all. On the other hand, demotive factors began to emerge within weeks of commencing the programme. Parents realized, for example, that they would need to play a significant supporting role or teachers found that children were having problems responding to the challenges being set for them. Many children were quick to pick up these signals and demotivation followed. In some cases, it was clear that children had already been subjected to demotive influences in earlier musical experiences, as in, say, the case of Iris's recorder experience (Chapter 7).

Early experiences in the band programme either served to negate the impact of previous experience and even turn it to an advantage, as it did in Lily's case, or served to reinforce those perceptions and demotivate for challenging musical engagement—sometimes for good. For other individuals, such negative factors arose much later. Sometimes there was a steady trickle of demotive factors over many years that gradually wore down students' resolve. For others, including most of the nine children in the study discussed in Chapter 4, whose parents separated during the early years of their training, there were catastrophic events where demotive factors became critical.

Often it was a combination of multiple demotive factors rather than just one or two: for Lily, it was the absence of a clarinet, lack of parental support, growing emotional conflict around practising, and totally inadequate arrangements for transition between primary and high school. Little, if any, attempt seems to have been made to address her abilities and needs, and there is little evidence, here as elsewhere, of communication between primary and high school about her musical experiences and achievements. The ensuing misalignment with her psychological, social, and biological experience proved irreconcilable. For Sarah, her relatively neutral attitude about the French horn did not impact on her progression for several years until the unavailability of a French horn teacher at her new school became the crucial demotive for that particular area of musical engagement, only for it to provide space for the promotion of greater musical commitment elsewhere. For Tristram, it was the frustration of having to work for almost a year on the same repertoire because of year 12 Higher School

Certificate (HSC) examination expectations, when he longed to learn new repertoire and continue the creative experiments in music and literature that were so dear to him. For Emily, it was a teacher that she felt treated her unfairly, and so on.

How promotive and demotive factors wipe out prior competency

Our study suggests that nothing has more significance for children's musical development than how other regulation around musical engagement aligns or misaligns with children's social, biological, and psychological experiences. Several of our young learners' comments about their teachers, quoted at the end of Chapter 4, reveal an intuitive understanding that this is what matters:

> She's really nice. She gives me the right kind of pieces, the right standard and level, she's always in a nice mood, she's not frustrated.
>
> He teaches well with children. He helps me improve my technique and pieces.
>
> Our new teacher is more interested in us and in what we want to learn. I like my new teacher because she's genuinely interested in what I want to learn to play.
>
> She is good because she goes through the tricky pieces a lot and pays attention to see what we're playing wrong.

Whilst this principle is particularly true of early experiences, it continues to impact our participants' musical lives in often dramatic ways as they move away from home, commence university or work, and exercise full autonomy for their social and private lives, for work and play. Whether transactions have had promotive or demotive agency in their lives appears to end up making the question of natural musical talent among our participants more or less irrelevant to subsequent competency. Sameroff and his fellow researchers have already provided compelling evidence that this is true in other domains (Gutman *et al.*, 2003). Their longitudinal research, cited in Chapter 5, revealed that low-risk, low-IQ children consistently achieved better than high-risk, high-IQ children when looked at from primary school through to high school. Prior competence was either fostered or wiped out. We believe that our study reveals very similar trends. Gutman *et al.*'s (2003) investigation developed an ecological model with six contextual sub-systems: family processes, including family climate, parental involvement, support for autonomy and emotional climate; family management, including social and economic pressures and resources; peers, which looked at association with antisocial and prosocial peers; and community, which included information about neighbourhood and school. Other measures were also used to look at psychological adjustment, self-competence, and academic performance.

In our study, many of the sub-systems that Sameroff (Gutman *et al.*, 2003) and his colleagues indentified are relatively stable across our sample, although as Emily reminded us there were differences in economic and social conditions that impacted the quality of provisions and the value attached to it. Nevertheless, we believe that the general similarity of provision and culture enabled us to target the impact of interactions within and across ecological systems fairly precisely.

We have identified three key systems, like Gutman *et al.*'s (2003), where transactional relations regulate our participants' musical experiences and have agency in musical development in promotive and/or demotive ways:

1. family and parenting processes, including siblings and extended family
2. teachers and teaching processes
3. other individual and group processes, including other key individuals, peers, and local community/cultural groups.

Interactions within and across these systems either promote or demote the growth of individual musical talent.

As ecological models like Bronfenbrenner's (1979) would predict, these agents do not behave discreetly and there is very considerable movement between and across systems. Indeed, misalignments across some of them, in particular between parents and teachers, are repeatedly implicated in the demotive impact of various factors. Many parents highlight this shortcoming in decisions to quit and none more than parents who had attempted to highlight the need for teachers to respond to particular social, biological, or psychological conditions, like the mother who shared with us the frustrating experience she had with her son and his special needs and the politics of the school wind band discussed in Chapter 2. Her pleas fell on deaf ears because school systems were prioritized over the individual, and the bands' needs above those of learners.

From our extensive data we have developed the following taxonomy of regulatory sites around musical development where significant transactions at each of the three key systems occur and acquire promotive or demotive status. The categories we have formulated are the sites and subjects of transactions. Transaction, for our present purposes is not limited to verbal interaction, but includes any kind of behaviour around musical experiences whether verbal, gestural, musical, or other non-verbal direct forms of communication. This also includes the arrangements that are made for musical experiences, for example in the provision of material resources such as an instrument or in wider cultural practices and beliefs. Whilst transactions are classified here according to separate systems and sites, there is considerable overlap or multi-level transaction around many of them (Sameroff, 2000, p. 16).

Around each of the site or subject issues the quality of interpersonal interaction, along with intrapersonal conditions, moderate the promotive or demotive impact of the transactional regulation on musical development. Site or subject issues relate, for example, to whether an instrument is well or poorly maintained, music files well- or disorganized, musical likes and dislikes recognized, the provision and quality of performance opportunities and so on. Interpersonal interaction includes the level of emotional conflict or sense of positive relatedness and the general behaviour of teachers, parents, peers, and others towards and around learners. Intrapersonal conditions relate to buoyancy and resilience, but also to personality traits and emotional and personal development. In each case, descriptors normally describe extremes at opposite ends of a spectrum of possibilities, or points across that spectrum.

The first system—*parenting and family processes*—exposes sites and subjects of transactional regulation around five key issues: the provision of physical resources for music learning, music practice and performance, child competency and autonomy, music works, and teachers and schools.

Family and parenting processes

- ◆ **Transactional regulation around the provision of physical resources for music learning**
  - *The instrument*
    - none–borrowed–owned
    - old–new
    - well maintained–needing repairs
    - clean/polished–dirty/unpolished
    - poor tone–nice tone
    - valued–not valued
  - *Practice space*
    - public–private
    - quiet–noisy
    - distracting–focusing
    - uncomfortable–comfortable
    - not valued–valued
  - *Physical accessories*
    - functional furniture (chair/stool)
    - music stand
    - lighting
    - woodwind reeds/brass valves
    - cleaning materials/lubricants
    - not valued–valued
  - *Music: printed and recorded*
    - none–borrowed–photocopied–owned
    - disorganized–organized (files/folders)
    - not valued–valued
  - *Storage*
    - disorganized–organized
    - insecure–secure
    - not valued–valued
  - *Transportation arrangements*
    - heavy–light, bulky–small
    - public–private

- *Listening resources*
  - none–borrowed–owned
  - old–new
  - poorly maintained–well maintained
  - inaccessible–accessible
  - not valued–valued
- **Transactional regulation around practice and performance**
  - *Emotional climate*
    - negative–positive
    - fraught–relaxed
  - *The instrument*
    - negative views–positive views
    - horrible noise–nice sound
    - not valued–valued
  - *Parents' time: supervising/listening/attending/driving to rehearsals/meetings/camps/practice/performance/concerts*
    - is not given–is begrudgingly given–is happily given
    - is tiring–is inspiring
    - is a distraction (i.e. from watching TV or other activities)–is an attraction
    - not valued–valued
  - *Performance opportunities*
    - no audience–audience (family, friends, public)
    - tense–relaxed
    - inconvenient time of the day/year–convenient time of the day/year
    - inattentive–attentive
    - critical/judgemental–favourable/positive
    - insignificant–meaningful ignored–celebrated
    - not valued–valued
  - *Making music (singing/playing/dancing) together*
    - absent from family scripts/culture–part of family scripts/culture, never–often
    - a source of anxiety–pleasure
- **Transactional regulation around child competency and autonomy**
  - *Attitudes*
    - criticizing
    - doubting
    - questioning–praising, believing, affirming
  - *Representations and prophecies*
    - using family (stereotypical) scripts to predict or explain failure–success

- *Discipline*
  - enforcing–encouraging
  - indifference–interest
  - punishments–rewards
  - demanding–responsive
  - positive feedback–negative feedback
- *Personal facilitation*
  - discouraging–encouraging initiative
  - discouraging–encouraging self-regulation
  - discouraging–encouraging other regulation
  - discouraging–encouraging experimentation (i.e. in interpretation/expression/improvisation)
  - controlling–empowering
  - withholding support–providing or arranging support
- *Authority*
  - no child power–child power over instrument
  - no child power–child power over repertoire
  - no child power–child power over performance forms
  - no child power–child power over scheduling
  - no child power–child power over strategies or interpretation
- **Talk**
  - didactic–dialectic
  - telling–asking
  - closed–open-ended
- **Transactional regulation around music works**
  - *Views of children's repertoire*
    - negative/positive comments about pieces children are playing
  - **Views of music styles/genre**
    - judgmental/prejudiced views of various music styles/genre–positive/open-minded, views of various music/styles
  - *Personal valuing of music*
    - insignificant–meaningful
    - not listening to music–listening to music
    - no personal participation (singing/playing)–personal participation (singing/playing)
    - not attending concerts–attending concerts
  - *Beliefs about wider music values*
    - academic

- vocational
- economic
- recreational
- cultural perspectives

◆ **Transactional regulation around teachers and schools**

- *Undermining/affirming respect for teachers, ensemble directors, school policies, traditions, practices and performances*
  - valued–not valued

As indicated above, more than one regulatory system may impact on the same issues to configure the promotive or demotive factors around them. The regulative transactions around the provision of resources, and around competency and autonomy, therefore operate at multiple levels (see Bornstein, 2009) of both family and parenting on the one hand, and at the level of the teacher and teaching processes on the other, even though the particular emphasis and impact will vary. In addition, however, teaching content, style, and strategies and general teacher behaviour are crucially important sites of transaction whose significance, our study suggests, is critical for the creation of syzygies that are conducive to sustainable musical development.

Teachers and teaching processes

◆ **Transactional regulation around provision of physical resources for music learning**

- *As in family and parenting processes (p. 193)*

◆ **Transactional regulation around child competency and autonomy**

- *As in family and parenting processes (see p. 194)*

◆ **Transactional regulation around music teaching content, style, and strategies**

- *Availability of teacher*
  - lack of continuity–continuity
  - no arrangements for transitions (between teachers/between schools)–arrangements for transitions
- *Teaching/learning/personality match*
  - mismatching–matching of teaching with learning capacities (cognitive, physical, musical, biological)
  - social, personal, and psychological experiences
- *Sequencing of learning activities*
  - random–planned
  - llogical–logical
  - easy–challenging
- *Forms of musical performance (sight-reading, playing rehearsed music from notation, playing by memory, playing by ear, improvising)*
  - devaluation of some–valuing of others

- teacher centred–student centred
- *Repertoire/musical styles/genre/works*
  - a little–a lot
  - repetitive–novel
  - restrictive–varied
  - discriminating against–privileging
  - teacher choice–student choice
  - easy–challenging, consolidating–expanding
  - teacher preference–student preference
- *Teaching routines, drills, student tasks*
  - many–few
  - repetitive–novel
  - restrictive–varied
  - challenging–easy
  - consolidating–expanding
  - disorganized–well organized
  - teacher centred–student centred
- *Practice follow-up*
  - no follow-up–follow-up
  - no feedback–feedback
  - no feed-forward–feed-forward
- *Expression and communication*
  - inattention to communicative purpose/expression–attention/monitoring of communicative purpose/expression
  - unimportant–important
  - didactic–dialectic
  - imitation–experimentation
  - teacher centred–student centred
- *Accuracy, precision*
  - not valued–valued
  - teacher monitored–student monitored
  - a means to an end–an end in itself
- *Ensemble opportunities*
  - absent–present
  - frustrating–fulfilling
  - predictable roles in ensembles–varied roles in ensembles
  - playing an insignificant part/voice–playing a meaningful part/voice
  - teacher/school centred–student centred

- *Emotional climate*
  - negative–positive
  - fraught–relaxed
  - not musically mediated–musically mediated
- *Performance opportunities*
  - never–often
  - no audience–audience
  - tense–relaxed
  - inattentive–attentive
  - critical/judgemental–favourable/positive
  - insignificant–meaningful
  - ignored–celebrated
- **Transactional regulation around general teacher behaviour**
  - *Personality and teacher talk*
    - disengaging–engaging
    - uncommitted–committed
    - mercenary–generous
    - moody–constant
    - lack of self-control (especially anger management in rehearsals)–controlled
    - ill-disciplined–self-disciplined
    - didactic–dialectic
    - telling–asking
    - open-ended–closed
  - *Personal habits*
    - antisocial habits–personable behaviours
  - *Relationships*
    - aloof–approachable
    - lack of meaningful connections–meaningful connections
    - unsupportive–supportive
    - lacks empathetic–empathy
  - *Fairness and integrity*
    - unreliable–reliable
    - noticeable favourites and victims–equal treatment
  - *Management*
    - poor–good, unpunctual–punctual
    - ineffective–effective instructions
    - poor–good organization/management of resources

- *Vocal and gestural communication*
  - poor use of voice and gesture (especially in band rehearsals)–good use of voice and gesture
  - shouting–speaking softly
- *Attitude to pupils' music making*
  - tolerating–celebrating
  - mundane/boring–exciting/special
  - unambitious–ambitious
  - incompetent–competent
- *Beliefs about wider music values*
  - academic
  - vocational
  - economic
  - recreational
  - cultural perspectives
- *Celebration*
  - attaching no significance/meaning–attaching significance/meaning
  - no performance–performance
  - no recording–recording
  - forgetting–remembering
- *Other teachers' values*
  - not valuing–valuing music learning
  - not respecting–respecting music teachers/band directors
  - music lessons get in the way of important stuff–music lessons are important stuff (see local community processes below)

Peers and local community processes

- ◆ **Transactional regulation around key individuals, friendship/peer/gender/cultural/sub-cultural groups, local and wider community**
  - *Musical values, practices, associations and preferences*
    - non-negotiable–negotiable
    - subdominant–dominant
    - minority–majority
    - constraining–liberating
    - exclusive–inclusive
    - presence–absence of role models
    - orientation of role models
  - *Instrumental choice*
    - negative–positive view of instrument

- absence–presence of role models
- orientation of role models
- *Commitment to music making/learning*
  - level of significance
  - negative–positive view of music making/learning
  - social benefits and costs
  - absence–presence of role models
  - orientation of role models
- *Prioritising music as a recreational activity*
  - valued–not valued
  - social benefits and costs
  - presence–absence of role models
  - orientation of role models
- *Values around music as a school subject*
  - negative–positive
  - music as elective is useless–useful
  - social benefits and costs
  - absence–presence of role models
  - orientation of role models
- *Musical preferences and (sub)cultural/group associations (clothing, lifestyle)*
  - alignments with music learning opportunities/provision/engagement
  - presence–absence of role models
  - orientation of role models
- *Musical competency*
  - alignments with various music skills (playing by ear/improvising/from notation)
  - presence–absence of role models, orientation of role models

We wish to emphasize again that care should be taken in assigning promotive or demotive labels to a particular regulative transaction without careful contextualization. Our evidence suggests that denying children the instrument of their choice, conflict around children's practice, the failure to match learning tasks to pupil competencies, teacher/director anger or impatience, and peer group prejudice about specific instruments are all likely to have a strongly demotive impact on musical development. Other constructs such as teacher praise, pupil autonomy over repertoire, valued social networks within wind ensembles, choice of instrument, peer group preference for particular music or songs and families attaching important meaning to music and music making are all likely to have a strongly promotive impact on musical development. However, all of these transactions depend on context and psychological, social, and biological experiences for their impact. One person's challenge is another person's breaking point. One person's pleasure at the recognition of achievement is another person's acute embarrassment. It is ultimately only at the level of the individual that we are able to understand the impact of behaviours and interactions because of the ways in which social, biological, and psychological experiences enhance and transform each other (Sameroff, 2009, 2010).

A developmental theory of music in our lives must be able to account for this detail of individual lives and not just an average of lots of people's musical lives. Realigning theories of musical development generated from a psychological framework of individual difference with theories built from idiomatic accounts of real lived experiences has emerged as the most challenging task for us in attempting to understand the journeys of over 150 individuals that we have followed for well over a decade. We believe, however, that our data indicate that experiences or transactions are transformed into factors that *promote* musical development rather than *demote* it when key psychological needs are met through those transactions or experiences.

Promotive or demotive impact on a developing musical self

Understanding how transactions act as promotive or demotive agents is essential then to effective other regulation that is likely to promote an emerging self-regulating musical learner and, subsequently, highly skilled musicians. In theory it seems relatively straightforward—maximize promotive factors and minimize demotive factors. Our case studies in the previous four chapters, and numerous examples in Chapter 5, have all shown in detail how transactions met or failed to meet our music learners' psychological needs—senses of competency, autonomy, and relatedness. Our findings suggest that other regulators, and teachers and parents in particular, would do well to plan for and assess experiences and transactions around the site issues outlined above on the basis of their impact on these three key psychological needs.

From a detailed analysis of the impact of transactions on our music learners across the span of our study, we have developed the figures (Figures 11.2-11.5) below that set out, as decision trees, key questions for teachers and parents to ask themselves in the planning for and/or assessing of music experience and the transactions around it. These are not decision trees in the statistical sense, since they are built primarily from qualitative accounts of learning experiences, but they do include our reading of the extensive quantitative data. Remember our data are from the learners themselves as they learn, from parents, and from retrospective accounts of specific learning experiences and of wider musical engagement in more general terms.

Essentially, it makes no difference whether the questions below are applied to the teaching of a new scale or a new piece of music, to a band rehearsal or performance, to supervising practice at home, or even to thinking about private practice sessions carried out behind closed doors. The questions asked of these music experiences and their transactional regulation are exactly the same questions we can ask in order to understand the role music plays in people's lives in wider contexts too. It helps us to understand all the music in people's lives, not just some of it. So, from our participants' personal iPod playlists to their attendance at clubs and concerts, from their

Competency

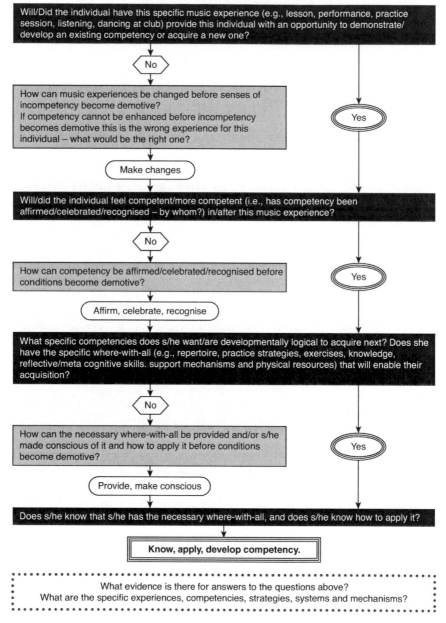

Figure 11.2 Transactions for musical development 1: meeting competency needs.

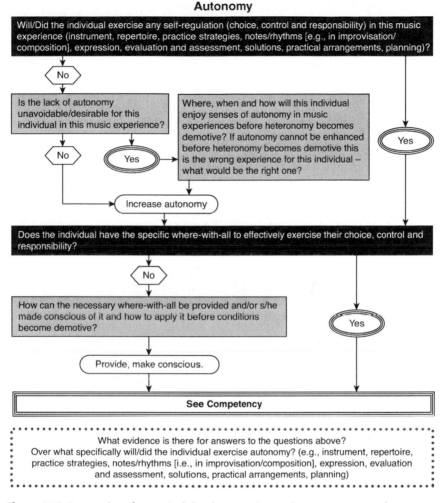

Autonomy

Will/Did the individual exercise any self-regulation (choice, control and responsibility) in this music experience (instrument, repertoire, practice strategies, notes/rhythms [e.g., in improvisation/composition], expression, evaluation and assessment, solutions, practical arrangements, planning)?

No

Is the lack of autonomy unavoidable/desirable for this individual in this music experience?

Where, when and how will this individual enjoy senses of autonomy in music experiences before heteronomy becomes demotive? If autonomy cannot be enhanced before heteronomy becomes demotive this is the wrong experience for this individual – what would be the right one?

No   Yes

Yes

Increase autonomy

Does the individual have the specific where-with-all to effectively exercise their choice, control and responsibility?

No

How can the necessary where-with-all be provided and/or s/he made conscious of it and how to apply it before conditions become demotive?

Yes

Provide, make conscious.

See Competency

What evidence is there for answers to the questions above?
Over what specifically will/did the individual exercise autonomy? (e.g., instrument, repertoire, practice strategies, notes/rhythms [i.e., in improvisation/composition], expression, evaluation and assessment, solutions, practical arrangements, planning)

Figure 11.3 Transactions for musical development 2: meeting autonomy needs.

dancing to their informal music-making activities, their musical passions, their musical hates, the motivation or demotivation for all and any musical behaviour can be thought of in terms of the impact of transactions around the sites outlined above on these psychological needs.

Given the extraordinarily diverse kinds and levels of musical competency that our case studies reveal, we need to clarify that musical competency is not synonymous here with high-level technical expertise. In traditional models of competency such as the one devised by Maslow (1943), learners typically move from unconscious incompetence to conscious incompetence, then to conscious competence and eventually to unconscious competence and expertise. It is this unconscious competence that leads

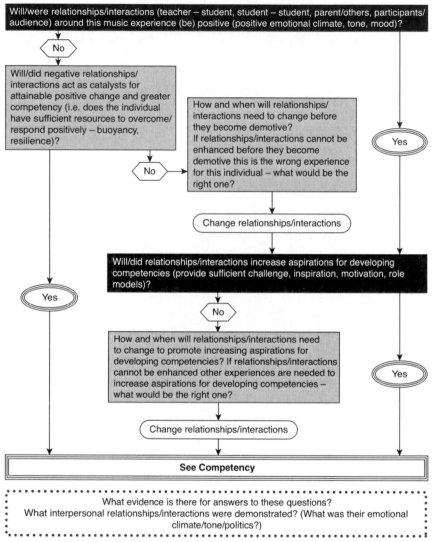

Figure 11.4 Transactions for musical development 3: meeting interpersonal relatedness needs.

to the kind of automaticity that is a key feature of expressive music performance—a theme to which we will return in the final chapter. In a sense, however, our study suggests that the most important point about musical skills relates to what it is that competency is measured against, and by whom. In other words, does competency allow a meaningful transaction between music and self or between music, self and other? Are individuals incompetent because they have very basic piano skills that are able to

Relatedness: Intra-personal

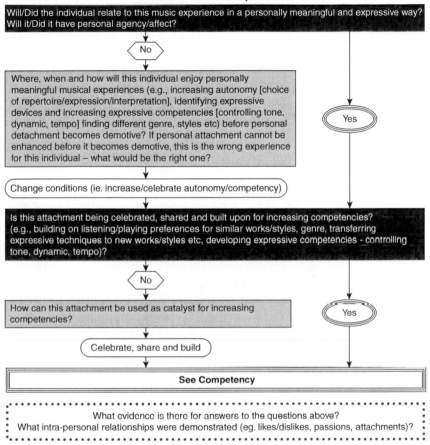

Figure 11.5 Transactions for musical development 4: meeting intrapersonal relatedness needs.

provide, when they want them to, meaningful private music experiences that have personal affect? Are they incompetent because the extent of music in their lives stretches little further than an iPod play list, but which they manage unconsciously, systematically, and flexibly to regulate mood and behaviour throughout the day and share with their best friends and even, through social networking, make new ones?

What these examples from our data suggest to us is that there is a clear hierarchy with regard to the significance of the individual psychological needs of competency, autonomy, and relatedness in relation to the value that people attach to music in their lives. First and foremost it appears that it is musical engagement's meeting of relatedness needs that explains how musical development is sustainable in the long term: meeting these needs is competency's purpose. The principle applies equally to listening and performing at whatever level and in whatever context. Wherever and whatever music functions communicatively, expressively, and affectively in our participants' lives, it has significance for them, regardless of genre, medium, or sophistication, because of the kinds of transactions that communication and expression in music are able to regulate.

Competency is about the skills that are needed for music to be fit for this kind of inter- and intrarelatedness purpose. Contrary to what music educators might like to think, we can see no evidence in our study for a relationship between the overall value that is attached to music in people's lives and their technical or perceptive competency as musicians. Programmes that prioritize particular forms of technical skills and competency as ends in themselves may prove frustrating for many and even most students if they leave communicative, affective, and expressive dimensions to chance. Precisely for this reason, high-level technical expertise turns out to be a cul-de-sac for some of our participants: there is a disconnect between technical skills and the ability to apply them in communicative, expressive, and affective transactions at inter- and ultimately intrapersonal level, where they fulfil personal needs for relatedness.

This is not at all to deny that experiencing a sense of competency is positive in itself, or that demonstrating competency has a promotive impact on the demonstrator. The desire for competency in itself has taken some of our participants a very long way indeed on their musical journeys. Competency is always relative, and it was very demotivating indeed for many of our participants to discover that there were other people far more competent than they, or that they were not competent enough for the job that had been assigned to them. One of two key demotivating factors for Tristram— the other being the frustration with the constraints that a school examination placed on his musical development for nearly 2 years—was an unfavourable comparison with another young musician in the same state wind ensemble. Many of our participants discovered this competency deficit from very early on in their wind band experience and nearly all quit because they were not provided with the where-with-all to develop competency or with the experiences that would at least have enabled what competency they had to enact a meaningful musical transaction. There is limited evidence that teachers or band directors significantly differentiated tasks to match individual levels of competency.

Furthermore, like a good many areas of achievement, there is a strong sense that competency in music is measured, as we measured it ourselves in some of this research, relative to other people's competence, such as the externally assessed music examination that some of the participants undertook, or that their teachers encouraged them to undertake, or the audition processes discussed above. Such a view reinforces competitive competency rather than a task-value focused competency. This is often true of formal educational settings in general. Several of our high-achieving performers and even the ensemble programmes themselves might be compromising the task-value of musical engagement by appearing to pursue competency *per se*, not least in competitive arenas. Where the value of music making for its own communicative and expressive sake is not already embedded in individuals' lives, it is very likely that feelings of incompetency will become strongly demotive when such comparisons turn out to be less than positive. In contrast, individuals who already hold strongly positive attitudes towards music making from previous experiences are more likely to respond positively to feelings of incompetency and to have access to the necessary where-with-all that will see the present deficit as a challenge to be overcome. In any case, where individuals exercise some choice over the task, they are extremely unlikely to choose a task for which they are incompetent or, at least, for which they are unlikely to be able to develop adequate competency. In the worst event they will probably exercise that autonomy and adapt the job to fit competency levels.

The discussion thus far focuses towards asking about the nature of the task or activity and we find ourselves asking what the musical task really was for most of our participants and whether it was deemed worthy of investment to acquire the necessary competency, even if they thought they could acquire it. It is clear that most of the school music programmes went to extraordinary lengths to provide social 'relatedness' dividends for their learners that were highly valued. These experiences are extremely significant because they focus transactional relations on shared musical activities themselves, so that the transaction is not just about or around music, but in and of music itself.

Group music making has extraordinary potential to create and sustain very special kinds of relationships. Taking part as a group in big social and cultural events ranging from local school concerts, Eisteddfords and national competitions, to international tours of extraordinary proportions was often cited by our participants as hugely important for ongoing commitment and consequent musical development. Some of our participants engaged in the most extraordinary social and personal adventures on overseas tours to perform in leading national and international venues. The friendships that were created and sustained by such intense and often longstanding musical partnerships were highly valued by many of our participants and their promotive impact cannot be over-stated.

It is confusing then, that so many of these young people used tours like this not as a springboard to even greater engagement but as an opportune and memorable moment to 'stop on a high note'. It is almost as if the grand tour became the prime motivator for music learning in high school and once the tour was over, the motivation for engagement ceased. Lots of participants found new social networks through music, either whilst at high school or at university, that fulfilled social 'relatedness' needs. This is precisely an argument raised against music researchers who make claims about the impact of music making on social wellbeing, say in amateur choral societies. The objection is that any other productive sociable activity might do the job just as well. It is hard to refute the similarity of social experience on the basis of many of our participants' accounts of fun and camaraderie that might describe a sports team or a social club. Musical engagement, however, does have the potential to provide a unique version of relatedness that is concerned with intra-action—affect and agency, personal meaning, and aesthetic experience that is not just about social networking. Participants repeatedly attested to this power in music, although not always in relation to their experiences in the instrumental programmes themselves.

We might call the relatedness in music we have observed and described a kind of 'meta-relatedness', so that music is both the practice of human relationships through shared musical experiences and a metaphor for ideas about human relationships too. Not surprisingly, we learn about music's special potential to fulfil relatedness needs through real musical transactions like infant–adult communication that remind us of music's origins in communicative, relational functions, and through making music with other people and by ourselves in so far as that music making has an expressive and communicative purpose. We are left with the impression from our data that for most of our participants, organized musical activities, especially those in schools, met individual needs at the level of general social interaction and relatedness, but that they were far less successful at providing transactions between music's communicative, expressive, and affective function and the intrapersonal.

Sustainability through musical transactional regulation

Participants like Anthony, Alistair, Sarah, Tristram, and Bryan testify to music's inter- and intrapersonal agency as being ultimately the kind of work for which they have aspired to acquire competency. This explains why we have divided the traditional psychological needs category of relatedness into two subclasses: interpersonal related-ness and intrapersonal relatedness. The former, for our purposes, is about interaction with other people through and in music experiences, for example teachers, parents, fellow players, and audiences. The latter is about meta-relationships or the idea of relationships that music is able to carry as a holder, bearer, or *phero* of those ideas, and which comes from personal intra-action in music itself. The dialectic around related-ness in music thus becomes the space between social interaction and relationships with people through and in music on the one hand, and personal intra-action, rela-tionship, and affect in music on the other. The experiences that music educators pro-vided for our participants focused very heavily indeed on competency and social interaction or inter-personal relatedness. Neither appeared capable of sustaining musical development to self-regulated places in individual's musical lives because ultimately the developing musical self is not about how people learn to self-regulate music learning, but about how people learn to music-regulate self, whatever the level of competency. Individuals will engage in self-regulation of musical behaviour (includ-ing learning) to the extent that they find it useful and pleasurable to regulate self through music. This musical regulation of self is totally dependent upon music's meta-relatedness, its communicative, expressive, and affective potential. It is only dependent upon competency and skills in so far as they are instrumental to fulfilling that potential. Ultimately, the aim of other regulation in musical development ought to be to mobilize music's transactional power and regulative potential. Configuring the musical transactional regulation of musical development becomes a key priority.

This is not to suggest for a moment that music education, or the support of music learning in any form, should ignore the teaching of skills. It is to remind us, however, that when those skills are divorced from affect and therefore from personal self-regu-lation, they are likely, sooner or later, to become demotive experiences that will limit future musical development.

The music educator's task, therefore, becomes the matching of transactions in musical engagement with individual biological, social, and psychological experiences and competencies, for communicative, expressive, and affective purposes. The notion that learning tasks and experiences will match those criteria on the basis that they match general ideas of maturation that are extracted from phased or staged models of development—whether they are general models of development or models of music development—is not supported by our evidence. In particular, we find our attention focusing on the critical presence or absence of genuinely musical transactions between self- and other regulation, especially when other is teachers, parents, or other key figures.

The question with which we began an earlier chapter concerned when a child is ready to learn a musical instrument. The question takes on very different dimensions in this context. How will instrumental teachers be able to square the questions asked above about levels of competency, autonomy, and inter- and intrarelatedness with formalized teaching of very young children, for example? Moreover, how will they be able to answer those questions through musical interactions rather than quasi-musical or even extra-musical ones? How will interaction need to adapt to individual circumstance and how can teachers develop the skills to do so? What kind of musical transactional regulation would enable the ongoing promotion of the innate motivation to music, rather than its demotion?

As we conclude this book, we would like to give pre-eminence to the idea that the extent to which transactional regulation around musical engagement is genuinely directed at and by music's communicative, expressive, and affective transactional power will ultimately determine whether transactions are demotive or promotive of musical development. In other words, music is the very means of transaction and communication at both interpersonal and intrapersonal levels.

Whatever the incontrovertible significance of meeting competency and autonomy needs, experiencing the particular version of relatedness that music uniquely offers as a communicative, expressive, and affective medium is paramount to sustaining musical development, whether it is in formal or informal settings, in infancy, childhood, or adolescence. What might musical experiences look like then, if they are to realize music's remarkable transactional potential and prioritize the music regulation of self and, in prioritizing that regulative power, encourage self-regulated music learning? Tackling this question will be the subject of the final chapter of our study into music in our lives.

Chapter 12

Musical transactions, the power of expression, and the self-regulation of musical development

Arriving at our final chapter, we believe that we have been able to offer a reasoned summary of over 150 musical lives, showing how each has unique and complex paths to varying types of participation from listening to performing. We now conclude by examining the ways in which these stories might assist us to bring a more coherent and informed agenda to understanding musical ability, development, and identity.

Reflecting back . . .

In their study into the development of musical expertise—one of the most significant precursors and catalysts for the research project that has led to this book—Sloboda and Davidson (1996) observed that individuals who achieved high levels of expressivity were often those who had engaged in performance activities involving expressive trial and error, or what some of their subjects referred to as 'messing about'. From these observations they predicted that instrumentalists for 'whom music "is all work and no play"' (p. 187) would fail to reach a high level of musically expressive performance and that activities such as improvisation and free activity are 'more likely to generate the kind of pleasurable emotional ambience for new learning of emotion structure links, than are achievement-oriented forms of technical or repertoire practice' (p. 186).

In this way, Sarah, Tristram, and Bryan's accounts of having been motivated to engage in loosely structured activities such as improvisation and free activity for the aim of enjoyment and personal satisfaction rather than refining technical skill are highly significant, not just for helping to frame early learning, but as a key for understanding ongoing musical development. The personal satisfaction these participants derived from this form of musical engagement was a crucially important sphere in the syzygy. In Chapter 6, when referring to similar results in sport, we noted the importance of *deliberate play* and the need for students to be exposed to a diverse range of activities during the sampling and specialization stages of development. Our results also remind us of our description of early forms of situational interest as detailed in Chapter 1, where attention and emotional reactions are triggered by activities that are meaningful to the learner. We now believe also that at the most intense levels these playful and pleasurable experiences offer extraordinary potential to heighten creativity, the capacity to focus on problem solving, and intensify a pure desire for performing music from the heart. An example of this is described in our analysis of Clarissa in Chapter 2, where the young clarinettist was so intrinsically driven to perform a jazzy version of Golden Wedding that her practice video showed a twelve-fold improvement in purposeful practice of a type we observed in no other learner (Renwick & McPherson, 2002).

Thinking back to Chapter 3 and the outcomes of the first three years of instrumental music learning we are struck by the paucity of *deliberate play* and diverse visual, aural, and creative forms of musical expression in the teaching and learning programmes we observed, and in our learners' early practice sessions. Only one of the five forms of music performance—performing rehearsed music—improved consistently, although far from universally, among our participants during those foundational years. Other performance skills that may be critical to long-term, sustainable, and self-regulated musical development, such as playing by ear, improvising and sight-reading, were rarely the focus of systematic teaching (although sight-reading sometimes was) and improvement was patchy at best. As detailed in Chapter 3 (Tables 3.7 and 3.8), the visually oriented form of learning our young musicians were exposed to probably explains why we observed steep declines of up to 44% from one year to the next in some of our learners' aural and creative performance abilities.

Sloboda and Davidson (1996) suggest that the opportunity that engagement like improvisation and free activities presents enable the understanding and the capacity to generate expressive intentions. A wide range of musical transactions can be mediated in experiments where teacher- or self-talk in such activities becomes 'What happens if . . .?': 'What happens if we slow down, get louder or use a different pitch or harmony? In the UK, Swanwick (1999; Swanwick & Tillman, 1986) and Paynter (1992) have made a convincing case for this kind of approach to composing in the classroom, but our study suggests that it rarely figures in strategies and planning for instrumental teaching and learning.

Infant–mother and therapeutic music interactions show that these questions do not even have to be verbalized for individuals to experience and playfully experiment with and monitor expressive intent: the simplest of infant–adult vocal and gestural games like 'peek-a-boo' illustrate the point. Musical development by osmosis is inevitable when expressive and communicative music acts as the transactor between self- and other regulation. Focusing on genuinely musical interaction may be a more effective teaching strategy than any other kind of transactional regulation because it focuses attention on music's communicative, affective, and expressive purpose. It is not sufficient, however, that the teacher or 'other regulator' determines the activity, piece, performance, process, or interpretation, as is the case in most Western instrumental teaching, and as we have observed for our music learners. The test is whether an individual's engagement with the activity, or with the 'other' through it, constitutes a musical transaction where competency enables an autonomous expressive response to create a reciprocal relationship. A key element is that the learner him/herself needs to realize the expressivity in their output.

Research has shown the importance of music teachers encouraging students to engage in meta-cognitive practices such as speaking out loud about their music, to encourage them to think about expression, or for that matter to think about technical

issues and practice strategies. Our observations would indicate that too much emphasis on the verbal too early could be detrimental because it comes at the cost of the
dynamic musical transactions themselves that are by their nature affective and expressive experiments. Infants do not have to be able to think about the experience of
mother–infant interaction to be affected by them. It is this affect that is motivating.
Exploring, modelling, experimenting with, and monitoring musical expression without having to verbalize them represents the sort of musical transactions between self
and other that may help to develop a reservoir of meaningful 'playing about playing'
experiences.

Nurturing sensibilities around musical engagement can highlight music's self-
regulative power and can provide a range of experiences from which meta-cognitive
processes can later reach beyond purely technical and acoustic concerns to make connections with communicative and expressive possibilities. Whilst some of the participants in our study did appear to have been engaged in some activities like this, they
were neither widespread nor systematic. Even primary school music before the instrumental ensemble project often focused on visually oriented skill-based transactions
such as playing the recorder and music literacy, with a focus on learning to read traditional staff notation. There is little evidence that these activities were valued, or even
planned, for communicative and expressive transaction. Mostly, they were seen as
primers for the serious business of learning to play a 'real' instrument. There are very
serious educational issues here about how to promote the role of music in early childhood and primary settings and interface them with programmes like the ones we
observed. The problem is that instrumental programmes often claim to offer a common experience, but in fact it is clear from our study that common provision and
common opportunity are not the same thing at all. The last thing that could possibly
be said about our participants' experience is that it was a common one, except at a very
superficial and pragmatic level. If participants arrived at the band programme with the
same grounding in musical experience, that would be at least one form of equalizing
context, but they did not. It was certainly not the case that expressive and communicative transaction was common to the experience. In exceptional cases like Anthony,
Alistair, and Lily expressive and communicative transaction occurred seemingly
because of the speed with which they became technically fluent and offered the spare
cognitive capacity to direct attention towards expressive and affective outcomes.

Looking across the entire age range of our participants, it is clear that the extensive
iPod playlists that nearly all of our participants have are valued as self-regulative technologies because a similar kind of experimentation has enabled the prediction of
expressive and affective outcomes so that music can then be selected and applied to
everyday settings—for focusing concentration during study, for entraining rhythm and
tempo when going on a run and so on. This is an advantage of our contemporary society, that listeners can indeed be creative in arranging and selecting music to suit their
mood, personality, and circumstance. What is more amazing is that without exception,
all those interviewed in the follow-up study between 2007 and 2011 used iPods extensively in their everyday lives. James, Lucy, Sarah, and Tristram all explained the conscious and creative application of this kind of musical engagement to their personal and
social lives in ways almost unimaginable when our research study first began.

Of course, our study brought to the fore the power of creative listening, performance improvisation and music sharing in the lives of the Hulme family. Despite the fact that all three children studied had ceased playing their instruments by adulthood, it was evident that their practical musical experiences had offered them important musical skills and broader opportunities. Most importantly, they had taken skills from their playing experience into their highly active world of music listening. Without doubt James is a connoisseur listener with profound knowledge and a highly refined musical taste, certainly enhanced by his knowledge of the scores and musical styles he has played. Of course, a broader discussion than the context of this book might lead us to ask whether or not Lucy's ongoing and professional level dance activities are not in part products of her practical musical experiences. The case most certainly demonstrates that musical instrument learning, even when eventually terminated, does leave the learner with enduring skills.

In terms of ongoing musical development, however, as our study reveals, there may be no or very limited opportunities to carry musical and expressive experimentation forward, and this was precisely Bryan's criticism of commercial popular music. In other words, popular musical forms often stick to broad rules.

For many people competency levels may be fit for everyday purpose and there may be no incentive to develop higher levels of musical skills or to engage in further experimentation. But, in truth, repeated experience, exposure, and education reveal there is so much more to music's expressive power than a few chords eliciting a shiver or a chill (Sloboda, 1991). There is a context, a cultural bearing, as well as the thrill of a structural expectancy being denied or deflected.

Encouraging opportunity for expressive experimentation, whether it is in music making or in listening, is one of the key challenges for music educators. It is clear that most of the participants, teachers, and parents in our study were not often involved in musical transactions that experimented with musical expression or illustrated how music might regulate self.

Music as a key form of self-regulation is at the heart of our participants' motivation for ongoing personal engagement in private music making, even though the level of competency in technical terms was often fairly low. The case of a participant who was learning to play the piano so that he could play popular movie and television themes when he came home from university illustrates the point. Our study also revealed a number of cases where students found playing at a far lower standard of technical competency than that which they had actually demonstrated through graded examinations as being far more meaningful for them at a personal level. We found this in the early years of the study when we asked the children at the end of their third and fifth years of learning to name some of the pieces that they most liked playing. Often their choices were some of the simplest and least technically difficult pieces they had learned in the first few months of learning. Years later, several of the high-achieving instrumentalists whom we revisited in their late teens claimed not to have played any of their examination pieces since completing the exam, months and even years previously.

At the end of the study, we are left with the impression that examinations represented an end that had little to do with personal attachment to music. Instead, it was more important that participants' competency enabled them to play tunes they knew or liked, and which, like their iPod lists, could be employed for communicative and affective ends. The gap between technical competency and its application at intrapersonal levels is often glaring. Much of the solo repertoire from students' graded examinations or instrumental lessons in general failed to make meaningful impact that might have enabled this repertoire to have regulative role in self-management. Such a fact could explain why individuals like Tristram and Sarah, who have engaged in the most wide-ranging trial and error experiments in making and responding to music through their playful approach to composing, improvising and performance, had by far the most extensive and diverse playlists.

Sloboda and Davidson (1996) noted that students at the specialist music school in the UK who engaged in extremely high levels of improvising and experimentation did not develop such high-level performance skills as those who did not. In thinking about our model of musical transactions, the question that ought to be asked is whether such students in the intensive Western classical atmosphere of the specialist music school engaged in musical transactions that challenged them to develop skills in areas of playing by ear and improvising in the same way that they were in Western art music? Were they encouraged to translate and adapt improvisatory and aural skills to areas of traditional Western art music practice, or were they simply left to their own devices without support for these learning areas, as participants in our project nearly always were?

The other critical and related question is why the learning of music from notation need necessarily exclude the very same kind of opportunity to generate and monitor expressive intentions (Mills & McPherson, 2006). In bands and orchestras the expressive intention is by its nature focused on the conductor-directed rather than the individual player's expression. In professional arenas, such arrangements have been shown to undermine orchestral players' motivation and senses of autonomy (Levine & Levine, 1996; Parasuraman & Purohit, 2000). In educative arenas there can hardly be any excuse to ignore expressive learning process for the sake of product. There is little evidence that the ensembles in our study engaged students directly or personally in decisions about musical expression. In private practice and solo performance repertoire the priorities for our participants were consistently to play the right notes at the right time. In both ensemble rehearsals and individual instrumental lessons very little opportunity was provided for exploring expressive and communicative possibilities in ways that encouraged our participants to develop intra-actional attachment with the music they were learning and for a piece of music itself to become important to self.

The absence of musical transactional regulation around many of these teaching and learning activities is impossible to ignore. In its absence, transactional relations between self and other become more mundane than musical and more concerned with practicalities, practice regimes, and note perfection than with music's communicative and expressive power. Surely, other scenarios are possible given that our learners were often in receipt of both individual instrumental lessons and group ensemble sessions—or was it the case that expectations around individual lessons and practice were frequently directed at the same over-riding priorities, i.e. the school ensemble and its performance of pre-selected repertoire, which left little space for the development of wider musical competencies and expressive and communicative ones in particular?

We need to recognize and celebrate the fact that for a few participants, like Anthony and Alistair, such was the fit between provision and opportunity on the one hand and biological, social, and psychological experience on the other, that they were quickly engaging with music's expressive and communicative elements from a position of competency. Early accounts of their musical engagement suggest a skill level that facilitated a playfully experimental approach to other dimensions of performance. It may not be the case then that activities which provide opportunities to generate and monitor expression are limited to improvisation, but that they include any handling of musical materials where individuals manipulate and monitor expressive, communicative, and affective parameters. Anthony and Alastair's orientation to learning and practice recalls American satirist Evan Esar's comment that 'Play is work that you enjoy doing for nothing'. The transactions between these two students and their teacher also reminds us of Wayne Booth's (2000) comment: 'That's the best possible sign: if practicing feels like the thing you want to do, you've found a good teacher' (p. 99).

Enjoyment and having fun were key predictors of ongoing engagement from the very outset of our study and a key component of that enjoyment—beyond the delight in competency for its own sake—is found in competency that unlocks music's expressive, communicative, and affective powers. Whilst we believe that playing by ear and improvising have a key role to play in unlocking that power, it might be helpful to think of these aspects of performing not just as experimenting with parameters of melody and rhythm, but as an approach to all expressive musical performance. The very word improvise (*im-proviso*), for example, suggests the making of provision, or providing, for future circumstances, and the future circumstances that matter are communicative and expressive impact. Musical activities that aim to encourage musical development need to make provision for communication, expression, and affect as central to musical cognition. In the early phases of music learning that provision must enable interest to accrue and for dividends to be paid from short-term investments, so that as much musical engagement as possible is identified with expressive, communicative, and affective outcomes.

In ensemble contexts, surely simple exercises such as putting sub-groups of students together to decide on the timing, phrasing, dynamics, and overall mood of a section of a work would be an excellent lesson in such expressive education, as well as a good opportunity for peer collaboration.

Taking time and matching competencies for generating and monitoring expression

Whilst Anthony and Alastair attained high levels of music performance, there is a sense in which even their impressive musical experiences appear less essential to self-regulation and senses of intra-relatedness than they are to Tristram and Sarah, or even, presently, to Bryan. There is a more 'matter of factness' about their attitude to performance and the far greater emphasis on notational and technical skills that we observed earlier. It may well be the case that personality traits are at work here too, but such priorities may be less conducive to the kinds of responsive experiments that we are suggesting are so significant, unless teachers give students the tasks and the time to be able to respond to music rather than just decode and reproduce it. Such an approach demands that instrumental fluency is focused on expressive outcomes.

An analogy with early literacy is pertinent here: fluency in literacy is seen as marking a transition from the decoding of individual words to the decoding of sentences. Remarkable numbers of our participants' individual practice sessions repeatedly stayed at the level of decoding words or notes with little of their private practice in the very early phases of learning showing evidence that they were able to decode the structurally meaningful entities within the music itself that might allow them to feel the music more deeply at a personal level (Bamberger, 1991, 2006). We observed many examples in our video analysis of the children's practice in the first weeks and months of learning where they stumbled over individual notes and continued playing, sometimes so slowly and hesitantly that they seemed unable to perceive the music they were attempting to play as a complete phrase or melody. As we observed in Chapter 2, right from their first practice sessions, the children's frustration with this approach to learning was clearly evident (see also Bamberger, 1991, 2006; McPherson & Gabrielsson, 2002).

Our videos of the children's practice across their first 3 years of learning also revealed very few instances where they played with any musical expression. Rather, much of their practice seemed to focus on learning the notes and playing pieces through the same way from beginning to end with few instances where we observed the learners thinking about or trying to actualize a personal, individualized interpretation. The only instance we observed in our video analyses of something quite different was the example of Clarissa, the 12-year-old clarinettist mentioned earlier in this chapter (and also in Chapter 2). Recall that in one segment of Clarissa's practice she scaffolded herself to a twelve-fold increase in practice efficiency. When we interviewed her soon after the session, we found out that her strong motivation to learn the piece was the result of an unusually effective transaction with her teacher who, in an attempt to motivate her to learn the classical version of *La Cinquantaine*, demonstrated how he could play a 'jazzy' version in the style of Woody Herman's *Golden Wedding*. Her teacher's performance immediately captured Clarissa's attention, such that she asked him to sketch out the new version in her practice diary, which she then used in a remarkably efficient and personally intense practice session to learn the piece by ear. Unfortunately, however, this powerful example of the effect of interest and choice on self-regulated learning and the use of master-oriented strategies was the only instance Clarissa could later recall of being allowed to select her own repertoire (Renwick & McPherson, 2002; see also Coyle, 2009).

In our study, the acquisition of fluency was most often through ensemble rehearsals and repertoire performed where directors, rather than pupils, took the initiative in decoding phrases and giving directions about performance style to the students. Along with up to about 20 of our participants, Anthony and Alastair managed at an early stage, seemingly because of the observable impact of transferable skills they had already acquired in previous musical experiences, to acquire a fluency that enabled transactions around musical syntax and meaning. Predictably, they had early and informal experiences of performances that were particularly inspiring to them. In Anthony's case in particular these were often unplanned performances with his mother as accompanist; for Sarah, it was through impromptu song and dance routines at home. These are precisely the kind of experiences that would facilitate the dynamic and communicative experiments, a musical transactional regulation, typical of infant–mother interaction and music therapy approaches, to a musical matching, reciprocity, and responsiveness. It is our strongly held belief, having arrived at this point in the study, that the syzygistic alignment of this sphere of experience in musical engagement is of critical importance to musical development.

In the context of this study, Anthony and Alastair's exceptional levels of technical competency meant that they were better able to match the technical demands made by the instrumental programme than most others. The previous chapter modelled competency matching and mismatching through other regulation and teaching, and it illustrated how transactions around it acquire promotive or demotive status. We saw earlier how transactional regulation around Anthony's sense of competency became strongly promotive from his very first lesson. It is possible that this initial advantage enabled Anthony and Alastair to enjoy a level of stability and automaticity in performing most of the musical challenges they faced. Such competency and self-efficacy would have given them far greater freedom and flexibility to respond expressively than almost all their peers. Put simply, Anthony and Alastair would have frequently found themselves with mind space that individuals struggling with the technical mastery of the challenge never had. This space capacity can be directed towards expressive ends that are promotive for ongoing musical development (see Lehmann & Davidson (2002), who discuss how different levels of representation of musical knowledge permit different levels of engagement, achievement, and so enjoyment.)

Various studies about musical development have focused on the emergence of exceptional performance skills like those that Anthony and Alastair display. In such frameworks, as we noted above, participants' over-emphasis on improvisatory and expressive experiments have been observed as limiting the development of formal skills and even repertoire (Sloboda & Davidson, 1996, p. 183). Sarah and Tristram's musical life stories illustrate precisely this point in slightly different ways, although there is an irony here in that Tristram gave up both bassoon and percussion after achieving a very high level of competency because his learning of repertoire was limited by the 'other' regulation of examination demands. Nevertheless, Sarah in particular appears to have found, through her large, eclectic, multi-aged and multi-interests collection of 'musician' and 'artist' friends and mentors, the kind of musical transactional regulation that provides her with the challenge for ongoing development that has not limited her skill, development, or repertoire. There is, in Sarah's regular frequenting of pubs and clubs to listen to other bands and musicians, a sense of Louis Armstrong sitting on the steps of New Orleans brothels to listen to jazz musicians.

Whilst recognizing that large amounts of improvisatory activities could act to limit the development of high-level performance, as Sloboda and Davidson (1996) observed, the more important point from our study is that high-level technical skills should not be confused with rich and self-regulated musical lives that testify to a dynamic and developing musical self. The particular set of skills and the particular ways of teaching, learning, and applying them that dominated the programmes we observed do not seem to have had very much impact on the musical lives of more than a few of our participants. If expressive and communicative components of musical experiences are ultimately essential for the promotion of self-regulative music behaviour because they reveal music's potential for individuals to regulate personal and social life in meaningful ways through music, we need to look in more detail at expressive performance at any level of music making and ask why it might be so significant long before performers become expert.

Expression, communication, and the sustainability of musical development

In the first chapter of this book we reminded the reader of research by Sloboda and Davidson that highlighted five key characteristics that 'attest to the rationality' or essentially rule-governed the nature of expressive performance:

1. It is *systematic*: there is a clear relationship between the use of particular expressive devices (e.g. slowing, accenting) and particular structural features of the music, such as metrical or phrase boundaries (Todd, 1985).

2. Expressive performance displays *communicability*, in that listeners are better able to infer structural features of the music when expression is present than when it is absent (e.g. Sloboda, 1985)

3. *Stability*: a given expert (or ensemble of experts) can very closely reproduce the timing of performances separated by months or even years (Clynes & Walker, 1982).

4. *Flexibility*: an expert performer can attenuate, exaggerate, or change the expressive contour to highlight different aspects of the music (e.g. Davidson, 1993; Palmer, 1989).

5. *Automaticity*: skilled performers are not always able to explain how they produce expression (e.g. Gabrielsson, 1988).

It would be hard to make a case for any of our young adults as the kind of high-level performers that Sloboda and Davidson (1996) used to develop their theory, but we believe that some of the key individuals in our case studies, along with up to another ten individuals, have clearly demonstrated that potential. Many participants, however, never had the kind of musical transactional regulation that was able to impact their musical development in spite of the very best intentions of music educators and their access to high-quality instrumental music learning programmes. There is plenty of evidence that the provision that schools and parents made for music education often missed the mark in ways that were not only unhelpful for students, but were even demotive to the development of their musical talent. Why? First, we believe that this was because of a widespread failure to 'match' music making and teaching to individual psychological needs, environmental opportunities, and musical abilities in ways that the previous chapter attempted to model. Second, and related to the question of psychological needs, there was a failure to demonstrate and engage with expressive, communicative, and affective elements in music at a meaningful and personally valuable level. Instead of musical transactional regulation, 'other' regulation was most often concerned with the business of getting learners to self-regulate their learning to play the right notes at the right time, i.e. technical regulation. This is what participants learnt as being of most value to 'others' as comments about practice strategies from parents, pupils, and teachers alike repeatedly confirmed. It is difficult to find any data in our study that suggest that the students were explicitly learning about the communicative and expressive potential of playing those notes during the early years of their learning. Much of the teaching appeared instead to comprise a learning agenda that was imposed upon it by the culture of the instrumental programmes and involved competitive task values where children had to match teacher-directed collective institutional needs and expectations rather than the other way round.

For many children, musical experiences were marked by a serious absence of opportunities to develop intrapersonal relationships with music itself. Low levels of communicative intent and the absence of flexible strategies that might have facilitated expressive experiments were evident in both home and school settings. The shortage of genuine musical interaction undermined the potential to have meaningful intraaction in the music itself. Add to this the emotional tensions with teachers and parents around the technical and literacy challenges that individuals often found difficult and even impossible to meet and a wide range of resource and support issues discussed in the previous chapter, and it is easy to see why music may have offered little in terms of relatedness that could not be gained elsewhere and at far less cost. In excluding the possibility of fluency—because tasks were not properly matched or differentiated—automaticity, communication, and expression are excluded too, or at best very seriously restricted. Automaticity implies the spare cognitive capacity that communicative and expressive purpose demands. Many students had neither the musical or cognitive 'readiness' to engage with music notation and the instrumental technique demands that dominated the projects, nor were adequate support systems available to them that might have helped bridge the gap.

Some might argue that the communicative and expressive elements noticeably missing from many of our children's experiences can only come after the establishment of technical competency and that competency is prerequisite to them. This was most definitely the view of at least two of our participating musical directors. Whilst technical competence is important, our view is more in line with (Mainwaring, 1941), who asserted that playing by ear and improvising 'so frequently derided by the ignorant as some inferior form of musicianship' are, in fact, 'more genuinely a criterion of real musicianship than is a highly developed executant skill dependent on the mechanised reproduction of a complex series of manipulatory processes' (p. 210). In Mainwaring's view, musical ability is best defined by the process of acquiring the ability to immediately and spontaneously produce what is heard inwardly—whether recalled, spontaneously conceived, or seen in notation—and grafting on to this the blend of knowledge and experiences plus musically creative imagination that can produce a real, ongoing love of music (see also Mainwaring, 1933, 1951; McPherson, 1993, 1995b).

Many of the challenges that were presented to our learners appeared not to recognize the learner's voices or responses, either because they failed to encourage attention to them or because they demanded skills that left little capacity to focus on them.

In adult–infant communication the pleasure of the present musical relational transaction becomes the challenge that promises even greater rewards and promotes further effort and higher levels of skill. This is the genuine artfulness of musical transactional regulation—the kind of scaffolding of which Vygotsky (1978) speaks in his learning theory (Santrock, 2009). Indeed Vygotsky (1978) can provide us with a useful analogy here because what we are calling for is indeed something akin to his proximal zone of development. We believe that a proximal zone of development in music is defined by a nearness and immediacy where experience encapsulates cause and affect, musical proficiency with musical purpose—rather than the remote zone of development with which formal music teaching confronted many of our participants.

A case can be made that the same rules that govern expressive music performance govern adult–infant communication and that they should govern music education too. In the absence of meaningful proximal communication from parents or carers, infants fail to put in the effort to develop competency and serious developmental problems may ensue. We see this as being analogous with later music learning too. Why would the motivation to develop musically suddenly become disconnected from music's communicative and expressive function? Our study indicates that it was the maintaining of this motivation and music's functioning to ends of inter- and intrarelatedness that were key to investment and commitment, leading to significant and sustainable musical development. Examples we have already documented illustrate the point: our case study clarinet player and the impact of self-selected repertoire on her practice; a comparison of the commitment made by Sarah to the French horn, as opposed to her other musical life of singing, song writing, and performing; the musical relationship that Anthony struck up with his trombone teacher from his first lesson and the impetus that came from his performances whether at school or with his mother at home; Bryan's late musical development in a genre and informal context far removed from the painful mismatch of his early school experience.

Some participants did manage to develop high levels of skills through being compliant to parental wishes or even from a desire to be technically 'very good', but they rarely if ever seemed to establish real personal attachment to the music itself because they appeared to experience little personal transaction with it. Instead they acquired strong senses of achievement and/or valued social networks. A good example is the participant, cited earlier, who acquired two Grade 8 instrumental examinations, but who rarely plays now except for some Disney tunes on the piano. In her more advanced technical playing as a young adult, which we observed, there were few signs of expression, communicability, automaticity, or flexibility. There seems to be a wide chasm between systematic technical accomplishment and personal attachment to music.

What music does in our lives

For reasons that we have already explored, it may transpire that none of our participants actually fulfil the considerable potential several of them have shown, although the possibility that a couple of them might achieve high-level performance status still remains. That Anthony has recently auditioned with two leading Australian orchestras clearly indicates that he has maintained a very high level of expertise even if he is pursuing another area of study after completing university. He would not be the first orchestral player or high-level performer to have taken a degree in a subject other than music.

All of the authors are presently teaching tertiary students like Anthony and several other participants in the project, who embarked on degrees in other subjects because of parental persuasion or future economic considerations exactly like the ones that Anthony articulated. After their first or second years, or on completion of their under-graduate degree, they found that what they really wanted to do, regardless of the risk involved, was to pursue a music career pathway. Bryan and Sarah, similarly, show the potential to develop into high-level performers, although in very different musical spheres. Martha still has the option of some kind of a career in music open to her on completion of her music and arts degree. Lucy may very well follow a career path entangled with musical engagement, either as a dance instructor or in early childhood education. Predicting where any of these people, or any of our participants for that matter, may be musically in another decade would be pure speculation, just as, when we look back to the early months of the project, we would have been unlikely to predict the kinds of musical lives that we have witnessed. Whether participants fulfil that high-level performance potential may be far less significant than whether they continue to live the fulfilling musical lives that they are presently, or indeed whether other participants in the study have yet to embark on a musically rich phase of their lives.

There are certainly plenty of high-level performers in the music profession who appear not to find their musical lives fulfilling, not least because of a lack of opportunity to demonstrate, at a personal level, exactly the kind of characteristics that we noticed were absent in the lives of so many of our participants—expressivity, com-municability, and flexibility. Many professional musicians, especially orchestral players, find their desire to exercise musical and creative autonomy subject to the regulation of others where automaticity becomes auto-pilot and musical experiences become frustrating, precisely because extraordinarily skilled musicians are unable to exercise autonomy (Levine & Levine, 1996; Parasuraman & Purohit, 2000; see also Woody & McPherson, 2010). No wonder that many orchestral players often turn to smaller ensembles, which they find far more promotive and rewarding—if not financially, then at least in personal psychological and musical terms.

A developmental theory of music in our lives must look at what music *does* in people's lives, the relationship they have with it, rather than *what* music is in people's lives by virtue of the technical skills they may have acquired for it. Our study suggests that it is not true that the higher level of skills an individual acquires the richer his or her musical life will be. The quality of a toolkit, or even declamatory knowledge about how to use it, is no indication of a person's ability to apply technical skills to solve real-life problems. This may be the litmus test for effective music education: ultimately it is surely impossible to justify educating people musically except that they learn how music can work for them and learn how to make music that works for them. If music educators are serious about the merits of educating young people for participation *in* music—as the educators in our project all seem to have been—then our evidence indicates that music cannot work for long in young people's lives from inflexible places where incompetency and heteronomy exclude personal expression, communication, affect, and music's special form of relatedness.

The latest major data collection of our participants has left us with the impression that many of the participants learnt how to live fulfilling musical lives in spite of formal music education opportunities. New technologies are filling the holes that music education continually leaves behind. Personal sound systems and social networking technologies provide musical experiences that tick the boxes of autonomy, competency, and relatedness.

There is a sense in which these kinds of musical behaviour do tick the five boxes of systematicity, communicability, stability, flexibility, and automaticity. It is true that the low level of tension in these kinds of musical transactions is often not conducive to significant musical growth nor high levels of musical skill. Nevertheless, any discussion with, or observation of, how young people engage with their music through iPods or other media, as we discussed in Chapters 5 and 9, illustrates the shallowness of claims that listening like this is just a passive music behaviour and therefore not worthy of serious consideration in relation to music development. The characteristics that testify to the rationality of expressive performance may be defining characteristics of personally meaningful musical engagement at any level and in any area of musical experience: the relatively low skills levels of say infant–mother vocal interaction, our teenage beginner pianist, any beginner on an instrument like our participants, our high-level performers and those examined by Sloboda and Davidson (1996), private practice behind closed doors, and even simply listening to music.

If we want young people to develop high levels of musical skills there must not be the kind of disjuncture between the processes by which they acquire those skills and the characteristics of meaningful music performance that so many of our participants experienced. This slippage accounts for a great deal of the frustration and disillusionment that followed children's initial, general, and often keen enthusiasm. It illustrates the acute need for instrumental teachers to reconcile expressive and technical elements, as highlighted elsewhere (Davidson *et al.*, 2001).

The slippage between the reality of music education and the potential of music

As our results clearly show, there is a gap between parental and even institutional expectations, values, and beliefs about music education and what many music educators would claim for the subject. This slippage extends to the myths surrounding the origins of musical talent that music educators unwittingly help maintain when the music programmes they provide prove more demotive than promotive for many and even the majority of students. Inevitably high levels of fall-out ensue, as our results clearly indicate. Evidence from an international comparison of children's and adolescent valuing of school music suggests that our results in Australia are indicative of most Western settings (McPherson & O'Neill, 2010). The extremely high drop-out rate merely reinforces the notion that music is a special talent for a select and naturally gifted few and prophecies that 'my child is not very musical' fulfil themselves. Recall, for example, our comments about some mothers giving up on their child before he or she had come to feel the same way, based on perceptions that they did not believe their child had what it takes to become a musician.

Whilst most parents really do see the value of providing their children with the opportunity to sample instrumental music opportunities as young children, parental responses leave us in no doubt that, for the vast majority, music's value remains firmly in the realm of the recreational and that its purpose is enjoyment or, to use the word used again and again by participants, to have 'fun'. There is no need to underplay the importance of recreation—it is a word, in its fullest sense, which goes to the heart of human identity, needs, capacities, and art itself. Music educators cannot expect parents to support their children's commitment to an activity whose value—in spite of all the rhetoric of extra-musical benefits—is seen primarily as being about the quality of life and its enjoyment if pupils do not enjoy what is offered to them. There is no reason for us to be surprised; the notion that teachers can motivate children to do any activity for which there is no relatively short-term personal benefit has long been acknowledged as unlikely in education more generally, as teachers have struggled with disaffected children in areas as fundamental as literacy and numeracy. Furthermore, how many adults or music educators engage in recreational activities that they do not enjoy? We will not convince parents of the value of music education unless their children enjoy it as a lively and vital experience where challenges are worth the investment in relatively short-time scales. Matching educational responses to students' needs, rather than expecting students to match demands that take little or no account of them at a personal level, is surely a prerequisite.

Specialization, generalization, and ways of performing

This highlights a further interesting comparison with research by Sloboda and Davidson (1996) as cited above. Whilst their earlier research with Howe and Moore looked at the biographies of young classical musicians whose journeys and musical accomplishments end up looking not dissimilar to Anthony and Andrew's, the later research, which identified the five characteristics of expressive music performance, looked at less traditional musical journeys. In one of the case study analyses that form Sloboda and Davidson's (1996) later research, Louis Armstrong's learning on street corners and brothel doorsteps, unsurprisingly, emphasizes playing by ear and improvising. It turns out to have far more in common with, say, Bryan's learning experiences with guys at the Legions Club, Sarah's in pubs and clubs, or listening to CDs. In contrast Martha, Anthony, and Alastair's expert performance of rehearsed music learnt from notation and playing music at sight shares much more with the musicians in Davidson *et al.*'s (2001) earlier study of young musicians. But just like Bryan and Sarah, Martha, Anthony, and Alastiar report transactional regulation of huge personal significance because this was musical transactional regulation, even if the impact was limited to traditional Western notions of instrumental competency and music literacy.

Playing by memory might have been expected to be a priority for our high-standard classical musicians too, but it needs to be remembered that there are strong instrument-specific expectations around playing by memory in classical music. Wind players traditionally are not expected to perform by memory even if they are performing as soloists. We found virtually no evidence that students were taught how to memorize pieces, or that there was any expectation that they should, even for those who were taking graded music examinations. Once again a strategy that may have been able to lead to the freeing up of thought and attention for other expressive and communicative tasks—with the proviso that memorization is secure and therefore has been a regular feature of music learning from the outset—is marginalized.

In contrast to Martha, Anthony, and Alastair, and at the other end of the scale to Bryan's exclusively aural mode of learning, Sarah and Tristram found themselves developing levels of expertise more comprehensively across all the five ways of performing music. Tristram, like Alastair and Anthony, still had a strong emphasis on notation, whilst Sarah appears stronger in areas closer to aural traditions. Another of our high-level achievers, Geoff, whom we visited recently, branched out into jazz at high school, joined the school jazz band, and performed a standard jazz piece for us, complete with a highly original and technically demanding solo, to an expert performer level on the saxophone. Where the few participants like Geoff made this transition, it was nevertheless competency that had been acquired through 'music literacy first' programmes. The failure of programmes to engage, if they engaged at all, with more than just two of these ways of performing music (performing rehearsed music and sight-reading) is significant, not just because of the way it limits musical experiences, but because the aural and creative aspects of performing music that it ignores are ways that may provide greater access to expressive and communicative musical transactions.

The dynamic exploration of music's expressive and communicative function could and should also feedback into and enrich the areas of music performance that schools chose to prioritize and in which they promote learners' specialization. We are not calling for schools to abandon such programmes, but to engage in far greater reflexive and reflective practices in assessing their impact and in developing and refining their regulation of musical development in ways that would incorporate a wider range of music performance and skill areas to meet a greater range of biological, social, and psychological experience.

The skills that Sarah and Tristram have developed force us to question the notion of specialization that was central to the models of talent development that we adapted from sports models earlier and which the music programmes in our study tended to reinforce. The breadth versus depth of musical talent is rarely accounted for in one-dimensional models of expertise with their repeated assumption that specialization is somehow more desirable than generalization. In terms of music education, our evidence suggests that there is a grave danger in curtailing sampling stages of music learning in premature pursuit of specialization and also that generalization in terms of the five aspects of musical activity may be more likely to promote musical expertise because the kinds of experiences they offer learners are more likely to be those to which far more learners will become personally attached. Moreover, if high-level music performance largely depends on expressive and communicative skills, why would music education choose to favour areas of music performance where the development of those skills may be less easy to support?

Sloboda and Davidson's (1996) research showed that the rules of expression had been learned by expert performers, regardless of whether they had been taught formally or not, and that these rules were not restricted to Western classical music and the dominant forms of learning and performing that are associated with it. Indeed, whilst the exact weighting of those rules may be negotiated by cultural and stylistic conventions, we believe that they have wide application. Very often it was extra-musical social experiences through and around music that our participants found meaningful. But if expressive transactions are prerequisite for meaningful musical experiences and meaningful musical experiences to musical development then learning how to be expressive and the application of that learning in all or even just in some of the five aspects of music performance is paramount. Where individuals learn how to control expression in some areas and not in others, those particular forms of music performance are either privileged or alternatively discarded, as Bryan's rejection of notation-based forms of music learning and performance illustrates. Learning how to be expressive through music, in any of the five kinds of music performance and learning how to teach children to be expressive in music performance becomes a final question for us in this volume.

Looking at the five key characteristics of a rule-based model of expression may provide clues about how teaching and learning strategies and support systems can provide the reconciliation of technical (playing note) problems with expressive (playing music) problems.

The development of expressive and communicative musical lives

It is in the context of expressive, communicative, and affective musical transactions that our participants aspired to take control of their own musical lives and in some cases developed them to highly skilled and creative levels. Beyond the pleasure of acquiring a technical competency for mastery's sake, the processes and events that were most significant in sustaining musical journeys—whether self-regulated or trans-regulated with teachers, parents, peers, or other role models—were typically characterized by musical engagement that was valued as expressive and communicative.

Skilful 'others' provided models of ever more challenging musical possibilities and the scaffolding to reach them through musical experiences that not only support the development of technical competency but plan for music's expressive and self-regulative power in their application. The key to effective musical competency—which means autonomous and affective competency—is that whatever the skill and whatever its level, pupils need to demonstrate that they are able to apply it systematically, flexibly, communicatively, automatically, and with stability. This is what a highly promotive musical experience and highly promotive music teaching sound like: it is not the endless pursuit of new technical, instrumental, and notational skills where even the most tentative grip on a skill or a piece of music becomes an indicator to move on to the next one as if this equated to musical development. Our study clearly shows that it does not. Such strategies appear very unlikely to promote the long-term inclusion of the particular musical behaviour, skill, or piece of music in question in young people's musical lives because the behaviour, skill, or piece will not have proved to be of any genuine musical relevance to them. Their engagement with it will not show the real features of musical expression, even though they may make occasional references to them in the form, say, of playing softer or louder because they have been told to.

In our opinion, a reordering of music priorities demands a willingness from music educators to slow down, to utilize a broader array of learner-centred teaching techniques and learning styles, and to focus on ways of making music fun and enjoyable. Careful assessment of the impact of transactions around music teaching and learning as outlined earlier in the last two chapters would leave us in no doubt about whether the present experience and 'other' regulation is the right one or not.

It is perhaps as a diagnostic and reflective tool for teachers and parents that we hope our framework might have some use. It is not a diagnosis of the learner's skill level *per se*; our study spent a great deal of energy looking for clues about musical development in diagnosing children's skill levels and whatever useful insights those diagnosis have provided, we find ourselves returning again and again to Sameroff's (2010) argument that it is impossible to separate a child diagnosis from a relationship diagnosis.

None of the above would require music educators to lower their expectations. On the contrary, it is hugely significant that one of the musical directors in our study who had extremely high expectations and placed greatest emphasis on examinations and competitions still went to great lengths to explain that his ultimate teaching and learning aim was fulfilled when after a particularly good performance, he would ask his primary school students, 'Did you feel that, did you? . . . and they said that they did, maybe not all of them but maybe four or five more than last time.' This is precisely the expectation of how to experience music deeply that all our participants and their parents appeared to set off with. The question we are asking now is how can we, as teachers and parents, regulate musical experiences so that more young people feel music's expressive power and more often. Whilst ever higher levels of competency are our aim as educators, we cannot afford to wait until our students have achieved those levels before they feel the power of musical expression. In contemporary communities where children have access to many other types of activities, and where electronic games of all sorts are so freely available, we will have a hard time convincing young people that it is worth the wait when a whole myriad of other experiences (including musical ones) can provide a quicker return. There is no denying the fact that there are implications here for priorities in teaching if our concern is for individual musical development before the public face of school music ensemble performance.

Skills can only continue to beget skills when they are valued for their deeply personal significance by their owner. In the linear or even spiral models of musical development that have been so influential in thinking about musical development and teaching for it, values and personal attachment often come somewhere at the end of the line, at the top of the spiral, or around the corner from present teaching and learning experiences. It might even have been argued that values and personal attachment are not the concern of music teachers because they fall outside the direct sphere of teaching. The consequence for many young people, as our study shows, is that such personal attachment may never come at all except in limited musical behaviours and skills, and with limited repertoire, which hardly do justice to the musical potential that they all innately possess.

Such potential can only be realized when the rules of expert high-level expressive performance and the principles of communicative musicality in infant–adult interaction are applied to music education as the first priority. Taking time to 'have fun' and 'feel music deeply' is not at all to trivialize music education, but to celebrate present competencies and musical transactional regulation which, in the right context and with the right support, provide the only sustainable motive for the acquisition and refinement of greater skill levels and for ongoing musical development. This approach maximizes promotive factors and minimizes demotive factors in the inter-regulation of musical experiences as well as encouraging the self-regulation of musical development through self-regulation in music.

Nowhere is this more significant than in transactions around music with those— whether teachers or parents—who bear primary responsibility for the musical education of their pupils or children. These transactions, around a wide range of sites and site issues outlined in the previous chapter, need to be far more carefully monitored and matched against individual learners' biological, social, and psychological experience than any of our programmes appeared to. In other words, the evaluation of transactions in and around music must centre around the impact they have on the individual's sense of competency, autonomy and relatedness. In turn, competency and autonomy need to be monitored, ensuring that they are directed towards music's particular sense of relatedness, rather than as ends in themselves. When they are, music is able to do regulative work in our lives at expressive, communicative, and affective levels and becomes a meta-relatedness (in an epistemological sense), a *phero* or bearer of real, virtual, or imagined relationships. This can be true of musical experience whether it is provided in the bedroom, home, classroom, studio, or concert hall, on iPods in any location in which individuals care to take them, or even, if we are able to develop the aural skills to do so, to have 'musical ideas' in our heads akin to those that Sarah spoke of.

Teaching students how to generate and monitor expression is not a luxury, but an imperative. Whilst generating and monitoring expression may most easily be evidenced in playful improvisatory activities and experimentation, the same exploration of expressive and communicative possibilities needs to be attended to in the teaching of technical exercises and repertoire whether learnt from notation or not. Musical development can only be sustained by musical transactional regulation. Whilst neither teachers nor parents are able to make all the alignments needed to create the powerful syzygies required for sustained and significant musical development, they might be able to regulate transactions across a wide range of sites and subjects far more effectively than our study suggests they often do. The most effective strategies for doing so are musical ones that celebrate music's communicative and expressive power.

Writing *Music In Our Lives* has been an extraordinarily enriching journey for us as researchers. It has been a great privilege to share so many intimate details from the musical lives of so many young people. If there is one standout lesson for us, it is how astonishingly impactful transactions around music are for intra-actions *in* and *with* it. Adults may find it far more useful to spend less time thinking about musical talent and far more thinking about what constitutes talent that is genuinely promotive of musical development. In other words, understanding and promoting musical talent must re-focus on the detail of interactions that constitute the transactional regulation of musical development. Because we have not understood the complexities of those transactions and their impact, we have tended to emphasize the need for individuals to self-regulate their own learning and development. In the absence of their self-regulation, we may have excused ourselves, as music educators and parents, from responsibilities for providing opportunities that match, support, and extend biological, social, and psychological experience. We excuse ourselves with arguments about the nature of musical talents and gifts when we may need to take a much closer and critical look at how we nurture them. If we are serious about music's importance in our lives then there is no point in talking about the need for individuals to develop self-regulation for their music learning without dedicating ourselves to understanding the sensitive and intricate inter-action that is needed to promote that self-regulation and the kind of personal intra-action with music that is essential for its sustainability.

We have attempted to illustrate that the motivation to self-regulate musical behaviour at whatever level, in whatever form and with whatever music comes from this inter-active–intra-active nexus—the realization, practice, performance, and interpretation of music's expressive and communicative dimension. Music's role in our lives has always been about this dimension and the music that each of our participants continue to engage with today, or choose to tomorrow, will be music that is important to them because it does a job in their lives at expressive and communicative levels: it is transactional in personally meaningful ways.

There is no doubt that music will have a larger presence in our participants' lives, that they will enjoy greater control over it and wider access to it than any previous generation. What then of music in the lives of young children and infants just beginning their musical journeys in ways not even available to our study participants when they began theirs? What of the children of our own participants? If teachers and parents wish to play significantly promotive roles in supporting musical development then transactions around their attempts to do so need to be far more faithful to music's expressive, communicative, and regulative dimensions than our study suggests they often have been.

It is humbling to discover that the rich musical lives that many young people in our study continue to enjoy are hardly dependent on what formal music education has provided. It is encouraging to think how profoundly young musical lives might be enriched and how more musically talented many individuals could become if adults ensured that the musical experiences they provided genuinely matched and then carefully challenged social, psychological, and biological experiences. Such interactions celebrate competency, affirm autonomy, and rejoice in the musical transactional regulation that is at the heart of music making.

Musical development is an expressive, communicative, and inter-regulative project: it is a project that focuses always first on what individuals are doing, are able to do and want to do, and only then on what 'others' think they could or even should be doing—more on their musical lives and less on our own. Ultimately it recognizes that the answer to questions about how young people can become self-regulated music learners and about how their musical development can be sustained lies in understanding music's versatile and virtuosic power to sustain and regulate their lives just as it has our own.

References

Abbott, A., & Collins, D. (2004). Eliminating the dichotomy between theory and practice in talent identification and development: Considering the role of psychology. *Journal of Sports Science, 22*(5), 395–408.

Adorno, T. W. (1997). *Aesthetic theory*. (R. Hullot-Kentor, Trans.). Minneapolis: University of Minnesota Press.

Altenmüller, E. (2011). Apollo's gift: Music making as a stimulus for brain plasticity. *Karger Gazette, 70.*

Alvidrez, J., & Weinstein, R. S. (1993). The nature of 'schooling' in school transitions: A critical examination. *Prevention in Human Services, 10*(2), 7–26.

Bailey, B., & Davidson, J. W. (2003). Amateur group singing as a therapeutic agent. *Nordic Journal of Music Therapy, 12*(1), 18–32.

Bailey, B., & Davidson, J. W. (2005). Effects of group singing and performance for marginalized and middle-class singers. *Psychology of Music, 33*(3), 269–303.

Bamberger, J. (1991). *The mind behind the musical ear: How children develop musical intelligence.* Cambridge, MA: Harvard University Press.

Bamberger, J. (2006). *What develops in musical development? The child as musician: A handbook of musical development* (pp. 69–92). Oxford: Oxford University Press.

Barry, N., & Hallam, S. (2002). Practice. In R. Parncutt & G. McPherson (eds), *The science and psychology of music performance* (pp. 151–65). New York: Oxford University Press.

Baumrind, D. (1991). The influence of parenting style on adolescent competence and substance abuse. *Journal of Early Adolescence, 11*(2), 62.

Benner, A., & Graham, S. (2009). The transition to high school as a developmental process among multiethnic urban youth. *Child Development, 80*(3), 356–76.

Benson, P. L., Sharma, A. R., & Roehlkepartain, E. C. (1994). *growing up adopted: a portrait of adolescents and their families.* Minneapolis: Search Institute.

Blacking, J. (1976). *How musical is man?* London: Faber.

Bloom, B. (Ed.). (1985). *Developing talent in young people.* New York: Ballentine Books.

Booth, W. C. (2000). *For the love of it: amateuring and its rivals.* Chicago: University of Chicago Press.

Bornstein, M. H. (2009). Toward a model of culture-parent-child transactions. In A. Sameroff (ed.), *The transactional model of development: how children and contexts shape each other* (pp. 139–61). Washington, DC: American Psychological Association.

Borthwick, D. J., & Davidson, J. W. (2002). Developing a child's identity as a musician: A family 'script' perspective. In R. A. R. MacDonald, D. J. Hargreaves, & D. Miell (eds), *Musical identities* (pp. 60–78). Oxford: Oxford University Press.

Bouchard Jr, T., & McGue, M. (2003). Genetic and environmental influences on human psychological differences. *Wiley Periodicals,* 4–45. Published online in Wiley InterScience (www.interscience.wiley.com), DOI 10.1002/neu.10160

Bronfenbrenner, U. (1979). *The ecology of human development: experiments by nature and design.* Cambridge, MA: Harvard University Press.

Bull, M. (2007). *Sound moves: iPod culture and urban experience*. Abingdon and New York: Routledge.

Burdick, K. E., Lencz, T., Funke, B., Finn, C. T., Szeszko, P. R., Kane, J. M., et al. (2006). Genetic variation in DTNBP1 influences general cognitive ability. *Human Mollecular Genetics, 15*(10), 1563–68.

Burland, K., & Davidson, J. (2004). Tracing a musical life transition. In J. W. Davidson, (ed.), *The music practitioner: exploring practices and research in the development of the expert music performer, teacher and listener*. Aldershot: Ashgate Publishing.

Charmaz, C. (2000). Grounded theory: Objectivist and constructivist methods. In N. K. D. Y. S. Lincoln (ed.), *Handbook of qualitative research*. Thousand Oaks, CA: Sage Publications.

Clynes, M., & Walker, J. (1982). Neurobiologic functions of rhythm, time and pulse in music. In M. Clynes (ed.), *Music, mind and brain: the neuropsychology of music*. New York: Plenum, 171–216.

Cohen, G. (2005). *The mature mind*. New York: Basic Books.

Conard, N., Malina, M., & Münzel, C. (August 2009). New flutes document the earliest musical tradition in soutwestern Germany. *Nature, 460,* 737–40.

Connell, R. (1995). *Masculinities*. Cambridge: Polity Press.

Cooke, N. (1998). *Music: a very short introduction*. Oxford: Oxford University Press.

Cooper, H., Lindsay, J. J., & Nye, B. (2000). Homework in the home: How student, family, and parenting-style differences relate to the homework process. *Contemporary Educational Psychology, 25*(4), 464–87.

Côté, J. (1999). The influence of the family in the development of talent in sports. *Sports Psychologist, 13*(4), 395–417.

Côté, J., Baker, J., & Abernethy, B. (2003). From play to practice: A developmental framework for the acquisition of expertise in team sports. In J. Starkes & K. A. Ericsson (eds), *Expert performance in team sports: advances in research on sport expertise* (pp. 89–110). Champaign, IL: Human Kinetics.

Côté, J., Baker, J., & Abernethy, B. (2007). Practice and play in the development of sport expertise. In R. Eklund & G. Tenenbaum (eds), *Handbook of sport psychology* (3rd edn, pp. 184–203). Hoboken, NJ: Wiley.

Cox, G. (2002). *Living music in schools 1923–1999: studies in the history of music education in England*. Aldershot: Ashgate.

Coyle, D. (2009). *The talent code: greatness isn't born. It's grown. Here's how*. New York: Bantam Books.

Creech, A., & Hallam, S. (2003). Parent–teacher–pupil interactions in instrumental music tuition: A literature review. *British Journal of Music Education, 20*(1), 29–44.

Cross, I. (2009). Music as a communicative medium. In R. Botha & C. Knight (eds), *The prehistory of language* (Vol. 1, pp. 113–44). Oxford: Oxford University Press.

Czikszentmihalyi, M. (1996). *Creativity*. New York: Harper Collins.

Davidson, J. W. (1993). Visual perception of performance manner in the movements of solo musicians. *Psychology of Music, 21*(2), 103–113.

Davidson, J. W. (1999). Self and desire: A preliminary exploration of why students start and continue with music learning. *Research Studies in Music Education, 12*(1), 30–37.

Davidson, J. (2002). Developing performance skills. In J. Rink (ed.), *Musical performance: a guide to study and practice* (pp. 89–101). Cambridge: Cambridge University Press.

Davidson, J. W. (2004). Making a reflexive turn: Practical music-making becomes conventional research. In J. W. Davidson (ed.), *The music practitioner: exploring practices and research in the development of the expert music performer, teacher and listener* (pp. 133–47). Aldershot: Ashgate Publishing.

Davidson, J. W. (2005). Bodily communication in musical performance. In D. Miell, R. MacDonald & D. Hargreaves (eds), *Musical communication* (pp. 215–38). Oxford: Oxford University Press.

Davidson, J. W. (2007). The activity and artistry of solo vocal performance: Insights from investigative observations and interviews with western classical singers *Journal of the European Society for the Cognitive Sciences of Music, Special Issue*, 109–40.

Davidson, J. (2011). Musical participation: Expectations, experiences and outcomes. In D. I. a. D. JW (ed.), *Music and the mind.* (pp. 65–68). Oxford: Oxford University Press.

Davidson, J., & Borthwick, S. (2002). Family dynamics and family scripts: A case study of musical development. *Psychology of Music, 30*(1), 121–36.

Davidson, J. W., & Burland, K. (2006). Musician identity formation. In G. McPherson (ed.), *The child as musician: a handbook of musical development* (pp. 474–90). Oxford: Oxford University Press.

Davidson, J. W., & Faulkner, R. (2010). Meeting in music: The role of singing to harmonise carer and cared for. *Arts & Health, 2*(2), 164–70.

Davidson, J., & Faulkner, R. (in press). Music in our lives: Syzygistic influences for achievement in music. In S. B. Kaufmann (Ed.), *Beyond 'talent or practice?': the multiple determinants of greatness.* Oxford: Oxford University Press.

Davidson, J. W., & Good, J. M. M. (2002). Social and musical coordination between members of a string quartet: An exploratory study. *Psychology of Music, 30*(2), 186–201.

Davidson, J., Howe, M., & Sloboda, J. (1995/6). The role of parents and teachers in the success and failure of instrumental learners. *Bulletin for the Council of Research in Music Education, 127*, 40–45.

Davidson, J., Howe, M., Moore, D., & Sloboda, J. (1996). The role of parental influences in the development of musical ability. *British Journal of Developmental Psychology, 14*, 399–412.

Davidson, J., Howe, M., & Sloboda, J. (1997). Environmental factors in the development of musical performance skill in the first twenty years of life. In D. H. A. North (ed.), *The social psychology of music* (pp. 188–203). Oxford: Oxford University.

Davidson, J., & Pitts, S. (2001). People have talents: A case study of musical behaviour in an adoptive family. *British Journal of Music Education, 18*(2), 161–71.

Davidson, J., & Scutt, S. (1999). Researching music examinations. *British Journal of Music Education, 16*(1), 79–95.

Davidson, J. W., & Smith, J. A. (1997). A case study of 'newer practices' in music education at conservatoire level. *British Journal of Music Education, 14*(3), 251–69.

Davidson, J., Howe, M., Moore, D., & Sloboda, J. (1998). The role of teachers in the development of musical ability. *Journal of Research in Music Education, 46*(1), 141–60.

Davidson, J., Pitts, S., & Correia, J. (2001). Reconciling technical and expressive elements in young children's musical instrument teaching: working with children. *Journal of Aesthetic Education, 35*(3), 51–62.

Davis, M. (1994). Folk music psychology. *The Psychologist, 7*(12), 537.

Deci, E., & Ryan, R. (eds). (2002). *Handbook of self-determination research.* Rochester: University of Rochester Press.

Delzell, J., & Leppla, D. (1992). Gender association of musical instruments and preferences of fourth-grade students for selected instruments. *Journal of Research in Music Education, 40*(2), 93–103.

DeNora, T. (2000). *Music in everyday life*. Cambridge: Cambridge University Press.

Dinham, S. (2007). Authoritative leadership, action learning and student accomplishment. In C. Glascodine & K-A. Hoad (eds), *The leadership challenge: improving learning in schools. Conference Proceedings*. Melbourne: Australian Council for Educational Research.

Dinham, S. (2008). *How to get your school moving and improving*. Melbourne: Australian Council for Educational Research.

Dörnyei, Z. (2001). *Teaching and researching motivation*. Harlow: Longman Pearson Education Limited.

Dunn, J. (1993). *Young children's close relationships* (1st edn., Vol. 4). London: Sage.

Dunn, J., & McGuire, S. (1992). Sibling and peer relationships in childhood. *Journal of Child Psychology and Psychiatry, 33*(1), 67–105.

Dunn, J., Slomkowski, C., & Beardsall, L. (1994). Sibling relationships from the pre-school period through middle childhood and early adolescence. *Developmental Psychology, 30*(3), 315–24.

Elliott, C. A. (1982a). The music-reading dilemma. *Music Educators Journal, 68*(6), 33–34,59–60.

Elliott, C. A. (1982b). The relationships among instrumental sight-reading ability and seven selected predictor variables. *Journal of Research in Music Education, 30*(1), 5–14.

Ericsson, K. A. (1997). Deliberate practice and the acquisition of expert performance: An overview. In H. Jørgensen & A. C. Lehmann (eds), *Does practice make perfect? Current theory and research on instrumental music practice* (pp. 9–51). Oslo: Norges musikkhøgskole.

Ericsson, K. A., Krampe, R. T., & Tesch-Römer, C. (1993). The role of deliberate practice in the acquisition of expert performance. *Psychological Review, 100*, 363–406.

Evans, P. (2009). *Psychological needs and social-cogntive influences on participation in music activities*. Unpublished doctoral thesis, University of Illinois at Urbana-Champaign.

Evans, P. A. (2011). *Music, learning, motivation and achievment in the lives of children and adolescents over a ten-year period*. Unpublished Master of Music Education thesis, University of Western Australia.

Evans, P., McPherson, G., & Davidson, J. (in preparation). Psycholgocial needs and the motivation to cease or continue playing a musical instrument.

Faulkner, R. (2003). *Men's ways of singing* Paper presented at the Sharing the voices: the phenomenon of singing IV. St John's, NL: Memorial University of Newfoundland, June 26–29.

Faulkner, R. (2006). *The vocal construction of self: Icelandic men and everyday vocal behaviour.*, Sheffield: University of Sheffield.

Faulkner, R., & Davidson, J. W. (2005). Men's vocal behaviour and the construction of self. *Musicae Scientiae, 8*, 231–55.

Faulkner, R., & Davidson, J. W. (2006). Men in chorus: collaboration and competition in homo-social vocal behaviour. *Psychology of Music, 34*(2), 219–38.

Faulkner, R., Davidson, J., & McPherson, G. (2010). The value of data mining in music education research and some findings from its application to a study of instrumental learning during childhood. *International Journal of Music Education, 28*(3), 212–30.

Finn, J., & Rock, D. (1997). Academic success among students at risk for school failure. *Journal of Applied Psychology, 82*(2), 221–34.

Flowers, P., Smith, J. A., Sheeran, P., & Beail, N. (1998). 'Coming out' and sexual debut: understanding the social context of HIV risk-related behaviour. *Journal of Community & Applied Social Psychology, 8*(6), 409–21.

Folkestad, G. (2006). Formal and informal learning situations or practices vs formal and informal ways of learning. *British Journal of Music Education, 23*(2), 135–45.

Forgeard, M., Winner, E., Norton, A., & Schlaug, G. (2008). Practicing a musical instrument in childhood is associated with enhanced verbal ability and nonverbal reasoning. *PLoS ONE, 3*(10), 383–90.

Fortney, P. M., Boyle, J. D., & DeCarbo, N. J. (1993). A study of middle school band students' instrumental choices. *Journal of Research in Music Education, 41*(1), 28–39.

Gabrielsson, A. (1988). Timing in performance and its relation to music experience. In J. Sloboda (ed.), *Generative processes in music.* Oxford: Clarendon Press, 27–51.

Gagné, F. (2009). Building gifts into talents: Detailed overview of the DMGT 2.0. In B. MacFarlane & T. Stambaugh (eds), *Leading change in gifted education: the festschrift of Dr. Joyce VanTassel-Baska* (pp. 61–80). Waco, Texas: Prufrock Press.

Gagné, F., Blanchard, D., & Bégin, J. (2001). Beliefs about the heritability of abilities in education, music, and sports. In N. Colangelo & S. G. Assouline (eds), *Talent development IV: Proceedings from the 1998 Henry B. and Jocelyn Wallace national research Symposium on Talent Development.* Scottsdale, AZ: Gifted Psychology Press, 155–178.

Galton, M., & Hargreaves, L. (2002). *Transfer from the primary school: 20 years on.* London: Routledge.

Glaser, B., & Strauss, A. (1967). *The discovery of grounded theory: strategies for qualitative research.* Chicago: Aldine.

Gordon, E. E. (1982). *Intermediate measures of music audiation.* Chicago: GIA.

Green, L. (2001). *How popular musicians learn: A way ahead for music education.* Aldershot: Ashgate.

Green, L. (2008). *Music, informal learning and the school: a new classroom pedagogy.* London and New York: Ashgate Press.

Green, L. (Ed.). (2011). *Learning, teaching and musical identity: voices across cultures* Bloomington: Indiana University Press.

Gruson, L. M. (1988). Rehearsal skill and muscial competence: Does practice make perfect? In J. Sloboda (ed.), *Generative processes in music: the psychology of performance, improvisation, and composition* (pp. 9–12). Oxford: Clarendon Press.

Gutman, L., Sameroff, A., & Cole, R. (2003). Academic trajectories from first to twelfth grades: Growth curves according to multiple risk and early child factors. *Developmental Psychology, 39*(4), 777–90.

Haensly, P., Reynolds, C. R., & Nash, W. R. (1986). Giftedness: coalescence, context, conflict, and commitment. In R. J. Sternberg & J. E. Davidson (eds), *Conceptions of giftedness* (pp. 128–48). New York: Cambridge University Press.

Hallam, S. (1997). What do we know about practicing? Towards a model synthesizing the research literature. In H. Jørgensen & A. Lehmann (eds), *Does practice make perfect? Current theory and research on instrumental music practice* (pp. 179–231). Norway: Norges musikkhøgskole.

Hallam, S. (1998). *Instrumental teaching: a practical guide to better teaching and learning.* Oxford: Heinemann Educational.

Hallam, S., & Shaw, J. (2002). *Construction of musical ability*. Paper presented at the A world of music education research, The 19th ISME Research Seminar, August 3–9, Goteborg, Sweden.

Heidegger, M. (1977). *The question concerning technology and other essays*. New York and London: Harper and Row.

Hidi, S., & Renninger, K. (2006). The four-phase model of interest development. *Educational Psychologist, 41*(2), 111–27.

Hoksbergen, R. A. C. (1997). *Child adoption: a guidebook for adoptive parents and their advisors*. London: Jessica Kingsley.

Hong, E., & Milgram, R. M. (2000). *Homework: motivation and learning preference*. Westport, CT: Bergin & Garvey.

Hood, M. (1960). The challenge of bi-musicality. *Ethnomusicology, 4*(2), 55–59.

Howe, M., & Davidson, J. W. (2003). The early progress of able young musicians. In R. Sternberg & E. L. Grigorenko (eds), *The psychology of abilites, competencies and expertise* (pp. 186–212). Cambridge: Cambridge University Press.

Howe, M., Davidson, J., Moore, D., & Sloboda, J. (1995). Are there early signs of musical excellence? *Psychology of Music, 23*(2), 162–76.

Howe, M., Davidson, J., & Sloboda, J. (1998a). Natural born talents undiscovered. *Behavioural and Brain Sciences, 21*(3), 432–42.

Howe, M., Davidson, J., & Sloboda, J. (1998b). Innate gifts and talents: Reality or myth? *Behavioural and Brain Sciences, 21*(10), 399–407.

Ibarra, H. (1999). Provisional selves: experimenting with image and identity in professional adaptation. *Administrative Science Quarterly, 44*(4), 764–91.

Isaacson, C. E., & Radish, K. (2002). *The birth order effect: how to better understand yourself and others*. Avon, MA: Adams Media Corporation.

Jørgensen, E. (2001). A dialectical view of theory and practice. *Journal of Research in Music Education, 10*, 523–42.

Kohn, A. (1994). The truth about self esteem. *Phi Delta Kappan, 76*(4), 272–84.

Lehmann, A. C., & Davidson, J. W. (2002). Taking an acquired skills perspective on music performance. In R. Colwell & C. Richardson (Eds.), *The new handbook of research on music teaching and learning* (pp. 542–60). New York: Oxford University Press.

Lehmann, A., Sloboda, J., & Woody, R. (2007). *Psychology for musicians: understanding and acquiring the skills*. Oxford: Oxford University Press.

Levine, S. & Levine, R. (1996). Why they're not smiling: stress and discontent in the orchestra workplace. *Harmony. 2*: 15–25.

Levitin, D. J. (1994). Absolute memory for musical pitch: Evidence from the production of learned melodies. *Perception & Psychophysics, 56*, 414–23.

MacDonald, R., Hargreaves, D. J., & Miell, D. (Eds.). (2002). *Musical identities*. Oxford: Oxford University Press.

Mainwaring, J. (1933). Kinaesthetic factors in the recall of musical experience. *British Journal of Psychology: General Section, 23*, 284–307.

Mainwaring, J. (1941). The meaning of musicianship: A problem in the teaching of music. *British Journal of Educational Psychology, 11*, 205–214.

Mainwaring, J. (1951). Psychological factors in the teaching of music: Part I—Conceptual musicianship. *British Journal of Educational Psychology, 21*, 105–21.

Malloch, S., & Trevarthen, C. (Eds.). (2009). *Communicative musicality: exploring the basis of human companionship*. Oxford: Oxford University Press.

Maslow, A. (1943). A theory of human motivation. *Psychological Review, 50*(4), 370–96.

McCrae, R., & Costa, P., Jr. (1996). Toward a new generation of personality theories: Theoretical contexts for the five-factor model. In J. S. Wiggins (ed.), *The five-factor model of personality: Theoretical perspectives* (pp. 51–87). New York: Guilford.

McCrae, R., & Costa, P., Jr. (1999). A five-factor theory of personality. In L. Pervin & O. John (eds.), *Handbook of personality: theory and research* (2nd edn, pp. 139–53). New York: Guilford Press.

McPherson, G. E. (1993). *Factors and abilities influencing the development of visual, aural and creative performance skills music and their educational implications*. Unpublished doctoral thesis, University of Sydney.

McPherson, G. E. (1994a). Evaluating improvisational ability of high school instrumentalists. *Bulletin of the Council for Research in Music Education, 119*, 11–20.

McPherson, G. E. (1994b). Factors and abilities influencing sightreading skill in music. *Journal of Research in Music Education, 42*(3), 217–31.

McPherson, G. E. (1995a). The assessment of musical performance: Development and validation of five new measures. *Psychology of Music, 23*(2), 142–61.

McPherson, G. E. (1995b). Redefining the teaching of musical performance. *The Quarterly Journal of Music Teaching and Learning, 1*(2), 56–64.

McPherson, G. E. (2001). Commitment and practice: Key ingredients for achievement during the early stages of learning a musical instrument. *Council for Research in Music Education, 147*, 122–127.

McPherson, G. E. (2005). From child to musician: Skill development during the beginning stages of learning an instrument. *Psychology of Music, 33*(1), 5–35.

McPherson, G. E. (2009). The role of parents in children's musical development. *Psychology of Music, 37*(1), 91–110.

McPherson, G., Bailey, M., & Sinclair, K. (1997). Path analysis of a theoretical model to describe the relationship among five types of musical performance. *Journal of Research in Music Education, 45*(1), 103–26.

McPherson, G., & Davidson, J. (2002). Musical practice: Mother and child interactions during the first year of learning an instrument. *Music Education Research, 4*(1), 141–56.

McPherson, G. E., & Davidson, J. W. (2006). Playing an instrument. In G. E. McPherson (ed.), *The child as musician: a handbook of musical development* (pp. 331–54). Oxford: Oxford University Press.

McPherson, G. E., & Gabrielsson, A. (2002). From sound to sign. In R. Parncutt & G. E. McPherson (eds), *The science and psychology of music performance: creative strategies for teaching and learning* (pp. 99–115). New York: Oxford University Press.

McPherson, G. E., & Hallam, S. (2009). Musical potential. In S. Hallam, I. Cross & M. Thaut (eds), *The oxford handbook of music psychology* (pp. 255–64). Oxford: Oxford University Press.

McPherson, G. E., & Lehmann, A. (in press). Exceptional musical abilities—child prodigies. In G. E. McPherson & G. Welch (eds), *the oxford handbook of music education*. New York: Oxford University Press.

McPherson, G. E., & McCormick, J. (2006). Self-efficacy and music performance. *Psychology of Music, 34*(3), 322–36.

McPherson, G. E., & O'Neill, S. (2010). Students' motivation to study music as compared to other school subjects: a comparison of eight countries. *Research Studies in Music Education, 32*(2), 101–37.

McPherson, G. E., & Renwick, J. M. (2000). Self-regulation and musical practice: A longitudinal study. In C. Woods, G. B. Luck, R. Brochard, F. Seddon & J. A. Sloboda (eds), *Proceedings of the Sixth International Conference on Music Perception and Cognition.* Keele, UK: Keele University, Department of Psychology.

McPherson, G., & Renwick, J. (2001). A longitudinal study of self-regulation in children's musical practice. *Music Education Research, 3*(2), 169–86.

McPherson, G. E., & Renwick, J. (2011). Self-regulation and mastery of musical skills. In B. J. Zimmerman & D. Schunk (eds), *Handbook of self-regulation of learning and performance* (pp. 234–48). New York: Routledge.

McPherson, G. E., & Williamon, A. (2006). Giftedness and talent. In G. E. Mc Pherson (ed.), *The child as musician: a handbook of musical development* (pp. 239–56). Oxford: Oxford University Press.

McPherson, G. E., & Zimmerman, B. J. (2002). Self-regulation of musical learning: A social cognitive perspective. In R. Colwell & C. Richardson (eds), *The new handbook of research on music teaching and learning* (pp. 327–47). New York: Oxford University Press.

McPherson, G. E., & Zimmerman, B. J. (2011). Self-regulation of musical learning: A social cognitive perspective on developing performance skills (pp. 130–175). In R. Colwell & P. Webster (Eds.), *MENC Handbook of Research on Music Learning, Volume 2: Applications.* New York: Oxford University Press.

Miell, D., MacDonald, R. A. R., & Hargreaves, D. J. (Eds.). (2005). *Musical communication.* Oxford: Oxford University Press.

Miklaszewski, K. (1989). A case study of a pianist preparing a musical performance. *Psychology of Music, 17*(2), 95–109.

Mills, J., & McPherson, G. E. (2006). Musical literacy. In G. E. McPherson (ed.), *The child as musician: a handbook of musical development* (pp. 155–72). Oxford: Oxford University Press.

Münte TF, Altenmüller, E. & Jäncke L (2002). The musician's brain as a model of neuroplasticity. *Nature Reviews Neuroscience, 3*(47), 473–78.

Nielsen, S. G. (1997). Self-regulation of learning strategies during practice: A case study of a church organ student preparing a musical work for performance. In H. Jørgensen & A. C. Lehmann (eds), *Does practice make perfect? Current theory and research on instrumental music practice* (pp. 109–22). Oslo: Norges musikkhøgskole.

Nielsen, S. (1999). Learning strategies in instrumental music practice. *British Journal of Music Educational Psychologist, 16*(3), 275–91.

Norton, A., Winner, E., Cronin, K., Overy, K., Lee, D. J., & Schlaug, G. (2005). Are there pre-existing neural, cognitive, or motoric markers for musical ability? *Brain Cognition, 59*(2), 124–34.

O'Neill, S. A., & Boulton, M. J. (1996). Boys' and girls' preferences for musical instruments: A function of gender? *Psychology of Music, 24*(2), 171–83.

Palmer, C. (1989). Mapping musical thought to musical performance. *Journal of Experimental Psychology, 15*(2), 331–46.

Papoušek, H. (1996). Musicality in infancy research: Biological and cultural origins of early musicality. In I. Deliége & J. Slododa (eds), *Musical beginnings* (pp. 37–55). Oxford: Oxford University Press.

Parasuraman, S., & Purohit, Y.S. (2000) Distress and boredom among orchestra musicians: The two faces of stress. *Journal of Occupational Health Psychology*. 5(1): 74–83.

Paynter, J. (1992). *Sound and structure*. Cambridge: Cambridge University Press.

Pintrich, P., & Schunk, D. (1996). *Motivation in education: theory, research & applications*. Englewood Cliffs: Prentice-Hall.

Pitts, S. (2000). *A century of change in music education: historical perspectives on contemporary practice in British secondary school music*. Aldershot: Ashgate.

Pitts, S. (2005). *Valuing musical participation*. Aldershot: Ashgate.

Pitts, S. E., & Davidson, J. W. (2000). Supporting musical development in the primary school: An English perspective on band programmes in Sydney, NSW. *Research Studies in Music Education, 14*91), 76–84.

Pitts, S., Davidson, J., & McPherson, G. E. (2000). Developing effective practice strategies: case studies of three young instrumentalists. *Music Education Research, 2*(1), 45–56).

Plomin, R. (1999). Genetics and general cognitive ability. *Nature, 402*, C25–29.

Plomin, R., & Daniels, D. (1987). Why are children in the same family so different from one another? *Behaviour and Brain Sciences, 10*(1), 1–16.

Plomin, R., Fulker, D. W., Corley, R., & DeFries, J. C. (1997). Nature, nurture, and cognitive development from 1 to 16 years: A parent-offspring adoption study. *Psychological Science, 8*(6), 442–47.

Pomerantz, E. M., Grolnick, W. S., & Price, C. E. (2005). The role of parents in how children approach achievement: A dynamic process perspective. In A. J. Elliot & S. S. Dweck (eds), *Handbook of competence and motivation* (pp. 259–78). New York: Guilford.

Pomerantz, E. M., Moorman, E. A., & Litwack, S. D. (2007). The how, whom, and why of parents' involvement in children's academic lives: More is not always better. *Review of Educational Research, 77*(3), 373–410.

Priest, P. (1989). Playing by ear: Its nature and application to instrumental learning. *British Journal of Music Education, 6*(2), 173–91.

Renwick, J. M., & McPherson, G. E. (2000). 'I've got to do my scale first!': A case study of a novice's clarinet practice. In C. Woods, G. B. Luck, R. Brochard, F. Seddon & J. A. Sloboda (eds), *Proceedings of the Sixth International Conference on Music Perception and Cognition*. Keele, UK: Keele University, Department of Psychology.

Renwick, J., & McPherson, G. (2002). Interest and choice: student-selected repertoire and its effect on practising behaviour. *British Journal of Music Education, 19*(2), 173–88.

Rice, T. (1994). *May it fill your soul: experiencing Bulgarian music*. Chicago: University of Chicago Press.

Rideout, V. J., Foehr, U. G., & Roberts, D. F. (2010). Generation M2: Media in the lives of 8–18 year olds. Menlo Park, California: Henry J Kaiser Family Foundation.

Rowe, K., & Rowe, K. (1999). Investigating the relationship between students' attentive–inattentive behaviors in the classroom and their literacy progress. *International Journal of Educational Research, 31*(1/2), 1–138.

Sameroff, A. (2000). Developmental systems and psychopathology. *Development and Psychopathology, 12*(3), 297–312.

Sameroff, A. (2009). The transactional model. In A. Sameroff (ed.), *The transactional model of development: how children and contexts shape each other* (pp. 3–21). Washington, DC: American Psychological Association.

Sameroff, A. (2010). A unified theory of development: A dialectic integration of nature and nurture. *Child Development, 81*(1), 6–22.

Sameroff, A., & Fiese, B. (eds). (2000). *Transactional regulation: the developmental ecology of early intervention.* Cambridge: Cambridge University Press.

Santrock, J. (2009). *A topical approach to life-span development* (5th edn). New York: McGraw-Hill.

Schellenberg, E. (2006). Exposure to music: The truth about the consequences. In G. E. McPherson (ed.), *The child as musician: a handbook of musical development* (pp. 111–34). Oxford: Oxford University Press.

Schlaug, G., Forgeard, M., Zhu, L., Norton, A. C., Norton, A., & Winner, E. (2009). Training-induced neuroplasticity in young children. *The Neurosciences and Music III: Disorders and Plasticity: Annals of the New York Academy of Sciences, 1169*, 205–208.

Schlaug, G., Norton, A., Overy, K., & Winner, E. (2005). Effects of music training on the child's brain and cognitive development. *Annals of the New York Academcy of Sciences, 1060*, 219–30.

Schleuter, S. (1997). *A sound approach to teaching instrumentalists: an application of content and learning sequences.* New York: Schirmer.

Scott, C., & Dinham, S. (2005). Parenting, teaching and self esteem. *The Australian Educational Leader, 27*(1), 28–30.

Shaffer, D. R., & Kipp, K. (2009). *Developmental psychology: childhood to adolescence* (8th edn). Belmont, CA: Wadsworth.

Simonton, D. K. (1991). Emergence and realization of genius: The lives and works of 120 classical composers. *Journal of Personality and Social Psychology, 61*, 829–40.

Sloboda, J. A. (1985). *The musical mind: the cognitive psychology of music.* Oxford: Clarendon Press.

Sloboda, J. A. (1991). Music structure and emotional response: some empirical findings. *Psychology of Music, 19*(2), 110–20.

Sloboda, J. A. (2005). *Exploring the musical mind: cognition, emotion, ability, function.* Oxford: Oxford University Press.

Sloboda, J. A., & Davidson, J. W. (1996). The young performing musician. In I. Deliege & J. Sloboda (eds), *Musical beginnings: origins and development of musical competence* (pp. 171–90). New York: Oxford University Press.

Sloboda, J. A., Davidson, J., & Howe, M. (1994a). Is everyone musical? *The Psychologist, 7*(8), 349–54.

Sloboda, J. A., Davidson, J. W., & Howe, M. (1994b). Musicians: Experts not geniuses. *The Psychologist, 7*(7), 363–65.

Sloboda, J. A., Davidson, J., Howe, M. J. A., & Moore, D. (1996). The role of practice in the development of performing musicians. *British Journal of Psychology, 87*(2), 287–309.

Sloboda, J. A., & Howe, M. J. A. (1991). Biographical precursors of musical excellence: An interview study. *Psychology of Music, 19*(1), 3–21.

Small, C. (1998). *Musicking.* Hanover: Wesleyan University Press.

Smith, J. A. (1996). Beyond the divide between cognition and discourse: using interpretative phenomenological analysis in health psychology. *Psychology & Health, 11*(2), 261–71.

Smith, J. A. (1999). Towards a relational self: social engagement during pregnancy and psychological preparation for motherhood. *British Journal of Social Psychology, 38*(4), 409–26.

Smith, J., Harre, R., & Van Lagenhove, L. (1995). *Rethinking psychology*. London: Sage.

Stegemann, T., Brüggemann-Etchart, A., Badorrek-Hinkelmann, A., & Romer, G. (2010). The function of music in the context of non-suicidal self injury. *Kinderpsychol Kinderpsychiatr, 59*(10), 810–30.

Sternberg, R. J., & Reis, S. M. (eds) (2004). *Definitions and conceptions of giftedness*. Thousand Oaks, CA: Corwin Press.

Stipek, D. (1998). *Motivation to learn: from theory to practice* (3rd edn). Boston: Allyn & Bacon.

Stoeger, H. (2009). The history of giftedness research. In L. V. Shavinina (ed.), *International handbook of giftedness* (pp. 17–38). New York: Springer.

Sulloway, F.J. (1997). Born to rebel: birth order, family dynamics and creative lives. New York: Vintage Books.

Suzuki, S. (1983). Nurtured by love: The classic approach to talent education. Smithtown, NY: Exposition Press.

Swanwick, K. (1999). *Teaching music musically*. London: Routledge.

Swanwick, K., & Tillman, J. (1986). The sequence of musical development: A study of children's composition. *British Journal of Music Education, 3*(3), 305–39.

Tierney, W. G. (2000). Undaunted courage: life history and the postmodern challenge. In N. K. Denzin, & Y. S. Lincoln (eds), *Handbook of qualitative research*. (pp. 537–54). Thousand Oaks, CA: Sage Publications.

Titon, J. T. (1994). Knowing people making music: Toward a new epistemology for ethnomusicology, *Etnomusikologian vuoskirja [Yearbook of the Finnish Society for Ethnomusicology* (Vol. 6). Helsinki: Suomen etnomusikologinen seura.

Todd, N. (1985). A model of expressive timing in tonal music. *Music Perception, 3*(1), 33–58.

Trautwein, U., Kastens, C., & Köller, O. (2006a). Effort on homework in grades 5–9: Development, motivational antecedents, and the association with effort on classwork. *Child Development, 77*(4), 1094–1111.

Trautwein, U., & Koller, O. (2003). The relationship between homework and achievement: Still much of a mystery. *Educational Psychology Review, 15*(2), 115–45.

Trautwein, U., & Lüdtke, O. (2007). Students' self-reported effort and time on homework in six school subjects: Between-student differences and within-student variation. *Journal of Educational Psychology, 99*(2), 432–44.

Trautwein, U., Lüdtke, O., Schnyder, I., & Niggli, A. (2006b). Predicting homework effort: Support for a domain-specific, multilevel homework model. *Journal of Educational Psychology, 98*(2), 438–56.

Trautwein, U., Niggli, A., Schnyder, I., & Lüdtke, O. (2009a). Between-teacher differences in homework assignments and the development of students' homework effort, homework emotions, and achievement. *Journal of Educational Psychology, 101*(1), 176–89.

Trautwein, U., Schnyder, I., Niggli, A., Neumann, M., & Lüdtke, O. (2009b). Chameleon effects in homework research: The homework-achievement association depends on the measures used and the level of analysis chosen. *Contemporary Educational Psychology, 34*(1), 77–88.

Vygotsky, L. S. (1978). *Mind in society: the development of higher psychological processes*. Cambridge, MA: Harvard University Press.

Walker, S., & Plomin, R. (2005). The nature–nurture question: Teachers' perceptions of how genes and the environment influence educationally relevant behavior. *Educational Psychology, 25*(5), 509–505.

Wallin, N., Merker, B., & Brown, S. (2000). *The origins of music.* Cambridget, MA: MIT Press.

Watkins, J. G., & Farnum, S. E. (1954). *The Watkins–Farnum performance scale: a standardized achievement test for all band instruments.* Winona, MN: Hal Leonard.

Weber, R. (2001). *The created self: reinventing body, persona, spirit.* New York: W.W. Norton.

Weinert, R. (1995). The role of formulaic language in second language acquisition: A review. *Applied Linguistics, 16*(2), 180–205.

Westerlund, H. (2006). Garage rock bands: A future model for developing musical expertise? *International Journal of Music Education, 24*(2), 119–25.

Whaley, J., Sloboda, J. A., & Gabrielsson, A. (2009). Peak experiences in music. In S. Hallam, I. Cross & M. Thaut (eds), *The Oxford handbook of music psychology* (pp. 452–61). Oxford: Oxford University.

Winner, E. (1996). *Gifted children: myths and realities.* New York: Basic Books.

Woody, R., & McPherson, G. E. (2010). Emotion in the lives of performers. In P. Juslin & J. A. Sloboda (eds), *Music and emotion.* Oxford: Oxford University Press, 401–24.

Xu, J. (2008). Models of secondary school students' interest: A multilevel analysis. *American Educational Research Journal, 45*(4), 1180–1205.

Xun, Z., & Tarocco, F. (2007). *Karaoke: the global phenomenon.* London: Reaktion.

Zhu, Q., Song, Y., Hu, S., Li, X., Tian, M., Zhen, Z., et al. (2010). Heritability of the specific cognitive ability of face perception. *Current Biology, 20*(2), 137–42.

Zimmerman, B. (1994). Dimensions of academic self-regulation. In D. H. Schunk & B. Zimmerman (eds), *Self-regulation of learning and performance: issues and educational applications* (pp. 3–21). Hillsdale, NJ: Erlbaum.

Zimmerman, B. (1998). Academic studying and the development of personal skill: a self-regulatory perspective. *Educational Psychologist, 33*(2/3), 73–86.

Zimmerman, B. (2000). Attaining self-regulation: a social cognitive perspective. In M. Boekaerts, P. R. Pintrich & M. Zeidner (eds), *Handbook of self-regulation* (pp. 13–39). San Diego, CA: Academic Press.

Index